LONGMAN LINGUISTICS LIBRARY
Title no 28

PSYCHOLINGUISTICS
LANGUAGE, MIND, AND WORLD

LONGMAN LINGUISTICS LIBRARY

General editors
R. H. Robins, University of London
G. N. Leech, University of Lancaster

Psycholinguistics

Language, mind, and world

Danny D. Steinberg

LONGMAN
LONDON AND NEW YORK

LONGMAN GROUP LIMITED
Longman House, Burnt Mill, Harlow
Essex CM20 2JE, England
Associated companies throughout the world

*Published in the United States of America
by Longman Inc., New York*

First published 1982
Second impression 1984
Third impression 1986

ISBN 0-582-29113-5

British Library Cataloguing in Publication Data

Steinberg, Danny
    Psycholinguistics.–(Longman linguistics library: 28)
    1. Psycholinguistics
    I. Title
    401'.9   BF455
    ISBN 0-582-29113-5 Pbk

Library of Congress Cataloging in Publication Data

Steinberg, Danny D.
    Psycholinguistics: language, mind, and world.
    (Longman linguistics library; title no. 28)
    Bibliography: p.
    Includes indexes.
    1. Psycholinguistics.   I. Title   II. Series.
    P37.S78   401'.9   81-8159
                                (AACR2)

    ISBN 0-582-29113-5 (pbk.)

Produced by Longman Singapore Publishers (Pte) Ltd.
Printed in Singapore.

To my father and in memory of my mother

Preface

This book is concerned with the conceptual foundations of language and their application in two very important fields, reading and second language teaching. For the most part, the book focuses on a consideration of how human beings use and acquire language. Toward this end, basic ideas from a variety of disciplines, particularly linguistics, philosophy and psychology, are presented and evaluated. A mentalistic approach is used as the basis for the integration of such ideas into a unified language theory, and experimental research is included to the extent that it is illuminating to the basic issues under consideration. Because of its interdisciplinary emphasis, the book is appropriate for both students and professionals in psychology, linguistics, education, philosophy, communication and other language related fields.

I am indebted to the following persons for their valuable assistance and comments on various chapters of the book: Ms Claudia Sullivan, Ms Rita Dente, Professors Richard Schmidt and Ted Plaister of the Department of English as a Second Language, University of Hawaii, Professors Roderick Jacobs, Ann Peters and Stanley Starosta of the Department of Linguistics, University of Hawaii, Professor Steven Davis of the Department of Philosophy, Simon Fraser University, and the students of my psycholinguistics and syntax classes at the University of Hawaii. I would like to thank Ms. Evelyn Nakanishi for her special efforts in the typing of the manuscript.

I shall always be grateful to Professor Jack Richards of the Department of English as a Second Language, University of Hawaii for his efforts and support in bringing the book to publication.

Honolulu, Hawaii
May 1981

D. D. S.

Chapter 1

Fundamental language abilities of speakers

One fundamental problem for language theorists, particularly psychologists, is to explain how people are able to carry out the two common everyday activities of producing and understanding sentences. Essentially, two types of theories have been proposed to account for the abilities of speakers in accomplishing such feats. One theory involves the use of the concepts of stimulus, response, and connections within a behaviorist (anti-mentalist) framework. The other involves the use of abstract rules and rule systems which are conceived within a mentalistic framework. Psychologists, linguists, and philosophers have allied themselves with one or the other of these opposing frameworks. Allied with behaviorism are such notables as Watson, Skinner, Staats, Bloomfield, Fries, Ryle, and Quine, while with mentalism are such eminent thinkers as Chomsky, Piaget, Putnam, and Fodor.

While in later chapters of this book we will consider additional aspects of the nature of the disagreement between the two antagonistic conceptions, the present chapter is devoted to describing how theories involving the stimulus-response and rule principles attempt to account for the language abilities of speakers. An evaluation of the adequacy of these accounts will also be provided. For the behaviorist-oriented view, the theories of Watson, Skinner, Fries, and Staats are considered, while for the rule view, the theory of Chomsky is analyzed. The chapter begins with a general discussion of the basic language abilities of speakers, establishing what it is that a theory attempts to explain.

Basic language abilities of speakers

Suppose someone said to you, *A foreign princess who claimed that she had become pregnant as the result of eating reindeer meat sukiyaki which had been served by a steward during her flight from Helsinki to Tokyo filed a paternity suit against the airline.*

Suppose, too, that you were asked the following questions:

(1)   Did you understand what was said?

(2a) Do you think that you have ever heard of a princess who claimed that she was made pregnant by eating reindeer sukiyaki and had filed a paternity suit based on that claim? Or, more specifically, do you think you have ever experienced that particular sentence before?

(2b) Could you produce a sentence that in all likelihood no one including yourself had ever experienced before but which you and others could understand?

(3a) Is the sentence a well-formed English sentence? (Sentences like *Went played waitress*, *The table which the purchased was expensive*, and *The triangle elapsed* are not well-formed.)

(3b) If the word *claimed* were deleted from the sentence, would the remaining string of words provide a well-formed sentence?

(3c) If the word *foreign* were deleted, would the remaining string be well-formed?

(4a) The sentence is about 40 words long. Could you make it longer and still keep it well-formed?

(4b) Is there any fixed number of words beyond which you could not make the sentence longer and still keep it well-formed?

(5)   In the environment where you read the sentence, were there any relevant cues that assisted you in understanding the sentence? For example, was there a foreign princess around and did she claim pregnancy?

Undoubtedly, as would most speakers, you would have given an affirmative reply to questions (1), (2b), (3a), (3c), and (4a), and a negative reply to the others. Such a highly replicable empirical phenomenon serves to illustrate a number of important facts about the abilities of people who know a language (hereafter, *speakers*). It establishes that speakers can produce and understand sentences which they have never experienced before, both in terms of their unique content (*novelty*) and length, and can assess the well-formedness (*grammaticality*) of such sentences even without the presence of any relevant environmental context. The fact that speakers can make sentences longer without any preset limit as to length also implies another speaker ability, the ability to produce and understand an unlimited number of sentences, since, with each lengthening, a new sentence occurs. Without lengthening, the potential number of sentences would be finite, for, given the finite vocabulary of the language, any fixed length would make the number of possible sentences finite (although astronomically large) even if all possible substitutions of vocabulary items were permitted. Of course, the number of sentences any speaker will produce or understand in a lifetime is finite. However, it is the potential that is without limit, just as in counting there is no greatest number we can generate. One can always make an existing number greater and provide numbers which never before existed. So it is that finite means can provide for infinite ends.

Explaining speaker's basic language abilities

Nobody's Whole Sentence Theory

In approaching the problem of evaluating how well certain theories are able to account for the ability of speakers to produce and understand novel grammatical sentences, independent of relevant environmental context and with no preset limit on length or number, it might be instructive to begin with a very simple and clearly inadequate theory. Since it is one which no one has ever proposed, it will be called Nobody's theory. Following this theory, the actual theories of Watson, Staats, Skinner, Fries, and Chomsky will be considered.

Language knowledge acquired

Let us suppose that Nobody's theory proposes that speakers learning language essentially acquire whole sentences. They do this by memorizing every string of words (an utterance) that they hear along with the environmental context of the utterance so that it may have meaning. Thus, speakers would have stored in their memories a number of utterances and their meanings.

Adequacy of the language knowledge

For this, and each of the other theories which follows, adequacy will be assessed with respect to the basic abilities relating to *novelty, grammaticality*, and *no fixed length or number*. The important ability of speakers being able to produce and understand sentences *independent of relevant context* will be considered when necessary.

NOVELTY. A speaker who had only the knowledge which was proposed would *not* be able to produce a novel sentence. Only the utterances previously stored could be uttered. Such a speaker would not be able to say, for example, *While at Queen's Surf Beach, my wallet, which I left in the trunk of my car, was stolen*, if that sentence had not been previously experienced and stored Neither would a speaker hearing it for the first time have a meaning for it if someone else had uttered it out of environmental context.

GRAMMATICALITY The speaker would have no basis for assessing whether or not any of the utterances which have been learned or newly heard are grammatical or not. Since natural speech often involves hesitations, slips, and changes in the middle of a sentence, e.g. *First,*

Mary, uh well, it might have been Jean, anyway, some girl came, The boy were singing, Joe sent me a – wait a minute – is that Bill I see?, the speaker would not know what the basic sentences were and whether or not they were grammatical. Such a speaker would have no basis for assessing whether sentences like *Went played waitress* or *The table which the purchased is expensive* are well-formed or not. (The placement of an asterisk before a sentence is a linguistic convention signifying that the sentence is in some way malformed.)

Of course, what may be grammatical in one speech community may not be grammatical in another. In Hawaiian Pidgin (Creole), for example, mass or group nouns like *fruit, furniture*, and *staff* are treated as count nouns and are pluralized when more than one instance of the same kind is being referred to, e.g., *these fruits* and not *this fruit* would be used to refer to three bananas. The sense in which grammaticality is used here and throughout the book is not as an absolute term related to some ideal or standard language or dialect. Its application is relative to the speech norms of any specific speech community. Thus, varieties of English such as Hawaiian Pidgin, Boston Brahmin, Detroit Black, Toronto Jewish, and Liverpool Working Class all have their own grammars and standards for what is or is not well-formed in their speech.

NO FIXED LENGTH OR NUMBER. A speaker who knew only sentences which had previously been experienced would not be able to produce or understand a sentence longer than the longest one that had already been memorized. Yet, it is clear that the language knowledge which ordinary speakers possess does allow this even though at some point we may run into difficulty dealing with very long sentences. (We can hold in memory and analyze just so much without forgetting what was said or previously analyzed, even with the aid of writing. Obviously there are psychological factors which limit our ability to achieve our language potential.)

As for number of sentences, that number would necessarily be finite since only sentences already known could be generated. No person could store an infinite number of sentences.

CONCLUSION. Nobody's Whole Sentence Theory fails to meet any of the essential criteria for adequacy.

Watson's Word Association Theory

Language knowledge acquired
One of the simplest theories ever proposed to account for the language abilities of speakers was formulated around 1920 by John B. Watson, the founder of behaviorism. According to Watson (1924: 247) we acquire new verbal creations '... by manipulating words, shifting them

about until a new pattern is hit upon. Since we are never in the same general situation when we begin to think, the word patterns will always be different. The elements are all old, that is, the words that present themselves are just our standard vocabulary – it is only the arrangement that is different.' In his writings, Watson makes two essential claims about what language knowledge speakers acquire. (1) Speakers learn a number of words. Each word consists of a sound form connected to a meaning that relates to objects and events in the environment, e.g. the sound form 'boy' is connected with the object 'boy' in the environment. (2) When speakers learn a sentence they learn the interconnections between words. For example, if *The ice melted* were learned, the connections among all three words and between the component words would also be learned, i.e. *the-ice* and *ice-melted*. Also, if *The boy melted the wax* were learned, the connections between *the-boy*, *boy-melted*, *melted-the*, and *the-wax* would be learned.

Adequacy of the language knowledge
Watson's theory clearly allows for the generation of novel grammatical sentences. For example, on the basis of the above example, a sentence like *The boy melted the ice* can be produced, for, if we begin with the word *the*, then *boy* is allowed to follow since it is already connected with *the*. After *boy, melted* is allowed to follow since it is already connected with *boy*. After *melted, the* may follow because of a prior connection, and finally *ice* may follow *the* again because of a prior connection. Unfortunately, though, this same mechanism also allows for a novel but ungrammatical string like *The boy melted the ice melted the boy melted* to be produced. Consequently, the theory provides no means for ensuring that what will be produced is not nonsense. It does not specify when we should stop connecting words. Such being the case, it is no better than a 'theory' which specifies that sentences may be composed of words selected at random. Of course, some of the sentences generated in this manner will be grammatical. But what this theory and Watson's fail to do is to account for the fact that every speaker essentially produces grammatical sentences and is able to identify which sentences are or are not grammatical even in the absence of any relevant environmental context. (This is not to say that environmental context is not relevant in helping speakers to interpret sentences. What it does say, however, is that there is a great deal that speakers can judge about a sentence independent of any context with which it may be concerned.)

The problem of grammaticality also contaminates Watson's theory with respect to length and number of sentences. While it is true that Watson's theory can generate sentences which are unlimited in length and number (words can be connected with one another on into infinity), such a benefit is rendered useless if the system indiscriminately

generates grammatical and ungrammatical sentences. One can only conclude, therefore, that Watson's theory is inadequate for explaining
basic language abilities of speakers.

Staats' Word Class Association Theory

Language knowledge acquired

The work of Staats (1968) which appeared in the 1960s may be viewed
as an extension of Watson's ideas. Essentially he viewed a sentence as
being formed by the association of word classes (nouns, verbs, etc.)
with one another. Thus, while for Watson individual words are connected, for Staats it is words which represent word classes that are connected. To explain the theory let us use the same examples as in the
Watson theory. Thus, if *The ice melted* and *The boy melted the wax*
were learned, then, as with Watson, the connections between *the-ice,
ice-melted, the-boy, boy-melted, melted-the* and *the-wax* would also be
formed. Now, if prior learning had established that *the* belonged to a
class (articles), *boy, ice,* and *wax* belonged to another class (nouns) and
melted belonged to still another (verbs), then substitutions within a
word class may take place. In effect, *the-ice, the-boy,* and *the-wax* represent an Article-Noun combination while *ice-melted* and *boy-melted*
represent a Noun-Verb combination. As a result, not only could the
novel grammatical sentence *The boy melted the ice* be generated but so
could *The girl melted the ice,* as long as *girl* and *boy* had been previously learned as members of the same class. Watson's theory, based as it is
on only the connections of particular words, does not allow for a novel
sentence like this to occur. The idea of word class and substitutions
within a class is what makes Staats' theory different and more complex
than Watson's.

Adequacy of the language knowledge

However, Staats' theory suffers from some of the same deficiencies as
Watson's. The same mechanism which will produce novel grammatical
sentences will produce ungrammatical ones as well. The same nonsensical strings of words which Watson's theory produced, e.g. *The boy
melted the ice melted the boy melted* will also be produced by Staats
the only difference being that other similarly nonsensical strings will be
produced by substitution, e.g. *The girl melted the ice melted the girl
melted.* The fact that such strings can be judged as ungrammatical without the presence of any relevant context indicates that speakers must
have other essential knowledge which controls for the proper form of
sentences. This knowledge, whatever it is, is not specified in Staats'
theory.

Of course, the fact that Staats' theory is unable to account for an
unlimited number of lengthy novel grammatical sentences has no bear-

ing on the idea of grammatical word classes (noun, verb, etc.). All language theorists believe that words can generally be sorted into classes. However, what they do not agree on is what the basis for classification should be. Two bases have been proposed over the centuries, one syntactic, the other semantic. Staats is an advocate of the syntactic basis, as were most of the linguists during what has been called the era of Structural Linguistics in the United States. Staats approvingly quotes the following from Brown and Berko (1960: 2), theorists who, at that time, were greatly influenced by Structural ideas:

> The linguistic scientist defines the part-of-speech in purely syntactic or formal terms. He has shown that the English teacher's semantic definitions (e.g. 'a noun is the name of a person, place, or thing') are imprecise approximations to the underlying but less obvious syntactic facts. The noun, in descriptive linguistics, is a class of words having similar 'privileges of occurrence.' Nouns are words that can follow articles and can occur in subject and object positions and, in this respect, are distinct from such other classes of words as the verb, adjective, and adverb.

While, as the authors say, a semantic basis for word classes is often imprecise (a noun being the name of a person, place, or thing), in actuality it is a much superior definition to the purely syntactic one. For, if word classes are to be based on position (privilege of occurrence), a detailed consideration shows that such a notion is entirely inadequate. For example, let us consider the following five sentences:

	A	B	C	D	E	F	G
(1)	The	horse	likes	sugar	in	the	morning.
(2)	The	cow	in	the	meadow	slept	soundly.
(3)	The	dog	which	bit	little	girls	barked.
(4)	The	theory	the	professor	formulated	was	mine.
(5)	The	city	horse	chased	the	friendly	dog.

According to Staats, the words in column B, *horse, cow, dog, theory* and *city*, will form a class because they are in the same position and are elicited by a common element, the word *the*. The 'privilege of occurrence' notion seems to work so far because the B class words do form an intuitively satisfying group, one that we call nouns. However, what sort of class can the words under column C, *likes, in, which, the*, and *horse*, be said to form, since, according to Staats' principles, they form a class because they are in the same position and all follow nouns? By this same mechanism, classes can be formed for the words under columns D, E, F, and G as well. Actually, it turns out that all of the words in all of the columns form one giant class. For, (1) since the word *the* is a member of each of the classes A, C, D, E, and F, then, according to Staats' principle of generalization, all of the words in these classes become substitutable and will form but a single class (let us call it X); (2) since classes B and G both have the word *dog* in it, therefore, by generalization, each of these two classes will form a single class (Y). Now, since the word *horse* is a member both of class X (it appears in C) and of class Y (it appears in B), then by generalization these classes form a single class (Z). It is readily seen that all words of the language form a single class. This being the case, it is clear that privilege of occurrence is an inadequate notion for establishing word classes.

The reason why Staats' theory fails to work is because on a word to word basis, almost any word class can be found to follow any word class, with a few exceptions. Consider the following sets of examples which show that any major word class can follow a noun, verb, or preposition.

Noun + ...

The *building superintendent* shouted.	Noun + Noun
The *boys sang*.	Noun + Verb
The *boys weary* and worn fell asleep.	Noun + Adjective
The *boys unfortunately* gave the alarm.	Noun + Adverb
The *boy the* girl kissed ran.	Noun + Article
The *boy with* red hair sang.	Noun + Preposition
The *boy and* the girl danced.	Noun + Conjunction

Verb + ...

The boy *ran home*.	Verb + Noun
The dog which the girl *bought barked*.	Verb + Verb
The boy *became sick*.	Verb + Adjective
Tbe boy *sang loudly*.	Verb + Adverb
The boy *sang a* song.	Verb + Article
The boy *walked to* the store.	Verb + Preposition
The boy *sang and* danced.	Verb + Conjunction

Preposition + ...

He went *to school*.	Preposition + Noun
The school he went *to burned* down.	Preposition + Verb
He travelled *with green* socks.	Preposition + Adjective
The school he went *to unfortunately* burned down.	Preposition + Adverb
He went *to the* farm.	Preposition + Article
The girl he had talked *with at* school arrived.	Preposition + Preposition
He walked *to and* from school daily.	Preposition + Conjunction

Actually, a consideration of all possible word class combinations shows that only one combination, perhaps, that of Article + Article does not occur.[1] This being the case, that virtually any word class can follow any word class, then the word class association theory permits virtually any word to follow any word. Such a theory obviously cannot explain how speakers can produce and recognize well-formed sentences.[2]

Skinner's Sentence Frame Theory

Language knowledge acquired

According to Skinner (1957: 346), speakers learn 'standard patterns' or 'skeletal frames' as a basis for sentence composition. Frames are composed of 'key responses,' *nouns, verbs*, and *adjectives*. Knowledge of frames permits a speaker to order key responses. Once key responses are ordered, other words may be added, e.g. *a, the, some*, and *all* for 'quantification,' and *is, not, like*, and *as* for 'qualification.' Thus, for example, given the key responses *hungry* and *man* in composing a sentence, they will be ordered on the basis of the frame N + Adj as *man + hungry* and then quantified and qualified with *the* and *is* to yield *The man is hungry*.

Adequacy of the language knowledge

Chomsky (1959), in his review of Skinner's book *Verbal Behavior*, discusses several important reasons for the inadequacy of Skinner's frame notion. One failing of Skinner's theory is that it does not distinguish grammaticality from ungrammaticality in sentences which have the same frames. Consider, for example, *The bird the girl bought chirped*, **John Marsha bought chirped*, and **The shoe the triangle elapsed dined*. While all strings are identical in terms of the key response frame of N–N–V–V, only the first is an English sentence. Such judgments can be made independently of environmental context by any speaker of the language.

Suppose one argues that N–N–V–V for *The bird the girl bought chirped* is not a basic frame but that such a string is composed of two basic frames: N–V, for *The bird chirped*, and N–V–N, for *The girl bought the bird* (we know that the bird is what the girl bought). If such were Skinner's intention, a serious defect in his proposal is immediately made manifest, for Skinner does not mention if and how basic frames are to be identified. How, for example, does one know that *The girl the bird bought chirped* is not a basic sentence? Even if he did make such a specification, an even more serious problem remains, the problem of how basic frames are to be combined into wholes. For example, how are the basic frames of *The bird chirped* and *The girl bought the bird* to be combined to form *The bird the girl bought chirped*? Clearly, a simple conjoining of the two sentences, e.g. *The bird chirped and the girl bought the bird*, does not give the required result. If we wish *The girl bought the bird* to modify *The bird* in *The bird chirped*, certain changes are necessary. The modifying sentence must be embedded between the subject and verb of the main sentence, such that *The bird the girl bought the bird chirped results. However, another change or transformation is necessary for the sentence to become grammatical. The direct object of the verb in the modifying sentence, i.e. the bird (which follows bought) must be deleted. This then will give us the grammatical sentence The bird the girl bought chirped. Actually, there is an alternative transformation besides deletion that is permitted in English and that occurs in the sentence The bird which the girl bought chirped. For such a sentence to be produced, the following steps may be necessary:

Basic constituent sentences:
The bird The girl bought the bird chirped.

Pronominalization: The bird The girl bought which chirped.
Fronting of pronoun: The bird which the girl bought chirped.

Clearly, when basic frames combine, they do so in a complex way. Speakers have the knowledge which permits them to do this.

That it is necessary to posit that complex sentences are composed of simple or basic sentences is clearly illustrated by the sentence which was presented earlier in the chapter concerning the claimed pregnancy. The sequence of 40 or so words composing that entire sentence could not have been memorized as a sequence of word classes to form a single frame. Yet speakers have little difficulty in assessing the grammaticality of such a sentence – and even much longer ones. A host of basic sentences comprises the whole sentence, yet how those basic sentences are integrated to form the whole is not a simple process. It is obvious that speakers possess some sort of language knowledge which allows them to make such integrations. Chomsky calls this particular type of language knowledge 'transformational rules.'

The notion of the operation of transformations such as those described above is strongly rejected by Skinner. Such operations, Skinner fears, will lead away from behaviorism to mentalism because transformations are obviously not stimuli and responses in the usual sense of behavioristic theorizing. (see Chapter 5 for more details) Because of his opposition to any sort of abstract structural analysis, Skinner (1957: 35 –51) is even unwilling to recognize that sentences like Pass the salt, Wait, and Sing loudly share any common structure. (This is why Skinner often refers to Chomsky as a 'structuralist.') That each sentence is without an overt subject and that the verb is in the infinitive form are not features which are indicative of a command or request, according to Skinner. He maintains that these sentences are understood only because of the sort of reinforcement that a listener has received for them in the past. A listener understands Pass the salt, for example, because that person in the past received reinforcement for what was specifically named in the sentence, i.e. salt. However, as Chomsky (1959) insightfully points out, Skinner's theory fails to explain how it is possible for a listener to understand a novel request or command. If someone said, for example, *Streak through the pineapple fields*, how could a listener understand it as a request or command without having been appropriately reinforced for it in the past? Since such sentences are easily understood by speakers, there must be something about their structure which provides a clue. To some extent Skinner recognizes this problem. He asserts, 'The speaker appears to create new mands [a mand essentially being a command or request] on the analogy of old ones' (Skinner, 1957: 48). However, such a statement is not at all explanatory unless the precise meaning of 'analogy' ('generalization' is another often-used term) is specified in detail. How analogy could possibly operate without an analysis of structure, either in the case of these imperatives or in the problem of the integration of basic sentence frames cited above, has never been explained by Skinner or any of his supporters. MacCorquodale (1970), for example, fails to address himself to any such critical issues which concern the basic abilities of speakers. That Skinner can successfully explain certain other aspects of language behavior is notable but in no way alters the fact that the theory is deficient in a number of essential respects.

Fries' Sentence Frame Theory

Language knowledge acquired
Fries' (1952) theory is similar to that of Skinner's but with some important modifications. Fries believed that speakers learn the sequence of all of the word classes in a sentence frame, e.g. Article + Noun + Verb for *The boy ran* and not just the key responses such as Noun and Verb. More importantly, Fries believed that speakers learn and are cognizant of the structure of sentences.

Adequacy of the language knowledge
By allowing that speakers are cognizant of the structure of sentences, Fries' theory does not encounter, as does Skinner's, the problem of how a speaker can identify a sentence like *Streak through the pineapple fields* as being a command. However, Fries' theory does share the other basic inadequacy of Skinner's theory which is that no mechanism is provided for the integration of basic sentence types. Other problems which Fries' theory (as well as the other theories previously discussed) is unable to handle are those sentences which are structurally ambiguous or synonymous. For example, *Oswald's shooting is remembered* is an ambiguous sentence, for it has at least two different meanings. In one meaning what is remembered is that Oswald shot someone, while

in the other what is remembered is that someone shot Oswald. What is interesting about this sentence is that there is but one sentence frame or series of words for the two greatly different meanings. It is ambiguous in a way which involves different structural relations. Such structural ambiguity is to be distinguished from simple vocabulary ambiguity where a sentence like *Joe went to the bank* has two meanings because the word *bank* can signify either a place where money is kept or ground that borders a river. The Oswald sentence cannot be explained in such a way because each of the interpretations given above has the same overt sentence structure and meanings of words.[3] Chomsky's popular examples of *John is easy to please* and *John is eager to please* raise similar problems, for both sentences have exactly the same sequences of word classes (both *easy* and *eager* are adjectives). Yet, the meaning interpretations are greatly different since we know that who is being pleased and who is doing the pleasing are different in both sentences.[4]

Structural synonymy presents a similar problem to Fries and other theorists. Consider the sentences: (1) *The bird which the girl bought chirped* and (2) *The bird the girl bought chirped*. As speakers of English we know these are synonymous even though the sequence of word classes is different in each. Clearly, there is some principle of English which permits us to delete or retain the relative pronoun *which*. In such a sentence as *The bird which ate chirped* we cannot delete the relative pronoun, for **The bird ate chirped* would result. Why *which* can be deleted in one case but not in the other involves a matter of complex structural analysis. The essence of the solution lies in the fact that *which* represents the direct object in the first case but the subject in the second case. For a similar reason, we judge *The boy who laughed jumped* as grammatical but *The boy whom laughed jumped* as ungrammatical because *whom* is only used in the object context while *who* must be used in the subject context. (*Who* is often used, too, in the object context.)

It is worth noting that even theories which go beyond Fries' notion of a sentence as being composed of a sequence of word classes, e.g. Pike (1954), and posit that a sentence consists of phrases (which in turn are composed of word classes) also suffer from the same inadequacies of Fries' theory. Even if sentences like *The bird chirped* and *The girl bought the bird* are said to be composed of the phrases *the bird* and *chirped*, and *the girl* and *bought the bird* (or *bought* and *the bird*), simple association of these phrases will not provide for a grammatical sentence such as *The bird the girl bought chirped*. Again, principles which provide for the proper integration of these structures are required. Chomsky recognized this necessity and in his theory, which will be presented in detail in the following chapter, proposed a type of rule which would do this, the transformational rule.

Chomsky's Transformational Generative Theory

1957 was a notable year for language theory. In that year, two well-known theorists, Skinner and Osgood, published books, as did one unknown theorist, Chomsky. While Skinner's *Verbal Behavior* and Osgood's *The Measurement of Meaning* provided a framework for a behaviorist approach to the study of language, Chomsky's *Syntactic Structures* offered a radically new approach. As it turned out, Chomsky's (1957) ideas were to revolutionize linguistics and force many psychologists, anthropologists, and philosophers to question some of their most basic assumptions.

Chomsky's success derives from his ingenious and original conception of a grammar as a set of ordered rules. Chomsky currently holds that speakers who have learned their language have learned a set of ordered rules and that such knowledge allows for an explanation of basic speaker abilities. To illustrate the nature and power of Chomsky's conception, let us consider a simple artificial language.

Suppose we have a language in which sentences are composed of only two different words, *a* and *b*. As in any language, only certain sequences of the words make for well-formed or grammatical sentences while other sequences do not. The following is a list of grammatical and ungrammatical sequences of words in this language.

ab Language strings

Grammatical	Ungrammatical
bb	b
bbbb	bbb
bbbbbb	bbbbb
aa	a
aaaa	aaa
aaaaaa	aaaaa
abba	ab
baab	ba
abbbba	aba
baaaab	bab
aabbaa	abab
abaaba	aabb
bbaabb	bbabba

If you study the sets of sequences, you may test yourself as to whether you have acquired the knowledge of this language by judging if the following novel sequences are grammatical or not: (1) *aaabbaaa*, (2) *abbba*, (3) *bbaaaabb*, (4) *abbabb*, and (5) *aaabbbbaaa*. If you have judged the odd-numbered strings as being grammatical and the even-numbered ones as being ungrammatical, you have indeed acquired knowledge of the language. If you have made some errors, think over the problem again. Then try to judge two more novel sequences: (6) *aaabbaaa* and (7) *aabaaaba*. If you find the former grammatical and the latter ungrammatical, chances are that you have now become a member of the *ab* language speech community. (Hint for those still in trouble: consider the idea of mirror image or symmetry.) Thus, if you were now asked to produce and judge *ab* language sentences which were longer than any of the ones which you had experienced, you could do so and would consequently possess abilities similar to those you possess for your own language.

The observable facts are, then, that certain strings of words are grammatical while others are ungrammatical. Now, the problem arises as to how to account for such data. Let us first attempt a solution in the spirit of the behaviorists. They would say that a speaker would have learned to form grammatical strings through the association of the words *a* and *b*. Thus, for example, if a speaker had experienced and remembered all grammatical and ungrammatical sequences of the *ab* language which are four words or less in length, such a speaker would then have stored the following knowledge:

Sequences beginning with *a*	Sequences beginning with *b*
*a	*b
a – a	*b – a
*a – b	b – b
*a – a – a	*b – a – a
*a – a – b	*b – a – b
*a – b – a	*b – b – a
*a – b – b	*b – b – b
a – a – a – a	*b – a – a – a
*a – a – a – b	b – a – a – b
*a – a – b – a	*b – a – b – a
*a – a – b – b	*b – a – b – b
*a – b – a – a	*b – b – a – a
*a – b – a – b	*b – b – a – b
a – b – b – a	*b – b – b – a
*a – b – b – b	b – b – b – b

Note: So as to conform to our example above, where sequences as long as six words were presented as basic data, this list would have to be expanded greatly. For the sake of simplicity, only sequences four words in length are used.

The above data may be summarized as follows into what behaviorist theorists refer to as associative networks, e.g. Staats (1968: 170).

Thus, in the network on the left, for example, there is: one 1-word string *a**, and that is marked as ungrammatical (for convenience sake, the ungrammatical marker * is placed following a sequence rather

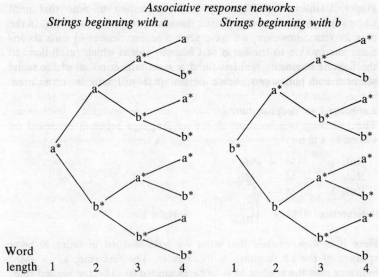

Associative response networks

Strings beginning with a   Strings beginning with b

Word length   1   2   3   4   1   2   3   4

than before it); two 2-word strings, *aa* and *ab**; four 3-word strings, *aaa**, *aab**, *aba**, *abb**; and eight 4-word strings, *aaaa, aaab**, *aaba**, *aabb**, *abaa**, *abab**, *abba, abbb**.

The problem for the associationist theorist is to explain, on the basis of the above data, the grammaticality of novel sequences which are longer than any before experienced. The main difficulty is that grammatical and ungrammatical strings do not combine through association to provide a predictable outcome. For example:

	Given	Add	Outcome
(1)	abbb*	ba*	abbbba
(2)	abbb*	bb	abbbbb*
(3)	abbb*	ab*	abbbab*
(4)	abba	ba*	abbaba*
(5)	abba	bb	abbabb*
(6)	bb	bb	bbbb

Here we see that when given an ungrammatical string, (1), (2), and (3), and an ungrammatical string is added, (1) and (3), the outcome is unpredictable, for the outcome string in (1) is grammatical while the outcome string in (3) is ungrammatical. Also, we see that when given a grammatical string, (4), (5), and (6), similar unpredictable outcomes occur, for when a grammatical string is added, (5) and (6), the outcome may be ungrammatical, as in (5), or grammatical, as in (6). No association theorist has ever been able to provide a solution to a problem such as this that is consistent with behavioristic precepts.

Despite such inadequacies in associationist theorizing and despite the formidable challenges of the Gestaltists and such eminent theorists as

Piaget, Lashley, and Vygotsky, it is interesting to note that until Chomsky came along, behavioristic theorizing continued to thrive. In the past 25 years, however, we have seen a severe decline in such theorizing, mainly due to the ideas of Chomsky, ideas which revolutionized the field of linguistics and have had a great impact on all of the social sciences and philosophy. Some of his ideas will now be considered.

Language knowledge acquired

The following is a solution to the *ab* language problem modelled on Chomsky's theory:

Rule 1   M → aMa
Rule 2   M → bMb
Rule 3   M → Ø

$$\text{Sentence} = M + \begin{bmatrix} \text{Rule 1} \\ \text{Rule 2} \end{bmatrix}^n + \text{Rule 3}$$

Here it is hypothesized that what we have learned in order to be a speaker of the *ab* language is three rules. The first rule, M → aMa, indicates that the symbol M is to be expanded to aMa; the second rule, M → bMb, indicates that the symbol M is to be expanded to bMb; the third and final rule, M → Ø, indicates that the symbol M is to be deleted. The symbol M may be conceived of as the notion of middle or midpoint. This abstract idea does not appear in any observed sentence of the *ab* language; only *a* or *b* appear as observed elements.

The construction of a sentence is made according to the basic sentence rule listed below the three rules. The symbol M is given as a beginning. To that symbol the Rules 1 or 2 may be applied in any order any number of times, after which Rule 3 applies. Sentences in the *ab* language are generated on the basis of this rule system.

Adequacy of the language knowledge

Let us test the adequacy of the rule system for the *ab* language. Suppose, we select Rule 2 + Rule 3 to be applied in accord with the formulation. The following would result:

Given	Apply	Outcome	Comment
M	Rule 2	bMb	The given M is expanded as bMb.
	Rule 3	bb	The M is deleted from the above string.

Let us apply Rule 2 + Rule 1 + Rule 3:

Given	Apply	Outcome	Comment
M	Rule 2	bMb	The given M is expanded to bMb.
	Rule 1	baMab	The M in bMb is expanded to aMa and the outside elements (b) are added to the sides.
	Rule 3	baab	M is deleted.

Let us apply Rule 2 + Rule 1 + Rule 2 + Rule 2 + Rule 1 + Rule 3:

M	Rule 2	bMb
	Rule 1	baMab
	Rule 2	babMbab
	Rule 2	babbMbbab
	Rule 1	babbaMabbab
	Rule 3	babbaabbab

As each Rule 1 or Rule 2 applies, M is expanded and the other surrounding elements are brought down. The result is a grammatical string of a length never before experienced. To test your ability to apply the rules, calculate what might be the output sentence for the following sequence of rules: Rule 1 + Rule 1 + Rule 2 + Rule 1 + Rule 2 + Rule 3. If your answer is *aababbabaa*, this is a good indication that you understand the operation of the rule governed system.

The above example demonstrates the power of a rule-governed system. It shows how a relatively simple system can generate an unlimited number of novel grammatical sentences of unlimited length. This system provides, in principle, the basis on which Chomsky and others have attempted to explain the language abilities for ordinary language. The next chapter will outline the grammatical theories of such theorists and consider their linguistic adequacy. The psychological adequacy of these proposals will be the topic of the succeeding chapter.

Summary

Various behaviorist oriented psychological and linguistic theories were assessed. These are Watson's *Word Association* theory, Staats' *Word Class Association* theory, and Skinner and Fries' *Sentence Frame* theories. All were found to be inadequate in explaining how speakers can produce and understand novel grammatical sentences independent of relevant environmental context and with no preset limit on length or number. The principle of association which all employed – word to word, word class to word class, or phrase to phrase – was shown to be insufficient for providing the necessary explanation.

The essence of Chomsky's rule system notion was demonstrated by means of an artificial language. It was determined that the rule system offered a viable mechanism that has the potential for providing a basis for explaining the language abilities of speakers. The description and assessment of the grammatical theory of Chomsky and others who employ the rule system notion were not considered in this chapter but are reserved for others which follow.

Notes

1. Even Conjunction + Conjunction and Article + Preposition combinations may occur, e.g. *He shouted but, and I wish to make this clear, not loud enough*, and *Appointed a member of the Privy Council by Kamehameha V, he had refused to attend meetings for the, to him, sufficient reason that they bored him!*' I recently came upon the latter sentence in a book on the history of Hawaii.

2. Staats is currently working on a revision of his theory which, aside from the principle of word association, includes a rule analysis in S–R terms. While such a relatively unabstract phenomenon such as affixation of a form of the plural morpheme (a *s*, *z*, or *iz* sound) to nouns can indeed be accounted for in behaviorist terms and regarded as a rule (Staats, 1971), abstract phenomena such as those which are involved in the deletion of a noun phrase in a complex sentence, e.g. *The girl sang and then danced* (where it is understood that *the girl* is also the subject of *dance* even though it does not appear), cannot be so accounted for without the operation of some sort of transformational rule of the kind which Chomsky proposes.

3. Actually, there is a third interpretation of the sentence which does involve vocabulary ambiguity. The word *shooting* has the meaning of *marksmanship*. Thus the sentence could mean that what was remembered was the marksmanship of Oswald.

4. The Immediate Constituent analysis which linguists applied in the 1950s is similarly unilluminating for such sentences. There is only one analysis which could be given to *Oswald's shooting is remembered*. A division would first be made between *shooting* and *is*, and then secondary divisions would be made between *Oswald's* and *shooting* and between *is* and *remembered*. Similarly, only one analysis can be given for both *John is easy to please* and *John is eager to please*. To assign such sentences the same analysis provides no insight into the true basic interrelations of constituents within the sentences.

Chapter 2

Chomsky's syntactic based grammar

This chapter will consider the grammatical ideas of Noam Chomsky as they are reflected in his recent *Trace Grammar* and less recent *Interpretive Semantics* theories. The following chapter (Semantic Based Grammar), which considers some opposing contemporary theories, will include a comparison and evaluation of Chomsky's basic ideas. In order to best comprehend Chomsky's current grammatical theorizing, it will be useful first to gain an understanding of a grammar which served as a forerunner of that theorizing, Chomsky's so-called *Standard Theory* or *Aspects' Theory* grammar (Chomsky, 1965). That grammar shall now be discussed in some detail.

Chomsky's Standard Theory

The sentence: subject and predicate
Consider the following sentences:

> *John laughed.*
> *The boy laughed.*
> *The little boy laughed.*
> *The little boy who played the ukulele laughed.*
> *The little boy who played the ukulele on the beach laughed.*

If you were asked to divide each sentence (S) into its most basic parts or constituents, you might analyze them as follows:

$$
\overset{\text{S}}{John \diagdown laughed}
$$

$$
\overset{\text{S}}{The\ boy \diagdown laughed}
$$

$$S$$
The little boy ⟍ *laughed*

$$S$$
The little boy who played the ukulele ⟍ *laughed*

$$S$$
The little boy who played the ukulele on the beach ⟍ *laughed*

You may feel, as does Chomsky, that each of the sentences may be divided as was shown into two basic constituents, one being *laughed* and the other (depending on the particular sentence) being *John, the boy, the little boy, the little boy who played the ukulele*, or *the little boy who played the ukulele on the beach*.

Suppose now you are asked to analyze the following sentences into their most basic constituents:

John laughed.
John laughed loudly.
John laughed loudly in the theater.
John laughed loudly in the theater at the joke.
John laughed loudly in the theater at the joke which Fred told.

You might divide them as Chomsky does:

$$S$$
John ⟍ *laughed*

$$S$$
John ⟍ *laughed loudly*

$$S$$
John ⟍ *laughed loudly in the theater*

$$S$$
John ⟍ *laughed loudly in the theater at the joke*

$$S$$
John ⟍ *laughed loudly in the theater at the joke which Fred told*

Again you might feel that each of the sentences may be divided into two basic constituents, one constituent being *John* and the other (depending on the sentence) being *laughed, laughed loudly, laughed loudly in the theater, laughed loudly in the theater at the joke*, or *laughed loudly in the theater at the joke which Fred told*.

Thus, each sentence is divisible into two basic constituents, one which has a noun (N), *John* or *boy*, at its core and another which has a verb (V), *laughed*, at its core. The constituent based on the noun traditionally is called the *subject* of the sentence while the constituent based on the verb is called the *predicate*, or as Chomsky terms it, the verb phrase. The basic noun and verb of a sentence may be elaborated to various extents. Around the noun *boy* we may have *little* or *who played the ukulele on the beach* and around the verb *laughed* we may have *loudly, in the theater, at the joke*, etc. To generalize, we may say that a subject of a sentence is represented by a noun phrase (NP) which consists of an N and, sometimes, other constituents. A predicate of a sentence may be said to be represented by a verb phrase (VP) which consists of a V and, sometimes, other constituents.

That a sentence (S) is composed of an NP and a VP may be illustrated with what is called a tree (branching) diagram:

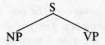

This same idea may be expressed in linguistic rule form as: S → NP + VP. Just what constituents may occur with an N or V in the NP and VP structure, is the topic of discussion of the next section.

The noun phrase

Often an article (*the, a*) or a pronominal determiner (*this, that, these, those*) may occur with a common noun (*boy, ship, dog*, etc.). Such grammatical classes are often referred to as determiners (D). One function of a determiner as in *this box* is to designate one member of the class which the common noun alone represents. In the case of a proper noun, such as *John*, which already designates a particular entity, or of a mass noun such as *milk*, determiners are not required.

The above information, that an NP is a structure which may consist of a D with an N or of an N alone, may be illustrated as follows:

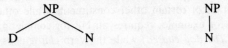

The first tree would adequately describe an NP like *the boy*, i.e.:

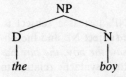

while the second would describe an NP like *John*, i.e.:

In rule form, this information may be combined into a single rule: NP → (D) + N. The parentheses indicate that the material enclosed may or may not occur, i.e. is optional. Thus, the expression of (D) indicates that D may or may not occur.

Another device which speakers may use to modify a noun is a sentence. For example, consider *The boy who laughed arrived, The boy who the girl kissed arrived, Harry pushed the boy who laughed,* and *Fred saw the boy who the girl kissed.* In all of these cases, we see that to the basic or head noun of *boy*, a sentence has been added, i.e. *who laughed* (representing the sentence *The boy laughed*) and *who the girl kissed* (representing the sentence *The girl kissed the boy*). Such modifying types of sentences are called relative clauses and they require that the NP in the modifying sentence which is the same as the head NP be made into a certain type of pronoun, e.g. *who*.

Summarizing the above information regarding determiners and sentences which may modify a noun, we have in rule form, according to Chomsky: NP → (D) + N + (S). Thus, every NP must contain an N, and, optionally it may be preceded by a D or followed by an S. Actually, this rule permits four different structures to occur: (1) N only, e.g. *Dentists fix teeth*; (2) D + N, e.g. *The dentist fixed the tooth*; (3) D + N + S, e.g. *The dentist who likes cheese telephoned*; and (4) N + S, e.g. *Dentists who like cheese are rare.*

The verb phrase

According to Chomsky, every sentence involves a verb which in turn is part of a larger unit, the verb phrase. This idea is expressed by the rule: VP → V. With respect to verbs, it is important to note that some require the addition of certain other constituents while others do not. The verb *chase*, for example, requires an NP for completion (*The dog chased the cat*, *The dog chased) while the verb *elapse* does not (*Much time elapsed*, **Much time elapsed the development*). Such a completion of the verb, in accord with tradition, is called the *direct object* of the verb.

A direct object, it should be noted, is an NP, just as a subject is. There is no difference in structure between the subject NP and the object NP, e.g. in *The boy jumped* and *The girl saw the boy, the boy* has the same NP structure. Where NPs differ is in their syntactic relation to the verb of the sentence. Because the object NP is thought by Chomsky to be more closely related to the verb and not as independent as the subject NP, it is regarded as forming a constituent with the verb. For example, in *The girl saw the boy*, the object NP of *the boy* is considered as forming a unit with *saw*, i.e. *saw the boy*. The subject and object NP relations with respect to the verb are shown in the following tree structure of that sentence:

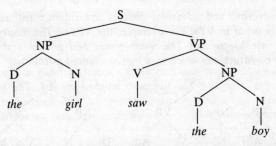

According to the tree structure, the NP which is the subject of the sentence (*the girl*) is immediately dominated by S, while the NP which is the direct object of the verb (*the boy*), is immediately dominated by VP.

Thus, the subject relation appears as:

$$\begin{array}{c} S \\ | \\ NP \end{array}$$

and, the direct object relation appears as:

$$\begin{array}{c} VP \\ | \\ NP \end{array}$$

The rule form for a verb with a direct object is, therefore: VP → V + NP.

Since, according to Chomsky, the complements of verbs are similar to objects in that they too form a close relation to the verb, such structures are shown in much the same way. For example, in *The police think a professor threw the bomb* the complement of the verb *think* is the sentence *a professor threw the bomb*:

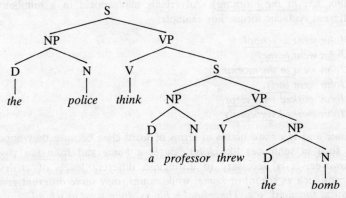

Thus, the rule form for a verb which takes a sentential complement is:

VP → V + S.

Adjectives, adverbs, and adverbial phrases are other constituents which frequently occur in VPs. For example, the VPs of *The money is blue, John became happy* and *The weather was bad* are all verb + adjective (Adj) constructions which may be represented as follows:

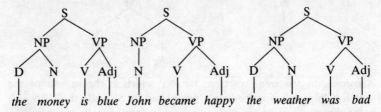

The rule form for a VP composed of a verb and an adjective thus would be:

VP → V + Adj.

Because a sentence may consist of only a verb and its subject NP, e.g. *John jumped*, structures such as the direct object NP, the sentential complement (S), or the adjective (Adj) appear only optionally in a sentence. This fact may be expressed in rule form as follows:

$$VP \rightarrow V + \begin{pmatrix} NP \\ S \\ Adj \end{pmatrix}$$

In describing the VP, one final important structure must be given consideration, the adverbial. Adverbials express such notions as 'manner' (*John ran quickly*), 'location' (*John ran to school*), and 'time' (*John ran in the morning*). Adverbials may appear in a number of different syntactic forms. For example:

John went to school.
John went home.
John went in the morning.
John went early.
John worked with vigor.
John worked vigorously.

Home and *vigor* are nouns in terms of word class because they appear as such in sentences like *John bought a home* and *John has vigor*. However, it is necessary to distinguish different levels of analysis. Words such as *school* or *home*, while nouns, may serve different grammatical *functions*, e.g. *The school is big* vs. *John went to school*.

Thus, adverbials in a sentence, hereafter called adverb phrases (AdvP), may appear as an NP alone (*home*), a preposition with an NP (*to school*) or a straight adverb (*vigorously*). Such information may be expressed in rule form as follows:

$$\text{AdvP} \rightarrow \begin{Bmatrix} \text{NP} \\ \text{PrepP} \\ \text{Adv} \end{Bmatrix}$$

The PrepP is a prepositional phrase which consists of a preposition and an NP. In rule form this is expressed as: PrepP → Prep + NP.

The VP rule which incorporates adverbials may therefore be expressed as follows:

$$\text{VP} \rightarrow \text{V} + \begin{pmatrix} \text{NP} \\ \text{S} \\ \text{Adj} \end{pmatrix} + (\text{AdvP}) + \ldots + (\text{AdvP})$$

This formulation indicates that adverbials optionally appear in sentences (there is none in *John jumped*) and that when they do one or more may appear. For example, a sentence like *The student danced gracefully at the disco on Monday* would be represented with the following tree structure:

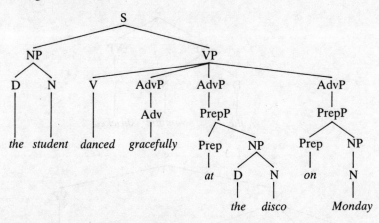

Operation of the system of base rules
The rules which have been used to describe sentence structures thus far are as follows:

1. S → NP + VP
2. NP → (D) + N + (S)
3. VP → V + $\begin{pmatrix} \text{NP} \\ \text{S} \\ \text{Adj} \end{pmatrix}$ + (AdvP) + ... + (AdvP)
4. AdvP → $\begin{Bmatrix} \text{NP} \\ \text{PrepP} \\ \text{Adv} \end{Bmatrix}$
5. PrepP → Prep + NP

It is important to note that a sort of loop may be created with respect to Rules 1 and 2, for example. Because the symbol S appears both on the input (left) side of Rule 1 (where S → NP + VP) and also on the output (right) side of part of Rule 2 (where NP → (D) + N + (S)), conditions are provided whereby Rule 1 can apply again to the S which Rule 2 generated. Rule 2 may then apply again after Rule 1, and so on. Such repetitive application has been termed a *recursive* process. Recursive loops can also be formed with the NP since it appears in both input and output positions. Such recursiveness allows for the infinite expansion of structures while at the same time maintaining well-formedness. The following sentences illustrate this principle of recursion: (1) *The vampire shrieked*; (2) *The vampire which attacks women shrieked*; and (3) *The vampire which attacks women who eat garlic shrieked*. In the second sentence, Rule 1 has been repeated once while in the third sentence it has been repeated twice, along with all the subsidiary rules. These structures may be represented as follows:[1]

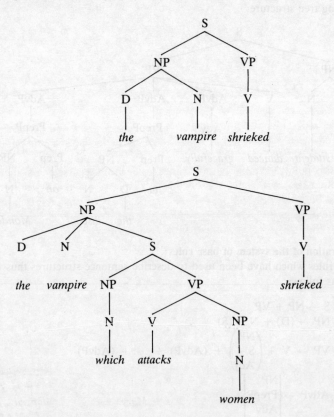

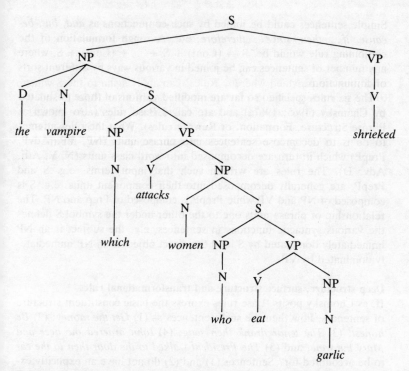

Further repetitions, of course, may also occur, e.g. *The vampire which attacks women who eat garlic which the Transylvanians grow in coffins that are moldy shrieked.*

At this point, it should be noted that, aside from recursiveness, there is another means which is provided for expansion and that is conjoining. For example, the sentences *John sang* and *Mary danced* could be combined to make a single complex sentence *John sang but Mary danced.* Such a sentence would be analyzed as follows:

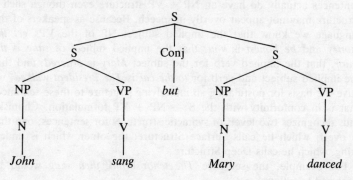

Simple sentences could be joined by such·conjunctions as *and, but, because, if... then, since... therefore*, etc. A rough formulation of the conjoining rule would be: S → (Conj) + S + ... + (Conj) + S, where any number of sentences can be joined in various ways by different sorts of conjunctions.

The six rules specified so far are modified versions of those postulated by Chomsky (1965; 1967a) and are called Base rules (also known as Phrase Structure, Formation, or Rewrite rules). What the rules attempt to do is to decompose sentences into phrase units (NP, VP, AdvP, PrepP) which in turn are decomposed into word class units (N, V, Adj, Adv, D). The rules are written such that input terms, e.g. S and PrepP, are generally decomposed into their component units, e.g. S is composed of NP and VP while PrepP is composed of Prep and NP. The relationship of phrase units one to the other under the symbol S defines the various syntactic functions in sentences, e.g. the subject is an NP immediately dominated by S, and the direct object is an NP immediately dominated by VP.

Deep structure, surface structure and transformational rules

If, as Chomsky posits, Base rules express the basic constituent structure of sentences, how then are such sentences as (1) *Get the money*; (2) *Be honest*; (3) *The tenor drank then sang*; (4) *John ordered the beer and Mary the wine*; and (5) *The President walked to the door then to the car* to be accounted for? Sentences (1) and (2) do not have an explicitly expressed subject NP for the verbs *get* and *be*, nor is there a subject NP for *sang* in the second conjoined sentence in Sentence (3). Sentence (4) does not have a verb for *Mary* in the second conjoined sentence and Sentence (5) has neither a subject nor a verb for the second conjoined sentence where only an adverbial phrase *to the car* follows the conjunction *then*.

Chomsky's explanation of what seem to be counter-examples to his basic S → NP + VP formulation is an insightful one. He holds that all sentences actually do have an NP + VP structure even though such a structure may not appear overtly in speech. Because as speakers of the language we know that the implied subject NP of the VPs *get the money* and *be honest* is *you*, that the implied subject of *sang* is *the tenor*, that the implied verb for the subject *Mary* is *ordered*, and that the implied subject and verb for *to the car* is *The President walked*, we have the basis for postulating an underlying structure to these sentences that is in conformity with the S → NP + VP formulation. Chomsky thus recognizes two levels of syntactic structures for sentences, one that is overt, which he calls Surface Structure; the other which is underlying, which he calls Deep Structure.

For example, the sentence *The tenor drank then sang* would be analyzed as follows:

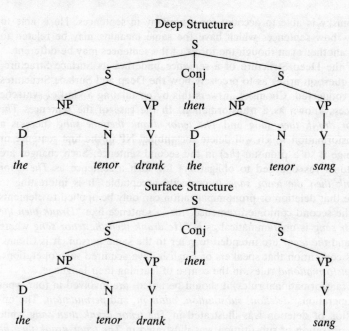

Deep Structure

Surface Structure

Thus, the Surface Structure has the NP of the second of the conjoined sentences deleted. Incidentally, consider how a sentence like *The tenor drank then he sang* might be analyzed (assuming that the person doing the singing is the same person who was doing the drinking). What would the Deep Structure be? According to Chomsky it would be the same Deep Structure as shown for *The tenor drank then sang*. However, the Surface Structure would be different. It would be:

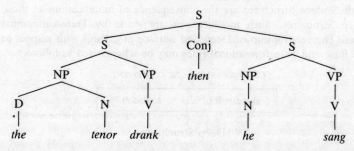

Surface Structure

Thus, while the two different sentences *The tenor drank then sang* and *The tenor drank then he sang* are assigned the same Deep Structure, they are assigned different Surface Structures. It is by this device that

Chomsky is able to account for synonymy in sentences. He is able to show how sentences which have the same meaning may be related to one another even though the forms of the sentences may be different.

If the Deep Structure of a sentence underlies its Surface Structure, the question arises as to precisely how the Deep and Surface Structures are connected. Chomsky answers this by postulating a kind of syntactic process known as a transformation. In the case of the sentences *The tenor drank then sang* and *The tenor drank then he sang* there is a transformation which will delete the subject NP in the first sentence or change it to a pronoun (*he*) in the second sentence. Such changes are optional (as opposed to obligatory) for such a sentence as *The tenor drank then the tenor sang* is perfectly acceptable. It is interesting to note that deletion or pronominalization can only be applied to elements in the second conjoined sentence, for, a sentence like **Drank then the tenor sang* is ungrammatical as is **He drank then the tenor sang* where *he* and *the tenor* are intended to refer to the same person. It is Chomsky's contention that speakers of English have acquired such operations, *Transformational* rules, in the course of learning their language.

Transformational rules, it should be noted, are involved in four types of operations: *deletion, substitution, addition,* and *permutation.* The operation of deletion was illustrated in *The tenor drank then sang* while the operation of substitution was illustrated in *The tenor drank then he sang* (a pronoun substitution). Addition will occur with certain negations or questions, e.g. the auxiliary *do* must be added in sentences like *The President did not lie* and *Did the President lie?* but not in ones like *The President is not happy* and *Is the President happy?* Permutation will occur with adverbials. *John sent the message quickly, Quickly John sent the message,* and *John quickly sent the message* are examples of such shifting or permutation.

Thus, according to the model, Deep Structures result from the application of Base rules and the insertion of lexical (vocabulary) items while Surface Structures are the consequence of modifications to those Deep Structures. Such modifications are made by Transformational rules. The relationship of Deep and Surface Structures with respect to the Base and Transformational rules may be schematized as follows:

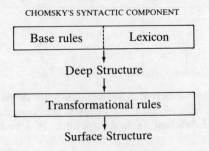

CHOMSKY'S SYNTACTIC COMPONENT

Base rules	Lexicon

Deep Structure

Transformational rules

Surface Structure

Chomsky's syntactic component of a grammar thus consists of two distinct sets of rules (Base and Transformational) with two resulting levels of structure (Deep and Surface). The Base rules permit an infinite number of Deep Structures to be generated. The Transformational rules function to render Deep Structures (which underlie sentences) into Surface Structures, which form the basis of observed speech. (For one specification and discussion of Chomsky's Base and Transformational rules, see Burt, 1971.)

Transformational rules serve to explain synonymy, ambiguity, and understood (deleted) elements in sentences and ensure that only well-formed Surface Structures will result after their application to Deep Structure. As an infinite number of Deep Structures may be generated by the set of Base Rules, so too may an infinite number of Surface Structures be generated through the application of Transformational rules to Deep Structures. It is through these essential devices, Base rules, Deep Structure, Transformational rules and Surface Structure that Chomsky attempts to make some contribution in accounting for the basic abilities of speakers.

At this point, clarification must be made as to the nature of the representation of the lexical items which appear in Surface and Deep Structures. Although orthographic representations of lexical items have been shown in the tree diagrams, what actually should have been shown is a type of sound representation. For, the immediate goal of linguistics is a description of the grammar of speech. The orthographic representations have been used for practical rather than theoretical reasons – they are more readily recognized by novices. An introduction to the sound system aspects of the grammar (phonology and phonetics) will form the basis of discussion in the section which follows.

Before moving on to that section, a word of caution should perhaps be injected here about Chomsky's notion of Surface Structure. Although the term *surface* is involved such a structure is nonetheless quite abstract. One might think Surface Structure is observed speech but this is not the case. It does not represent the pronunciation of a sentence. For example, suppose the Surface Structure of the sentence *Mares eat oats* is:

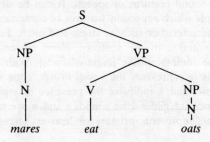

Apart from the words *mares, eat,* and *oats* none of the rest of the structure occurs in speech. That *mares* is the subject and *eat oats* is the predicate, with *oats* the direct object of *eat* is not explicitly stated for actual speech consists only of sounds. A syntactic structure obviously does not appear directly in speech but is rather an abstract construction of the mind. 'Surface' and 'Deep' are terms which involve varying levels of abstraction, one of which is relatively deeper or more abstract than the other.

Similarly, a word of caution should be noted here regarding Deep Structure. For Chomsky, such a structure is syntactic and not semantic. Consider, for example, the sentence *The needle hurt John.* While a Deep Structure syntactic analysis would provide something like

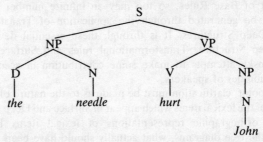

such an analysis is quite remote from its meaning or semantic interpretation. For such a sentence indicates that (1) two separate events were involved. 'The needle in some unspecified action' and 'John experienced pain'; and (2) the two separate events were related as cause and effect, the former event being the cause of the latter. How Chomsky accounts for the meaning of sentences in his model will be discussed in a later section of this chapter.

The phonological component
Just as a sentence is conceived of having two levels of syntactic structure so, too, is it conceived of having two systematic levels of sound. One of these speech levels is called *phonetic*, the other *phonemic*. The phonetic level of description is essentially based on a very careful listening to the sound features of speech. It can be described using a system of symbols which represent features of consonants, vowels, and other speech characteristics such as stress and pitch. For example, the phonetic representation of the sentence *Mares eat oats* when spoken quickly might be something like [mérzìydhôwts]. With regard to some of those symbols: *e* represents the vowel in *wet, i* the vowel in *key, o* the vowel in *flow,* and *h* indicates the presence of aspiration (expired air); *y* and *w* indicate glides (the sounds *i* and *o* are not abruptly cut off), the symbol ´ represents primary or heaviest stress, ˆ represents a

secondary or lesser stress, and ` represents tertiary or weakest stress. The square brackets [ ] around the entire string of symbols is a convention which indicates that the phonetic sound level is being described.

The phonemic level, on the other hand, is more abstract and oriented to particular languages. According to Chomsky, Halle, and others, it provides the basis for the phonetic level of speech. Thus, while the phonetic representation of *Mares eat oats* is [merziydhowts] (stress and intonation omitted), the phonemic representation might be /#merz#it#ots#/.[2] Around this string of symbols is a set of the slashes //. These indicate that a phonemic sound level is being described. The # sign indicates a word boundary. As might be expected, linguists differ greatly as to what the phonemic form of items should be. (See Chomsky & Halle, 1968; or Schane, 1971, for example, or Steinberg & Krohn, 1975, for a critical discussion of some of these issues.)

It is the phonemic representations of lexical items which appear in both Deep and Surface Structures. Thus, the Surface Structure of *Mares eat oats* would include the phonemic representation of each of its lexical items, i.e.:

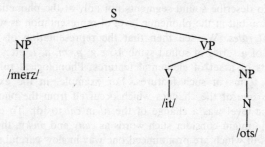

The change from phonemic to phonetic sound levels is accomplished by means of *Phonological* rules. Such rules specify how Surface Structures (syntactic structure with lexical items described in phonemic terms) are to be treated so as to result in a phonetic sound pattern. In the example sentence, for instance, phonological rules must at least perform the following operations: merge the phonemic sound patterns of the three individual words /merz/, /it/, and /ots/ into a single unit, change the *t* in /it/ to *d*, add *h* (aspiration) to *d*, add the glides *y* and *w* to the vowels of /i/ and /o/, and assign a stress pattern of ´ˆ ˆ to the whole string of sounds. By the time all phonological changes have been made, none of the original syntactic structures in the tree remains – only a string of phonetic elements which is essentially the pronunciation of the sentence is the result.

Sound feature analysis. Thus far, sound segments such as consonants and vowels have been represented by individual symbols, e.g. *p*, *b*, *i*, and *o*, undoubtedly giving the impression that indivisible entities are involved. Actually, such an impression is a misleading one for each sound segment (phonemic or phonetic) can be fruitfully regarded as being comprised of a set of atomic-like elemental sound features. Just as in physics, where matter which is unitary or whole at one level may be decomposed into constituent elements at another level, so too may a sound segment be decomposed into constituent components. Thus, we recognize that sounds like /s/ and /z/ share something in common, a continuous frication or hissing (a *continuant* feature), while /t/ and /d/ share something else in common, a sharp burst (a *stop* feature). On the other hand, the sounds /z/ and /d/ also have a feature in common that /s/ and /t/ do not share; /z/ and /d/ both greatly involve the use of vocal chords (a *voiced* feature) while /s/ and /t/ do not.

There are a number of other features which are said to comprise these consonantal sounds, and serve to distinguish them from other consonants and from vowels. (For a specification of the features for all speech sounds and for a discussion of their role in phonological rules, see Chomsky and Halle, 1968 or, for a more concise and understandable treatment, Schane, 1973.) The distinctive phonetic features posited are intended to describe sound segments not only at the phonetic level of representation but at the phonemic level of representation as well.

Phonological rules. We see then that the representation of lexical items consists of a series of sound symbols, e.g. *p, m, a, i,* etc., which in turn consists of a set of elemental features. Phonological rules are formulated in terms of such features. For example, in the example *Mares eat oats* one of the changes which occurred from the phonemic to the phonetic level was a change of the /t/ in *eat* to [d]. To explain this change one might consider such words as *catty* and *picky*, the middle consonants of which are pronounced one way in slow careful speech but in another way in conversation. Such unvoiced sounds tend to become voiced in the speech of ordinary conversation so that such words might become similar to the pronunciation of words like *caddy* and *piggy*. A consideration of these and other data seem to show that an unvoiced consonant tends to become voiced when it is both preceded and followed by a vowel. Such a phenomenon then is incorporated into the grammar as a phonological rule. The reason why such a rule will apply in a case like *eat oats* is because in rapid speech the two words are spoken together without a pause, as if they were a single word. That being the case, the /t/ in *eat* will have a vowel /o/ immediately following it. That, in addition to the /i/ vowel which precedes the /t/, provides the necessary condition for the phonological rule to apply.

Phonological rules comprise Chomsky's *Phonological Component* of the grammar, the purpose of such rules being the conversion of Surface Structures to Phonetic Representations. The relationship of Surface Structure, Phonological rules, and Phonetic Representation may be illustrated by the following schema:

CHOMSKY'S PHONOLOGICAL COMPONENT

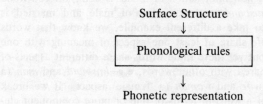

Surface Structure
↓

Phonological rules

↓

Phonetic representation

It must be noted that neither of the two levels of sound structure, phonemic or phonetic, is a description of the actual physical sound signal. Both are *psychological* rather than physical levels. The physical speech signal, which is described in terms of the physical properties of sound waves, e.g. frequency, amplitude, and duration, is very complex. The individual consonants and vowels which we perceive so clearly in speech do not appear as individual segments on a sound spectogram. An intricate complex blending is what is seen instead.

The lexicon
The lexicon, a part of the Base, is a crucial part of that sub-component. It is like a dictionary, consisting of a number of lexical entries. Entries are mainly morphemes, which are minimal strings of phonemic sound segments that carry a meaning. For example, the words *longer* and *longest* are each composed of two morphemes, /long/ and /er/, and /long/ and /est/, respectively. The word *mares* is also composed of two morphemes /mer/ and /z/ (the plural morpheme), as is *blackberry* which is composed of the morphemes /blæk/ and /beri/. Words are composed of one or more morphemes. While the word *elephant*, for example, is composed of a single morpheme, the word *antidisestablishmentarianism* is composed of at least seven. The morpheme is not to be confused with the syllable, a unit which is wholly sound based. The word *elephant* is instructive in this regard for, although it consists of three syllables, it is only a single morpheme.

Associated with each lexical entry is a variety of information. For example, the entry for *mare* might be: /mer/, Noun, +Animate, −Human, +Equine, +Female. Three types of information are provided here: the phoneme sequence provides phonological information; the Noun provides some syntactic information; while the features +Animate, etc. provide semantic information. (See Fillmore, 1971, for a discussion of types of lexical information.) The last type of information, semantic, will now be discussed.

Semantic feature analysis. First let us consider the meaning of nouns and why it is necessary to decompose their meaning into parts. Suppose we were to regard the meaning of a noun as an undifferentiated whole where each noun is considered to be uniquely different from every other noun. If so, we would not be able to explain how it is that in *This person is a man* new information of 'male' is being offered while in *This person is a husband* new information of 'male' and 'married' is being offered. Or, to take a different example, we know that words like *husband* and *wife* share at least one· aspect of meaning with one another ('married') but yet these same words share different aspects of meaning when compared with other words, e.g. *husband* and *man* (a 'male' aspect), and *wife* and *woman* (a 'female' aspect). If we break down the meaning of a word in terms of one or more component elements (much the same idea as sound segments being composed of features), we can explain how speakers recognize the similarity relations among words and how the meanings of words combine to provide the meaning of sentences. The notion of semantic features was developed in detail by Katz and Fodor (1963) and formed the basis of their semantic rules. These semantic rules later provided the foundation for the semantic component of Chomsky's grammar.

To gain a deeper understanding of the atomistic notion of meaning, consider a set of 10 nouns, *person, man, woman, spouse, husband, wife, sheep, ram, ewe,* and *chair.* It immediately becomes evident that certain of these words share elements or features in common. For example, with regard to the semantic dimension of sex, the words *man, husband,* and *ram* share a 'male' feature while *woman, wife,* and *ewe* share a 'female' feature. The words *person, spouse,* and *sheep,* on the other hand, are different in that sex is not specified. We might say that they share an 'either male or female' feature. As for *chair,* since sex is completely irrelevant for it, it would not be coded at all on this dimension, in effect being assigned a 'neither male nor female' feature.

The meaning of nouns, to a great extent, may be characterized by such codings on a number of semantic dimensions. The 10 nouns, for instance, may be differentiated from one another on the basis of four semantic dimensions: animateness (A), humanness (H), sex (S), and marriage (M). The basic meaning features which comprise each semantic dimension are: 'animate' (+) and 'inanimate' (−) for A, 'human' (+) and 'animal' (−) for H, 'female' (+) and 'male' (−) for S, and 'married' (+) and 'single' (−) for M. The basic features of a dimension (symbolized by + and −) are at once complementary and conflicting (antonymous). They are complementary in that the two features define the dimension, and they are conflicting in that the assertion of one feature implies the denial of the other. Thus, for example, the dimension of sex is defined by the features of 'male' and 'female.' The assertion of the feature 'male' implies the denial of the feature 'female,' and vice versa. In some cases, like that of color, more than two basic features may comprise a dimension, i.e. red, blue, green, etc.

Using semantic features, we may say that the meaning of the word *spouse*, for example, is specified by the coding +A +H vS and +M, where +A represents the feature of 'animateness,' +H represents 'human,' vS represents 'either male or female' (the symbol v indicating 'either...or...') and +M represents 'married.' (*Spouse* is a single morpheme, incidentally.) The meaning of the word *ram* on the other hand, would be represented as +A, –H, –S, and xM, where xM represents 'neither married nor single' (the symbol x indicating 'neither... nor...').[3] (Empirical validation for the assignment of these features is provided by Steinberg, 1975a.) It should be noted that, although four dimensions fully differentiate the 10 items from one another, such dimensions do not completely exhaust the meanings of these words.

Semantic features may be usefully regarded as representing elemental properties, relations, actions, or states, i.e. semantic predicates which are characteristics of an entity. Whether this entity is as concrete as a shoe or as abstract as an idea, semantic predicates or features may be used to describe it.

Verbs and adjectives, too, may be viewed as comprised of predicates, see e.g. Engelkamp (1975). Some may express a single elemental predicate while others may express more than one. The verb *cause* and the adjective *male*, for example, each seems to be composed of a single predicate. The verb *die*, on the other hand, is considered by many linguists to be a complex predicate being composed of at least two elemental predicates 'not' and 'live.' The verb *kill* is thought to be even more complex since it would include the predicate 'cause' as well as 'not' and 'live.' It may be that the meanings of such verbs are specifiable in terms of structures similar to trees. (For a discussion of issues relating to the representation of such lexical items, see McCawley, 1971; Postal, 1970; or Bierwisch, 1971.)

The meanings of lexical items are part of Deep Structure, along with their phonological specification.[4] Thus, for example, the lexical item *mare* might be represented in a Deep Structure tree as something like:

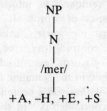

$$\text{NP}$$
$$|$$
$$\text{N}$$
$$|$$
$$\text{/mer/}$$
$$|$$
$$\text{+A, –H, +E, +S}$$

(The coding of +E represents the semantic feature of 'equine.') While the semantic specification of lexical items does not play a great role in the application of Transformation and Phonological rules, such a specification does play a critical role in the application of Semantic rules. Such rules comprise what Chomsky calls the *Semantic Component*.

The semantic component
The final component in Chomsky's grammar is the semantic component. As was noted earlier, its development began with the work of
Katz and Fodor. Continued development within the Chomskyan syntac-
tic-based framework has largely been carried on by Katz (1972). The
function of the semantic component is to provide a semantic interpretation for Deep Structures. This is carried out by the means of Semantic
rules. The Semantic Interpretation or Representation which results
from the application of these rules makes manifest the various semantic
aspects of a sentence. This section will consider some of the semantic
rules involved in the determination of such semantic aspects as the information and truth value of sentences.

Word meaning and sentence meaning. It is important first to recognize that the meaning of words is not the same as the meaning of sentences. While sentences such as (1) *This person is a man* and (2) *This
man is a person* are both composed of exactly the same words, they do
not have the same meaning. An English speaker knows that, at a literal
level, the first offers new information while the second does not. We
may say that the former has an *informative* (or synthetic) interpretation
while the latter has a *redundant* (or analytic) interpretation.

Furthermore, Sentence (1) evidently expresses an idea (proposition)
that may be either true or false, depending on the situation in the environment, while (2) appears to be true by virtue of the meaning of the
words involved. The truth of the proposition in (2), thus, does not
seem to be contingent upon context, given appropriate usage. And,
just as there are sentences which express propositions that are true independently of context, so, too, are there ones that are false independently of context. Such a proposition as that expressed by (3) *This wife
is a husband* is false, given the usual literal meaning of the constituent
words. It may also be said to be *contradictory* since conflicting information is offered.

Such characteristics of sentences as information or truth value are
obviously not characteristics of words. It makes no sense to ask
whether an individual word, e.g. *horse, vacate, the, with, thought, cold*
is informative, redundant, contradictory, true, false, etc. Rather, when
we consider the meaning of words, we consider their elemental constituents, such as was described in the semantic feature analysis.

Semantic rules. Why is it that some sentences are informative while
others are redundant or contradictory? In this regard, let us consider
the three sentences mentioned above. Given the constant syntactic
structure for each, *This _____ is a _____*, it is clear that the
differing interpretations must be a function of the interaction of the
meanings of the nouns which filled those slots, since these are the only
elements which vary. This being the case, let us consider the three
sentences, with their component nouns analyzed in terms of semantic

features. The analysis for the noun on the left is shown below in terms of features on the right. For example, *person* is + on both A and H while v on both S and M. The letters A, H, S, and M represent the semantic dimensions of animateness, humanness, sex, and marriage, respectively. The codings are such that +A represents the feature 'animate,' –A = 'inanimate,' +H = 'human,' –H = 'animal,' +S = 'female,' –S = 'male,' +M = 'married' and –M = 'single.' The v coding represents 'either + or –.'

	A	H	S	M	
(1) *This person*	+	+	v	v	
is a man	+	+	–	v	
	Ø	Ø	NEW	Ø	= Informative, True or False
(2) *This man*	+	+	–	v	
is a person	+	+	v	v	
	Ø	Ø	Ø	Ø	= Redundant, True
(3) *This wife*	+	+	+	+	
is a husband	+	+	–	+	
	Ø	Ø	CON	Ø	= Contradictory, False

Inspection of the feature coding combinations shows that certain patterns of feature combinations result in distinctive sentence interpretations. We see that for Sentence (2), which has a redundant interpretation, combinations of + +, + +, vv, and –v, occur on the various semantic dimensions, while for (1), which has an informative result, combinations of + +, vv, and v– occur. These combinations appear vertically in the schema above. The first coding of a combination represents the feature for the subject noun while the seond represents the feature for the predicate noun on the same dimension. Since the two sentences differ only with regard to the –v and v– combinations, it would appear that a v– combination is the basis for a result of new information (symbolized by NEW), while –v (along with + + + + vv) is the basis for (along with + + + + vv) a result of no new information (symbolized by Ø). A third type of feature interaction is one that occurs in Sentence (3). Here, a distinctive + – combination evidently is the basis for a conflicting information result (symbolized by CON) and an interpretation of contradictory and false.

Clearly a set of rules may be formulated on the basis of semantic feature combinations and patterns that will acount for sentence interpretations relating to information and truth value. (See Steinberg, 1975a, for a formulation of such rules.) Such Semantic rules and many others would be included in the semantic component. Such rules function to provide a Semantic Interpretation (also known as a Semantic Representation) for a Deep Structure.

The relations concerning Deep Structure, Semantic rules, and Semantic Representation are illustrated in the following schema:

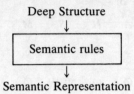

CHOMSKY'S SEMANTIC COMPONENT

Deep Structure
↓

Semantic rules

↓
Semantic Representation

Thus, on the basis of a syntactic structure which includes a semantic specification of lexical items, i.e. Deep Structure, Semantic rules are applied in order to derive the various aspects of the meaning of the sentence as a whole, i.e. to determine its Semantic Representation.

It should be noted that, while in Chomsky's theory the content of Semantic Representation may be universal to all languages, the content of Deep (and Surface) Structure is not. Such syntactic structures are language specific. For example, consider the Deep Structure of the English sentence *The boy ran to school*. According to Chomsky, the Deep Structure would include an article (*the*), a preposition (*to*) and a prepositional phrase (*to the school*). Since many languages do not have these constituents, they would not appear in the Deep Structure of those languages.

Summary
According to Chomsky, the grammar of a language establishes a relationship between sound and meaning, i.e. between Phonetic Representation and Semantic Representation. To discover this grammar is the primary goal of linguistics. One of Chomsky's attempts to accomplish this goal (Chomsky, 1965) is the Standard Theory grammar which has been outlined in the preceding pages. On the following page a schema of this grammar is shown.

We note that the grammar consists of three distinct components: the *syntactic* component, which consists of a Lexicon and two types of syntactic rules, the Base and the Transformational, the *phonological* component, which consists of Phonological rules, and the *semantic* component, which consists of Semantic rules. The syntactic component is given a primary determining role with the other two components serving secondary or interpretive roles, i.e. it is the syntactic Deep and Surface Structures which determine how the Phonetic and the Semantic

CHOMSKY'S STANDARD THEORY GRAMMAR

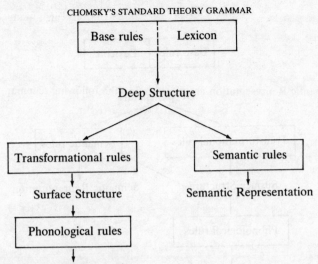

Representations shall be interpreted. This organization of the grammar reflects Chomsky's claim that syntax is 'autonomous' and independent of semantics.

Interpretive Semantics grammar

Interpretive Semantics (also known as the Extended Standard Theory) grammar which is based on a modification of the Standard Theory was developed by Chomsky (1971) and elaborated by Jackendoff (1972). The change involves a revision of the relationship of Surface Structure to Semantic Representation and the function of Transformational rules in introducing new meaning. Chomsky now sees Surface Structure serving as input to the semantic component as well as continuing to serve as input to the phonological component. Thus, the following schematic relations obtain:

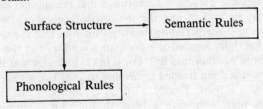

All other relationships among the various components remain unchanged. The resulting grammar, termed Interpretive Semantics, may be represented by the following schema:

CHOMSKY'S INTERPRETIVE SEMANTICS GRAMMAR

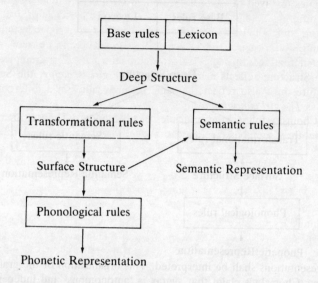

One principal reason that the Standard Theory was modified was to accommodate differences in meaning that are exhibited by emphasis. For example, consider the following sentences. (Capitalization of a word indicates that it receives main stress and serves as the point of maximal inflection of the pitch contour, i.e. it is the emphasis focus of the sentence).

(1) *Did John hand the book to* BILL?
(2) *Did John hand the* BOOK *to Bill?*
(3) *Did John* HAND *the book to Bill?*

To these questions, the following answers would be appropriate:

For (1) *No, he handed the book to Fred.*
For (2) *No, he handed the pen to Bill.*
For (3) *No, he mailed the book to Bill.*

Different semantic presuppositions (ideas that the speaker may hold to be true) may be said to underlie the original questions. Focus in (1), according to one interpretation, indicates the idea that the speaker presupposes that John handed the book to someone, but the speaker is uncertain as to whether it is Bill. Focus in (2) indicates that the speaker presupposes that John handed something to Bill, but is uncertain as to whether it was a book. Finally, focus in (3) indicates that the speaker presupposes that John gave a book to Bill, but is uncertain as to whether it was handed to him. Clearly, the meanings of these sentences are different depending on where emphasis is placed.

The essential problem which these data pose for Chomsky is what the Deep Structures of the sentences are to be. In particular, are they to receive the same or different Deep Structures? According to the principles involved in Chomsky's Standard Theory grammar, sentences with different meanings are to be assigned different Deep Structures and one function of Transformational Rules is to keep constant the meaning of a sentence from Deep to Surface Structure, i.e. new meaning is not added through Transformational rules. For example, if a Deep Structure reflects a meaning like *The girl is happy*, the Surface Structure must also reflect the same meaning and not a different one such as *The girl is not happy*.[5]

If Chomsky follows the principles of his Standard Theory, then each of the three emphasis sentences above would be assigned different Deep Structures since they have different meanings, and the Transformational rules would then maintain those same meaning distinctions in Surface Structure. (Some sort of emphasis marker must appear in the Surface Structure so as to allow for the Phonological rules to assign intonational stress for the Phonetic Representation.) Now, if different meanings are to be reflected in the Deep Structure for these sentences, the source of such distinctions must be through the Base rules since it is the Base rules which construct (along with lexical items) Deep Structures.

Focus or emphasis markers (f) would have to be included in the Base rules. The result of this, however, would make Base rules appear very odd since with every noun, verb, adjective, adverb, and even prepositions (*Did John walk to school?*) a focus marker could optionally appear, e.g. $N+(f)$, $V+(f)$, etc. This is perhaps one reason why Chomsky decided that such a course of action would lead to 'great artificiality' in the specification of Deep Structures (Chomsky, 1971: 201).

What Chomsky decided to do was to allow focus markers to be inserted by Transformational rules. The result of this was that a Surface Structure with a focus marker could have a different meaning from the Deep Structure that did not contain such a marker. Such being the case, if the meaning of a sentence were to be properly specified in the Semantic Representation, it would be necessary for the Surface Structure to serve as input to the Semantic rules. For, if only the Deep Structure served as input (as in the Standard Theory), then the meaning focus which appeared only in the Surface Structure would not be reflected in the Semantic Representation. It is for this reason that Chomsky decided to allow both Deep and Surface Structures to serve as input to the Semantic rules. The resulting model of grammar, with some Transformational rules introducing new meaning and with Surface Structure serving as input to Semantic rules, has been called the Interpretative Semantics Grammar.[6]

In passing, it might be mentioned that another feature which Chomsky and his proponents, e.g. Jackendoff (1977), introduced into the Interpretive Semantics framework was a so-called *lexicalist* treatment of nominalizations.

Thus, in a complex NP such as *John's refusal to go* in a sentence like

John's refusal to go surprised Mary, the early treatment by Chomskyans was to provide a Deep Structure analysis for that NP essentially like:

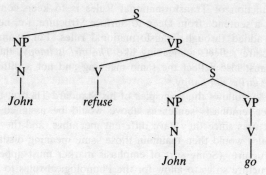

According to this analysis, a Transformational rule would apply to this Deep Structure to change it to an NP where, among other changes, the verb *refuse* is changed into the noun *refusal* for the Surface Structure. Similar verb to noun transformations would be required for such items as *destroy-destruction*, *hate-hatred*, *explode-explosion*, and *admire-admiration*. For a number of reasons (Chomsky, 1970; Jackendoff, 1972), one being that transformations which can change grammatical classes (e.g. verb to noun) are much too powerful, it was decided that the Deep Structure of an NP such as *John's refusal to go* should be something like:

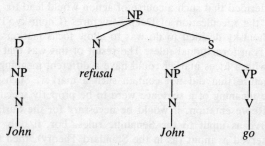

In effect, *John* becomes a kind of determiner for the *noun* refusal. Transformational rules will then be applied to this Deep Structure (e.g. add possessive to the determiner NP of *John* in order to generate *John's*) so that the desired Surface Structure will result. It should be noted that this lexical approach to nominalizations has been included in all of Chomsky's theorizing since its introduction and is included in his most recent theory, that of Trace Grammar.

Trace grammar

Chomsky's most recent theorizing (Chomsky, 1975a; 1975b) abolishes the connection between Deep Structure and the Semantic component. Instead, we find that Surface Structure alone determines how the meaning of a sentence is to be interpreted. As Chomsky (1975b: 82) puts it, 'all semantic information is determined by a somewhat enriched notion of surface structure.' Because the meaning-determining role now rests solely with Surface Structure, we find that Surface Structure is no longer as simple as it once was. For, included in such a structure are now *traces*. A notation of traces ensures that Surface Structure will be sufficiently detailed so that all of the meaning of the original sentence can be derived. Essentially, traces are markers which identify Transformational rules which have been applied to Deep Structure. By 'enriching' Surface Structure with Deep Structure traces, for semantic interpretation, Chomsky no longer requires Deep Structure to serve as input to the Semantic component as was necessary in his Interpretive Semantics Theory. A schema of Chomsky's Trace Grammar follows:

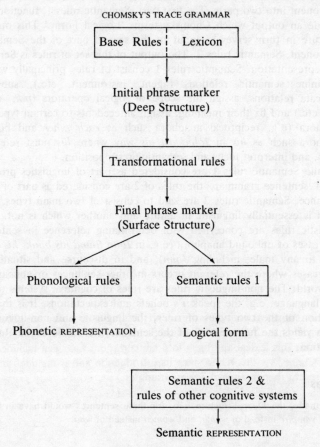

CHOMSKY'S TRACE GRAMMAR

Base Rules ┆ Lexicon

Initial phrase marker
(Deep Structure)

Transformational rules

Final phrase marker
(Surface Structure)

Phonological rules   Semantic rules 1

Phonetic REPRESENTATION   Logical form

Semantic rules 2 &
rules of other cognitive systems

Semantic REPRESENTATION

As an illustration of a trace, *t*, consider one of Chomsky's own examples:

Sentence: *John seems to be a nice fellow.*
Deep Structure: *Y (someone) seems [John to be a nice fellow]*_S
Surface Structure: *John seems [t to be a nice fellow]*_S

For the correct semantic interpretation of the sentence, it is essential that the Surface Structure indicate that *John* is the subject of the embedded sentence S, *to be a nice fellow.* According to Chomsky (1975b: 96), 'The position of the bound trace [*t*] in the Surface Structure allows us to determine the grammatical relation of "John" as subject of the embedded sentence.' Presumably, traces and Transformational rules would have to be numbered, so that the traces would be able to relate to the proper Transformational rules.

As an additional change, Chomsky breaks up his original Semantic component into two parts. The first part, Semantic rules 1, functions to provide an output which Chomsky terms 'Logical Form.' This output structure in turn serves as input to the second part of the Semantic component, Semantic rules 2. The output of this set of rules is Semantic Representation. Semantic rules 1 consist of rules principally which determine semantic relations (agent, instrument, etc.), subject-predicate relations, assign the scope of logical operators (*not, each, who,* etc.) and fix their meaning, assign antecedents to certain types of anaphora (e.g. reciprocal anaphora such as *each other* and bound anaphora such as *his* in *John lost his way* where *his* must refer to *John*), and interpret focus and semantic presupposition.

While Semantic rules 1 are considered as part of linguistics proper, i.e. of 'sentence grammar,' the rules of 2 are considered as part of performance. Semantic rules 2 are said to consist of two main types, one which is essentially linguistic in nature and another which is not. The linguistic rules are concerned with determining reference in sentence level cases of unbound anaphora (e.g. in *John found his book, his* may refer to any male, including *John*), and in discourse and situational level cases where the referent occurs in other sentences or appears in the world. The non-linguistic rules are rules of cognitive systems other than language, e.g. the speaker's beliefs and expectations. It is the interaction of the two types of rules, the linguistic and non-linguistic, which yields the full meaning of the sentence, i.e. its Semantic Representation.

Notes

1. Actually, the Deep Structure trees for these sentences would have in them *the vampire* instead of *which*, and *women* instead of *who*.

2. Chomsky and Halle's systematic phonemic representation for this sentence would be considerably more abstract than has been shown. Besides assigning different vowels in certain instances, the plural morpheme would be assigned the same phonemic representation.

3. The features v and x are actually not elemental, but derived. The features of *disjunction, conjunction*, and *denial* are involved in the v and x codings: v is the disjunction of + and −, and x is the denial of + conjoined with the denial of −.

   An additional derived feature, 'either v or x,' is required in the analysis but is replaced with v for the sake of simplicity. Since the word *person* may properly be applied to children or adults, and since the dimension of marriage is applicable only to adults, a coding of vM for *person* is incorrect. A feature coding of 'either v or x' would be in order. Without such a coding one could not explain why the sentences *The person is either married or single* and *The person is neither married nor single* are both informative and not redundant or contradictory.

4. Whether Chomsky would actually include the semantic features along with lexical items in Deep Structure is a matter of conjecture. His earlier work is not clear on just what are or are not semantic features, e.g. he calls 'Animate' and 'Humanness' syntactic features. McCawley (1968) criticizes that view. Certainly it would be untenable for Chomsky to hold that features like 'Marriage' are syntactic (a *spinster* vs. *bachelor* distinction). If so, the question arises as to when such features are included along with the lexical item. Either such features accompany lexical insertion when all lexical items are inserted into the Deep Structure, or such features are added as one of the first semantic rules to apply, i.e. to return to the lexicon to recover the semantic features (this was the position of Katz & Fodor, 1963). I think Chomsky might now go along with the solution which has been provided here, i.e. to include semantic features with lexical items in the lexical insertion function for creating Deep Structure.

5. Chomsky's original grammar in the 1950's, incidentally, did allow such changes of meaning through Transformations. But such a notion was abandoned with the introduction of his Standard Theory in 1965.

6. Exactly why Chomsky preferred to make such drastic revisions in the function of transformations and the relationship of Surface Structure to Semantic rules rather than revise his Base rules and have odd appearing Deep Structures perhaps is related to the climate of linguistics at the time. Chomsky's notions were particularly under severe attack by the Generative Semanticists who argued that Deep Structure (and Base rules) should be done away with. Such being the case, Chomsky may have thought it more prudent not to complicate Deep Structure more, especially with something like focus that is peculiar as an element of syntax.

Chapter 3

Semantic based grammar

The question of the adequacy of Chomsky's attempt to account for the relation between sound and meaning through his grammar is one of the central concerns of contemporary linguistics. Challenges have come from two main sources, both of which are semantically oriented. One is from a group of linguists who have been called Generative Semanticists. Prominent founders of this group include McCawley, Ross, Lakoff, and Postal. (See Lakoff, 1971 for an articulation of this position.) The other challenge comes from the insights of Fillmore and his conception of a grammar based on semantic cases. The views of these theorists will be presented and compared with those of Chomsky and an overall evaluation will be made. In addition, objections to Chomsky's theorizing by a group often referred to as Relational Grammarians will also be considered.

The basis of the semantic theorist's objections to Chomsky's grammar, whether Standard Theory, Interpretive Semantics, or Trace, is that a primary role is assigned to syntax while only a secondary or dependent one is assigned to semantics, i.e. syntactic form determines semantic representation. As they see it, the roles should be completely reversed, with semantics primary and syntax secondary. They argue that syntax cannot be done independently of semantics. Furthermore, they see little need for two levels of syntax. They advocate abandonment of Deep Structure and Base rules, holding that what a grammar must do is to relate the semantic level of structure (let us continue to call it Semantic Representation) to a syntactic level of structure, Surface Structure. They posit that this be done with a set of transformational rules and a lexicon. Transformational rules might usefully be regarded as constituting the 'syntactic' component of their grammar. The Transformational rules and the Lexicon are viewed as continually interacting so as to produce a final structure, Surface Structure. This view sharply contrasts with that of Chomsky where lexical items are inserted all at once into an already completed tree structure (Deep Structure).

Generative semantics grammar

The Generative Semantics schema for a grammar may be represented as follows:

GENERATIVE SEMANTICS GRAMMAR

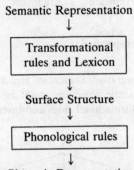

Semantic Representation
↓

> Transformational
> rules and Lexicon

↓

Surface Structure
↓

> Phonological rules

↓

Phonetic Representation

Another component which is implied and might be included in this schema is one labelled 'Semantic Elements and Structures.' Such a component would contain all of the stock out of which possible semantic representations are formed, i.e. natural logic and an inventory of semantic elements.

In considering how Generative Semanticists deal with sentences some examples are in order here. Consider such a sentence as *The collar hurts* and how the Chomskyans and the Generative Semanticists begin their analysis. For those theories the initial underlying structure might roughly be as shown below:

CHOMSKYAN DEEP STRUCTURE

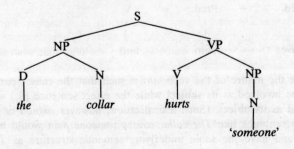

GENERATIVE SEMANTICS SEMANTIC STRUCTURE

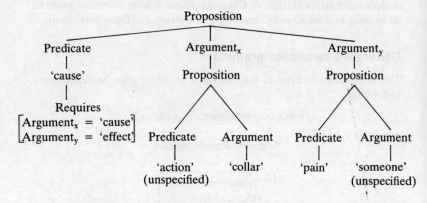

From the above Generative Semantics structure, the following intermediate English syntactic structure might be then derived through the application of transformational rules and insertion of lexical items:

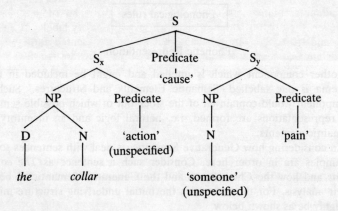

Further English lexicalization could occur:

Pred.	+	Pred.	=	V
cause		pain		hurt

where the nature of the verb *hurt* is such that the cause sentence (S_x) will be involved as its subject while the effect sentence (S_y) will be involved as its object. (Such lexicalization, however, would be optional, for, a sentence like *The collar causes someone pain* would be acceptable and have the same underlying semantic structure as *The collar hurts someone.*) Transformational rules would then provide the following Surface Structure:

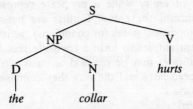

It may be noted that this Surface Structure does not include a VP node as does Chomsky's. Some of the reasons for this are described later (pp. 58–62).

It is important to consider that while in Chomsky's Deep Structure actual words of the language appear, in the Generative Semantics structure it is ideas which are represented (ideas are designated by single quotes). The ideas shown in the structure are not necessarily elemental idea, for, while 'cause' and 'pain' may be elemental, 'collar' and 'someone' are not, consisting of such elemental semantic features relating to animateness, humanness, clothing, etc. For the sake of simplicity, however, these latter complex ideas are given summary labels, i.e. 'collar,' and 'someone.' It is because ideas are represented rather than words and syntactic structures that the semantic structure is a universal one, i.e. is applicable to all languages. Different languages will express the idea of a collar hurting someone in different ways, e.g.:

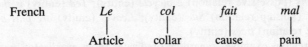

Because such different Surface Structures are required, every language of the world will have its own particular Transformational rules and lexical items.

Similar complex semantic analyses as those involving cause-effect relations would be provided by the Generative Semanticists for such syntactically simple sentences as *Mary frightened John* ([Mary + Unspecified Action, Situation, or Characteristic] CAUSE [John afraid]), *John beautified the yard* ([John + Unspecified] Action] CAUSE [yard beautiful]), *Mary cleaned the wound* ([Mary + Unspecified Action] CAUSE [wound clean]) and *John exploded the bomb* ([John + Unspecified Action] CAUSE [bomb explode]).

In the Generative Semantics semantic structure shown above some new terms, *Proposition*, *Predicate*, and *Argument*, have been introduced. A proposition is the thought or idea that underlies a sentence. It is not a string of sounds nor a set of syntactic constituents but it is the idea or thought that such elements are used to express. A proposition or complete thought is composed of two parts, a *predicate* and one or more *arguments*. In terms of meaning, an argument basically represents some sort of entity while a predicate represents some sort of aspect which concerns the entity. Entities are basically objects while predicates are properties, states (or conditions), activities, and relations which complement entities to form a complete thought or proposition. Entities and predicates may be physical or mental in nature. Examples of entities and predicates and the way they combine to form propositions are as follows:

Entity and Property:
The ball (entity) *is round* (property); Joe (entity) *weighs 150 lbs.* (property); The idea (entity) *is complex* (property).

Enity and State:
The boy (entity) *is bored* (state); The finger (entity) *is infected* (state); The shirt (entity) *is torn* (state); John (entity) *is happy* (state).

Entity and Activity:
The cat (entity) *jumped* (action); The rock (entity) *moved* (action); Mary (entity) *is thinking* (action).

Multiple Entities with Property, State, and Activity:
Harry (entity) *touched* (action) the ball (entity); Saul (entity) *sent* (action) Jean (entity) a present (entity); John (entity) *bought* (action) a radio (entity) for Mary (entity); John (entity) *hates* (state) Bill (entity); The baby (entity) *wants* (state) ice-cream (entity).

Multiple Entities with Relations:
The book (entity) *is on* (location relation) the table (entity); The boy (entity) *owns* (possessive relation) a bicycle (entity); Ted (entity) *is the husband of* (kinship relation) Sue (entity); Leaves (entity) *are part of* (part-whole relation) trees (entity).

As the previous examples regarding predicates show, predicates have various requirements regarding number of arguments. For example, predicates like *round, jump, infected*, and *bored* require only a single argument for completion (*The ball* is round, *The cat* jumped, *The finger* is infected, and *The boy* is bored). On the other hand, some predicates like *want, hit*, and *owns* require two arguments for completion (*The baby* wants *ice-cream, Harry* touched *the ball, The boy* owns *a bicycle*). Others still require three arguments, e.g. *sent* and *gave* (*Saul* sent *Jean a present, John* gave *a radio* to *Mary*).

Clearly different predicates have different requirements as to the number of arguments which they require for completion. Philosophers have traditionally referred to predicates which require a single argument (*John jumped*) as a 'one-place predicate,' those which require two arguments (*John hates Bill*) as 'two-place predicates,' and those which require three arguments (*Saul sent Jean a present*) as 'three-place predicates.' Such terminology is often used now in linguistic analyses. The number (and type) of the arguments which predicates require will be recorded in the lexicon of a grammar. Thus, a lexical entry for the predicates of verb and adjective will specify such information, e.g. the adjective *happy* requires a single argument (*John is happy*), one that concerns a living creature which can experience certain higher levels of consciousness (it would be odd to say *A worm is happy*), while the verb *want* requires two arguments (*The baby wants ice-cream*) concerns a living creature which has needs or intentions and another that concerns the goal of the intention or need in question. It is because verbs and adjectives have such requirements regarding the number and meaning of arguments that a sentence like *The baby wants* is incomplete or that a sentence like *The rock is happy* is odd. It should be recognized that although some verbs like *sing* require two arguments, the language may not require the expression of both, e.g. *Mary is singing* is just as acceptable as *Mary is singing a ballad* for it is understood that Mary is singing something in the former sentence. On the other hand, not just any argument can be optionally omitted from a sentence, e.g. **Singing a ballad* is not a complete sentence. It might be mentioned here in passing that arguments may consist of whole propositions as well as entities. For example, in *John claims the world is flat*, the verb *claim* requires two arguments, one of which (the complement) is a complex entity, i.e. an entire proposition. Other verbs like *regret, believe*, and *assert* have similar argument requirements.

It is important to recognize that languages of the world use two principal devices in conveying how a particular argument (realized as an NP) is to relate to a predicate (realized as a V or Adj). These are *word order* and what I shall call *morpheme indicator*. In English, we use both. For example, in *Sally pushed Terry*, the NP which precedes the verb (*Sally*) is the initiator or agent of the action while the NP which follows the verb (*Terry*) is the receiver or experiencer of the action. On the other hand, in *Terry was pushed by Sally*, the morphemes *by* and *was* indicate that the agent and experiencer roles are reversed. Consider, too, *Sally gave Terry Sam* (assume *Sam* is a baby). We interpret the first NP following the verb as the receiver or experiencer of the action and the second NP as the object which was received. On the other hand, in *Sally gave Terry to Sam*, the insertion of the preposition *to* has the effect of reversing those relations. In the case of Japanese, the order of NP constituents is not essential to conveying their role to the verb because each NP is followed (typically) by a morpheme (a postposition) which signals which role is involved. Thus, two appropriate Japanese versions of *Sally gave Sam to Terry*, are *Sally-ga Terry-ni Sam-o ataeta* (*gave*) and *Sally-ga Sam-o Terry-ni ataeta*, where the postpositions (like English prepositions) *ga, o*, and *ni* signal the role relations. The particular order of the NPs is not critical since it is the postposition that conveys the information. Generally, however, the Japanese prefer to place the NP with the *ga* postposition preceding the others with the *o* and *ni* postpositions. Still, a sentence like *Terry-ni Sam-o Sally-ga ataeta* is perfectly understandable.

Incidentally, the expression of the underlying semantic structure which is shown above as Predicate + Argument$_x$ + Argument$_y$ is intended to be neutral with respect to order. Such a formulation as Argument$_x$ + Predicate + Argument$_y$ could equally be shown as could many others. Furthermore, rather than trees, symbolic logic type notation could be used, e.g. Proposition = (Predicate, Argument... Argument). In none of the formulations is it intended that order is significant. First of all, there is no basis for believing that thought itself is linear (although language is since the words of sentences must be uttered in order). For, even though a majority of the world's languages begin sentences with an NP rather than a V (Greenberg, 1963), this is insufficient reason to believe that thought too is similarly ordered by having an argument precede a verb. If thought were really ordered with an NP first, there would be no way of explaining why some languages do begin sentences with a verb in opposition to the supposed thought order. Then, too, there is human politics, conquest, and genocide. The fact that languages which begin sentences with a NP predominate today is no reason to believe they dominated in the past or will dominate in the future. Peoples are conquered, languages disappear, and so what language types are dominant today is not a matter of the reflection of the order of thought but of the language communities which have been able to survive.

In comparing the Generative Semantics theory with that of Chomsky's, it is worth keeping in mind that although there are substantial differences between the two, in certain respects there are remarkable similarities. Chomsky's conception of a grammar as constituting a system of rules which relates levels of semantics, syntax, and phonetics is one that has been accepted and incorporated into Generative Semantics theorizing.

Semantic case grammar

Essential theory

Fillmore's Semantic Case Grammar theory (Fillmore, 1968; 1977), like that of the Generative Semanticists', focuses on representing the meaning of sentences. Actually, Fillmore might be called the original Relational grammarian since he was the first linguist to recognize and deal forthrightly with the problem of specifying the semantic relations among the basic constituents of sentences.

To illustrate Fillmore's basic ideas, let us consider the following sentences: (1) *The door will open*; (2) *The door will open with this key*; (3) *This key will open the door*; and (4) *The janitor will open the door with this key*. All sentences include the verb *open* and any of a number of NPs, *the door, this key*, and *the janitor*. As Fillmore points out, the basic semantic relations or roles of the NPs remain the same in these sentences with respect to the action of *open*. Thus, it is the door (the *Object* or recipient of the action) that opens, the key which is used for opening (the *Instrument* or means), and the janitor who causes the opening to take place (the *Agent*). These semantic roles of Object, Instrument, and Agent remain constant in the sentences, even though the syntactic relations of the NPs vary greatly. For, while *the door* is the syntactic subject in Sentences (1) and (2), it is the direct object in (3) and (4). And, while *this key* appears as an adverbial PrepP in (2) and (4), it serves as the subject in (3).

According to Fillmore, the principal factor which determines the particular syntactic relations and forms of NPs is related to the semantic roles which appear in particular sentences. If a sentence includes Agent, Object, and Instrument roles as in sentence (4), the Agent role (*the janitor*) will take precedence to become the subject (except in the case of passives) while the Object (*the door*) will become the direct object and the Instrument (*this key*) will become an adverbial. If a sentence does not contain an Agent as in (1), (2), and (3), then either the Object or Instrument may become the subject. Other similar selection principles are identified by Fillmore.

Fillmore represents the underlying semantic representation of the sentences and their syntactic counterparts essentially as follows:

1. *The door will open.*

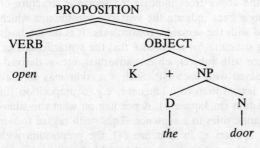

2. *The door will open with this key.*

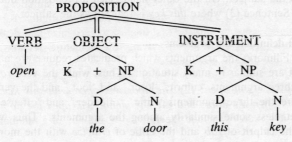

3. *This key will open the door.*

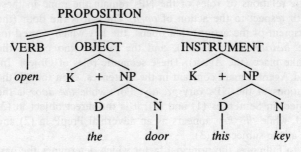

4. *The janitor will open the door with this key.*

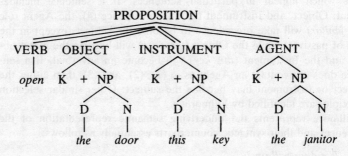

The double lines in the above trees indicate the semantic structure of the sentence. The single lines indicate the syntactic constituents which are directly associated with the semantic constituents. It is on the basis of such an underlying structure for a sentence that the syntactic Surface Structure of a sentence with subject, object, adverbial, etc. is derived. A K marker is associated with each NP. Such a marker may or may not be realized as a lexical item in a language, e.g. a preposition (in English) or a postposition (in Japanese), depending on what the situation is regarding semantic roles in a sentence. Thus, with regard to *this key*, when an Agent appears as in Sentence (4), the preposition *with* must be added, just as that preposition must be added in Sentence (2) where *door* is the subject. On the other hand, such a preposition does not appear in Sentence (3) where *this key* is realized as the subject.

Semantic case: definition and problems

According to Fillmore, the arguments which predicates require are not all unique but are similar in many situations. Thus, while the verb *rob* requires the three arguments 'culprit,' 'loser,' and 'loot,' and the verb *criticize* require the three arguments 'critic,' 'offender,' and 'offense,' there is nonetheless some similarity among the arguments. 'Thus we can identify the culprit of *rob* and the critic of *criticize* with the more abstract role of Agent, and interpret the term Agent as referring, wherever it occurs, as the animated instigator of events referred to by the associated verb. . . . in general it seems to me that for the predicates provided in natural languages, the roles that their arguments play are taken from an inventory of role types fixed by grammatical theory.' (Fillmore, 1971: 376) It is the role type that Fillmore refers to as semantic case relationships or, simply, cases. Aside from the case of *Agent*, other cases such as *Object* (the entity that moves or changes or whose position or existence is in consideration, e.g. sent *the bicycle*), *Instrument* (the stimulus or immediate physical cause of an event, e.g. *by car*), *Source* (the place from which something moves, e.g. *from home*), *Goal* (the place to which something moves, e.g. *to school*) and *Experiencer* (the entity which receives or accepts or experiences or undergoes the effect of an action, e.g. *John gave the ball to Mary*). The following sentence will illustrate these cases:

John	sent the *bicycle*	to *Mary*	from *home*	to *school*	by *car*.
Agent	Object	Exper.	Source	Goal	Instr.

How to identify cases often becomes a problem, however, as in the analysis of such sentences as *John ran to school* and *John went to school by running*. With such similar meaning, both sentences should be given essentially the same case analysis. However, what the case analysis should be is the problem. Should *run* be listed in the lexicon as being essentially composed of *go by running*, where *running* is an Instrument case? If so, then *John went to school by running* would reflect the true underlying case structure and *John ran to school* would be derived from it by a transformational rule which converts *went by running* to *ran*. Actually, this is a problem for all linguistic theorists since how to analyze the meaning of predicates must be considered in any complete semantic analysis of a sentence.

Semantic case grammar and generative semantics compared
Both the Case and Generative Semantics theories are the same in terms of the relationship between the Semantic Representation, Surface Structure and the Phonetic Representation of a sentence. The Semantic Representation serves as the primary initial unit with syntactic transformational rules and the lexicon applying to it to provide a Surface Structure. The Surface Structure then has phonological rules applying to it so as to provide a Phonetic Representation. In this writer's opinion, the theories do not differ in any essential way. The apparent differences in terms of the specification of the underlying meanings of sentences are really only terminological ones. For example, consider a sentence such as *John pushed Jim*. According to Semantic Case theory, the NPs of *John* and *Jim* represent the cases of Agent and Object with respect to the action verb of *push*. The semantic case relationship of these NPs to

the verb is specified directly, i.e. each NP is labelled with a semantic case. The Generative Semanticists, on the other hand, mark the semantic function of each argument indirectly. For example, the various arguments may be given an identifying notation such as X and Y.[1] The significance of the X and Y notation is specified in the meaning of the predicate, e.g., the predicate 'push' is an action such that it requires one argument that is an animate cause and another argument that is the receiver or object of the action. Since it may be argued that an 'animate cause' is the essence of Agent in the case framework and that a 'receiver' or 'object' is the essence of what is the Object case, it would appear that there is no substantive difference between the two semantic theories.[2] Actually, such a finding should not be surprising since one might well expect that the essential semantic relations between a predicate and its arguments would be regarded as similar given the aims and orientation which these semantic theories share.

Other challenges to Chomsky's Deep Structure and autonomy of syntax

Related to the Generative Semanticists' attack on Chomsky's notions of Deep Structure and the primacy of the syntactic component is one which has been launched recently by a group of linguists who are being called *Relational* grammarians because of their interest in accounting for the various syntactic and semantic relations which NPs may have with a verb. Such linguists include Postal, Johnson, and Perlmutter. What makes their objections to Chomsky's theorizing interesting is that they have applied criteria which Chomsky himself has advocated. We shall discuss here the two most serious objections which these theorists raise (Johnson, 1974): (1) the superfluousness of the VP notion for defining Direct Object in a VSO language, and (2) the failure of the VP notion to syntactically define the indirect object in English and Japanese. I would like to add another which Generative Semanticists have implied, (3) the subordination of the direct and indirect object to the subject. The purpose of raising these objections is to demonstrate that Chomsky's theory is unable, in a well-motivated way, to specify the essential structure of sentences in wholly syntactic terms. By doing so, the theorists hope to establish the primacy of semantics.

1. SUPERFLUOUSNESS OF VP IN A VSO LANGUAGE. Suppose a language has a Verb + Subject + Direct Object order of basic constituents, i.e. VSO. Thus, where English has a SVO order, e.g. *John kissed Mary*, and where Japanese has a SOV order, e.g. *John + Mary + kiss*, this language would have a VSO order, e.g. *Kiss + John + Mary*. Certain Polynesian, American Indian, Semitic, Celtic, and African languages are VSO languages. That being so, then Chomsky's notion of VP, where the verb and the direct object form a VP could not be applicable to this sort of

language. For, the verb and direct object NP would be separated by the subject NP. That is, in a VSO language, the order would be V + NP (subject) + NP (object).

To answer this criticism, Chomsky might claim that the notion of VP is one that is relevant only to certain languages, e.g. English. (Thus, the VP would not be a universal language concept.) However, if he does so, he runs into the problem of how to distinguish the subject NP from the object NP in the VSO language. For, if such a language does not have a VP, then both the subject and object NPs will be directly dominated by the S node, i.e:

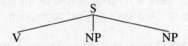

The result of this is that the direct object and the subject would be assigned the same structure, i.e.:

S
|
NP

It could not be said, therefore, that Chomsky had succeeded in his goal of independently defining basic linguistic notions in terms of syntactic structure.

If it were to be argued that the order of occurrence of the NPs might serve as a distinguishing criterion, i.e. the subject NP appears before the object NP, such would not provide a satisfactory solution. For, the very use of order implies that the notions of subject and object cannot be defined independently but with respect to one another. Then, too, if in the VSO language, the direct object is defined as:

S
|
NP

plus some order consideration, then this definition of the direct object would differ greatly from that of an SVO language like English where it is:

VP
|
NP

Chomsky could not then argue, as he has (Chomsky, 1967: 72), that basic syntactic relations such as subject and direct object may be universally specified. A further problem in this regard would arise, too, if order is to be considered. The rule S → NP + VP for one language, e.g. SVO, would have to be considered different in essence from S →

VP + NP for another language, e.g. VOS. Order could not be considered simply as incidental but as providing an entirely different structure. Such an outcome is incompatible with Chomsky's theorizing.

In order to maintain his theory, there is also the possibility that Chomsky might posit that all languages, including a VSO one, have an underlying Deep Structure form like SVO as in English. (Actually, I don't believe Chomsky himself would indulge in this form of linguistic imperialism.) This would allow Chomsky to say that a VSO Surface Structure is simply the result of a permutation transformation which has been applied to the non-VSO Deep Structure. Such a solution, however, would be *ad hoc* since there is no good reason for its postulation except for the preservation of Chomsky's original conception.

2. FAILURE TO DEFINE INDIRECT OBJECT IN ENGLISH AND JAPANESE. Consider the sentence *John gave Max a book*. If Chomsky defines the indirect object, *Max*, as an NP which is immediately dominated by the VP node, then the direct object, *a book*, would have the same structure, i.e.:

VP
|
NP

Obviously, the two types of objects are not distinguished from one another if they have identical structures and order is not considered a significant variable. However, if instead of defining the indirect object as an NP, Chomsky defines it as being a prepositional phrase (PrepP) in the Deep Structure (the preposition could be deleted for Surface Structure optionally), he would again run into difficulty. For, the PrepP indirect object (*to Max*) must be distinguished structurally from an adverbial phrase such as *in England* which also has the PrepP form. Suppose one says that the distinction can be made by having the adverbial PrepP dominated by an AdvP label. (Chomsky, 1965 suggests this solution and many of his followers, e.g. Burt, 1971, have adopted it.) The result is that the indirect object PrepP is distinguished from the adverbial PrepP as follows:

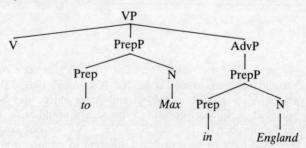

The problem with such a solution is that the adding of the AdvP node cannot be regarded as a satisfactory solution. For, simply adding such a node does not change the fact that the indirect object and the adverbial are both assigned the same basic form, i.e.:

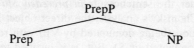

and that both are dominated by VP. There is no independent syntactic motivation for adding the AdvP label. On the same grounds, with regard to the VSO language problem it would be ludicrous to offer a syntactic solution where the subject and direct objects are labelled as such, e.g.:

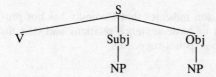

(Then, too, if such can be done for a VSO language, the same should be done for all languages, like English.) Unjustified labelling is clearly not an acceptable solution for the problem at hand.

A similar and perhaps more devastating problem arises for Chomsky's theory in Japanese. In that language, the subject, direct object, and indirect object can be marked by postposition particles such as *ga, o,* and *ni* respectively. Thus, in *John ga Max ni hon o ataeta* (John gave the book to Max), there are three NPs where each NP is composed of a noun and a postposition particle, *John ga, Max ni,* and *hon o.* Utilizing Chomsky's grammar, such a sentence could be represented as follows:

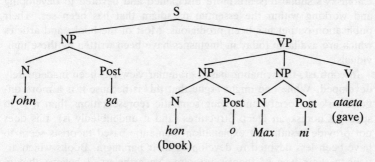

In such a case, the direct and indirect object NPs are not distinguishable from one another syntactically, for both NPs have the structure N + Postposition and are immediately dominated by VP. Chomsky's theory, therefore, does not adequately account for the direct and indirect objects in Japanese.

3. SUBORDINATION OF DIRECT AND INDIRECT OBJECT TO THE SUBJECT. Consider the sentences *John preceded Mary* and *Mary followed John*. In Chomsky's analysis, the direct object NP is placed in a subordinate position (being dominated by VP) with respect to the subject NP (being dominated by S). But, is it justified to say that there is such a constituent as *preceded Mary* or *followed John*? Why should *preceded Mary* form a unit, the VP, but not *John preceded*? Why should not the subject NP and the direct object NP (and the indirect object NP) be given equal status? Chomsky has not provided a justification for placing the direct (and indirect) object in a subordinate position under the domination of VP.

Conclusion. The above discussion indicates that Chomsky has not provided a syntactic specification of basic sentence relations and that his thesis that syntax is 'autonomous' is not supported.

Conclusions

The essential issue dividing Chomsky's type of grammatical theorizing and those of his opponents concerns the relationship and primacy of syntax and semantics. Chomsky and his proponents believe that basic syntactic structures can be specified independently of semantic considerations. His opponents, such as the Generative Semanticists and the Semantic Case theorists, disagree, holding that only semantic structure can be specified independently and that the selection of syntactic structure is governed by semantic determinations.

While over the years, support for the Chomskyan position has waned somewhat, that viewpoint continues to remain dominant. Chomsky's supporters are more disciplined and devoted to developing and working within the essential paradigm that has been set. Their publication output has been prodigious. Most of the books and articles which are available today in linguistics have been written by these individuals.

In contrast, the semantic based grammar view has been inadequately developed. While one might argue that this is because it is a more difficult task to specify underlying semantic representations than it is to specify Chomskyan Deep Structures (and it undoubtedly is), this does not provide a sufficient explanation. Semantic based theorists seem to have been less devoted to developing their paradigm. Books which articulate their type of theory are rare. Nevertheless, I believe that in time their ideas will prevail, for, as the next chapter shows, those ideas are more in accord with psychological reality than those of Chomsky.

Notes

1. Generative Semanticists often use representations which do not explicitly state the semantic function of arguments. For example, a formulation like *push: John, Jim* or a tree structure with a *John + push + Jim* order of constituents might be presented. In such cases, the theorist expects the semantic functions of the arguments to be intuitively grasped. Such formulations, it must be recognized, lack the theoretical specificity that is necessary for a comprehensive semantic analysis. They are acceptable as a practical shorthand only if the theorist somewhere makes manifest precisely what the semantic functions are that particular arguments serve. Too often, it seems to me, the cases of Semantic Case theory are criticized by Generative Semanticists who themselves fail to specify what semantic functions are involved.

2. It should be noted though that in certain ways Fillmore's theory is not wholly adequate in semantic terms. For example, in his propositional structure, rather than that of verb the more fundamental concept of predicate should appear since adjectives, too, serve a similar function with respect to arguments. (One often gets the impression, however, in reading Fillmore that he uses Verb in the general sense of predicate.) Then, too, the K marker should not be included along with NPs in the propositional structure since the K is a mere surface manifestation of the basic semantic relation which is already identified by the case name. The K marker is really a superfluous concept since the transformation rules which operate directly on the cases will reflect those cases in surface structure not only through morphemes, such as prepositions and postpositions, but also through constituent order, such as in *John pushed Jim*, where order determines the semantic case relations of the NPs. To have a K marker which accommodates a preposition but not word order is not sufficiently universal from a semantic view.

Chapter 4

Grammar, speaker performance, and psychological reality

This chapter is principally concerned with assessing the relationship of a number of current grammatical conceptions with respect to their possible role in the sentence production and understanding of speakers. The psychological validity of Chomsky's grammar, in particular, as well as the grammars of Generative Semantics and Semantic Case are evaluated from a psychological point of view.

Grammar, knowledge, and performance

Grammar: a description of language or knowledge

Whether or not a linguist's grammar should relate to speaker knowledge and performance has been a long-standing issue in linguistics. While, prior to Chomsky, some linguists like Bloomfield (1933) made strong psychological claims and some linguists like Twaddell (1935) made strong anti-psychological claims (Twaddell argued against the psychological reality of the phoneme while allowing that it was a legitimate unit for linguistic description), it seems that most linguists avoided the issue altogether.

Since Chomsky, one might say that linguistics has been highly psychologized. Most linguists share (or at least pay lip-service to) Chomsky's purpose of a grammar which is to describe the knowledge which speakers have of their language (Chomsky, 1965). Such a purpose, it is essential to note, is quite different from that of a grammar describing a language. A description of one's knowledge is clearly a psychological aim. A description of a language may or may not coincide with the knowledge which speakers have of that language. Given Chomsky's outlook, one can easily understand the basis for his assertion that linguistics is a particular branch of cognitive psychology

(Chomsky, 1968: 1). Interestingly enough, Chomsky did not always hold this position. In the 1950s, as will be detailed later in this chapter, Chomsky favored non-psychological formalistic theorizing and went out of his way to attack mentalistic conceptions of any sort.

Role of grammar in performance

Supposing that a grammar which a linguist writes represents a specification of certain language knowledge held by speakers, it is natural to ask what role the hypothesized knowledge plays in language performance, principally in the production and understanding of sentences. At the very least, it would seem that a theory of performance should explain how speakers convert ideas or meanings to speech sounds (the process of sentence production) and how speakers convert speech sounds to meaning (the process of sentence understanding or comprehension).

Essentially, two basic performance conceptions are possible. In the first conception – which I shall name *componential* – a number of components interact so that a speaker may produce or understand sentences. The grammar is *one* of the components. This is the sort of theory which Chomsky advocates. In the second conception – which I shall name *integral* – a grammar (or grammars) operates on its own to produce or understand sentences. This is the sort of theory which many people mistakenly believe that Chomsky advocates. It is also one which, to varying extents, some theorists think should be advocated (Fodor, Bever & Garrett, 1974; Derwing, 1973; Watt, 1974).

The componential role of grammar

A few analogies might be helpful here. Consider the problem of finding one's way around a strange city by the use of a city map. The map alone does not actually specify how to get from one particular point to another. For, even though the knowledge provided by the map will allow for the plotting of virtually an infinite number of different routes, the map itself does not specify how to plot a route. Additional knowledge, that is, knowledge of how to use the map, is required. It is the interaction of these two types of knowledge, the knowledge specified by the map and the knowledge of how to use the map that accounts for the ability to plot individual routes. Similarly, a grammar may be said to be like a city map but with infinite potential for the production and understanding of sentences. For language, a speaker's grammatical knowledge interacts with knowledge of how to use a grammar (such knowledge may be thought of as use rules, strategies, or heuristics) in order to produce a particular sentence. The grammar alone, however, cannot produce or understand a particular sentence, just as the map does not specify any particular route.

Another analogy, one which Chomsky (1961: 121) suggests and I elaborate here, involves the role of the so-called Multiplication Table in the solving of arithmetic problems. Knowledge of a Multiplication Table (such as a 10 × 10 or a 12 × 12 table which includes all products of all combinations) will not by itself allow a person to get the answer to a multiplication problem like 462 × 32. One must also know precisely what digits are to be multiplied together, in what order, etc. A set of guiding operations or *Use* rules is necessary. The Multiplication Table only provides knowledge which may be used for the solving of multiplication problems; it does not provide the entire multiplication process. Analogously, just as the Multiplication Table is a component in the process of multiplication, so, too, is Chomsky's grammar conceived of as one component in the process of language performance.

The Multiplication Table analogy is an especially useful one because it can be used to illustrate another important aspect of Chomsky's componential performance model. Just as the Multiplication Table serves as a component in multiplication, so, too, may that *same* table serve as a component in division. A division problem like 483 ÷ 9 requires the use of that table for a solution. What is different in doing division rather than multiplication is that a different set of *Use* rules is employed. The schema shown in Fig. 1 may thus serve to represent the arithmetic performance processes of multiplication and division. (For the sake of simplicity, other necessary knowledge such as that of addition and subtraction is not included in the model.)

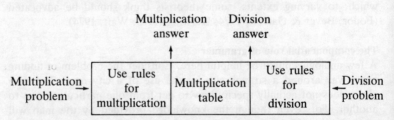

FIGURE 1. Componential model of arithmetic performance

Chomsky's view of the role of a grammar with respect to production and understanding is much the same as that of the Multiplication Table with respect to multiplication and division. One grammar serves *both* performance processes of production and understanding. And, as in the arithmetic example, two sets of Use rules are required: one set for production, the other for understanding. The schema shown in Fig. 2, represents Chomsky's conception of a language performance model. Essentially, production involves meaning or ideas as input, and speech as output, while understanding (sometimes referred to as 'comprehension' or 'perception') involves speech as input, and meaning as output. Given an input, one of the sets of Use rules will interact with the grammar to provide an output.

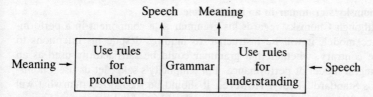

FIGURE 2 Chomsky's componential type performance model

It is interesting to note, that although it has been nearly 20 years since Chomsky has proposed his componential model, no workable performance model has ever been formulated. Even some of his most ardent supporters, e.g. Fodor, Bever, and Garrett (1974), have failed in the task. Other than providing an outline of the model, Chomsky has never formulated a working model himself. Actually, Chomsky may not feel impelled to do so for as he has stated (Chomsky, 1965) it is the task of linguistics to specify a grammar and it is the task of psycholinguists or psychologists to specify the details of a performance model which would use that grammar. Perhaps Chomsky feels that he has done his share by working on the grammar. One cannot help but wonder though why psycholinguists have not come up with a workable model. Two distinct possibilities come to mind. Either they are not smart enough or there is something wrong with Chomsky's particular grammar. I believe that the latter alternative is actually the case and will present arguments later in this chapter to substantiate that view. (This is not to deny that there may be some degree of truth to the first alternative. A psycholinguist of Chomsky's intellectual caliber has yet to appear.)

The integral role of grammar

It is the use of a component such as *Use* rules that distinguishes the componential model from the integral model. Essentially the integral model does not require *Use* rules in order to realize an output. The grammar itself does the whole job. The Generative Semanticist's grammar, for example, could be interpreted as a performance model for production in an integral sense, because, as was shown in Chapter 2, given meaning as a starting point, the grammar can provide a level of speech (phonetic representation) as output. *Use* rules would not be necessary. Such a grammar might be called an *integral production grammar*. An *integral understanding grammar* would be one which would take speech as input and, without the assistance of *Use* rules, provide meaning as output. (This, the Generative Semantics grammar cannot do.) In the integral grammar, therefore, not only does a rule of grammar represent knowledge, it also serves as an instruction for an activity or an operation in the mind. A rule of grammar, in this sense, is a specification not only of knowledge, but knowledge for action.

Chomsky's grammar in an integral role

Although Chomsky regards his grammar as a component in a performance model, it will be instructive to inquire, despite his intentions to
the contrary, whether that grammar could be satisfactorily used as an
integral model of performance. For simplicity's sake, let us use Chomsky's Standard Theory. However, it should be recognized that what will
be said for that theory is equally applicable to his Interpretive Semantics Grammar and his Trace Grammar theories. For, all of these grammars have the characteristic of constructing derivations beginning with
a Phrase Structure type of syntax. It is this characteristic which is crucial in the discussion which later follows.

In order to determine whether Chomsky's grammar could be used as
an integral model of performance, some examination of the organization of the grammar is necessary. Fig. 3 provides a schema of the organization of Chomsky's Standard Theory grammar. (While the Standard
Theory only is considered here, this grammar does not differ in essentials from the Interpretive Semantics and Trace Theory grammars.)
Each of the components (syntactic, semantic, phonological) or sub-
components (the Base and Transformational rules are sub-components
of the syntactic component) of the grammar are shown along with the
directional ordering of the rules within each component or sub-
component. The directional ordering of rules is shown with a dotted
arrow in each component or sub-component. In essence, rules are applied sequentially in that the output of one rule becomes the input for
a succeeding rule. Such ordering is established for all components and
sub-components except for the Base rules which in that sub-component
may be unordered. The vacuous symbol 'S' is Chomsky's input to the

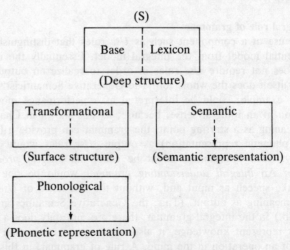

FIGURE 3. Directionality of rules in Chomsky's grammar

Base. Such a symbol will guarantee that every sentence will have an NP + VP structure.

However, not only is there an order of rules within each component or sub-component except the Base, there is an order among the components and sub-components as well. This ordering involves various input and output relations. Thus, because Deep Structure is the output of the Base which serves as input to the Semantic component and the Transformational sub-component, the set of Base rules is ordered to operate prior to the sets of Semantic and Transformational rules. Similarly, because the output of the Transformational sub-component is Surface Structure and this Surface Structure serves as input to the Phonological component, the Transformational rules are ordered to operate prior to the Phonological rules. The various principal output structures in Chomsky's grammar – Deep Structure, Surface Structure, Semantic Representation, and Phonetic Representation – thus have specified ordered interrelations because of the ordering of the various types of rules. That order appears in the schema shown in Fig. 4.

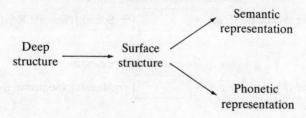

FIGURE 4. Principal output structures and order of structure construction according to Chomsky's trace theory.

Given the above facts about the organization of Chomsky's Standard Theory grammar, let us consider now whether that grammar could be reasonably used as an *integral* model of performance. On this question, Chomsky (1967a: 435–6) has said the following:

> We have now discussed a certain model of competence [Chomsky's Standard Theory grammar]. It would be tempting but quite absurd, to regard it as a model of performance as well. Thus, we might propose that to produce a sentence, the speaker goes through the successive steps of constructing a base-derivation [Deep Structure], line by line from the initial symbol S, then inserting lexical items and applying transformations to form a surface structure, and finally applying the phonological rules in their given order. . . . There is not the slightest justification for any such assumption. In fact, in implying that the speaker selects the general properties of sentence structure before selecting lexical items (before deciding what he is going to

talk about), such a proposal seems not only without justification but entirely counter to whatever vague intuitions one may have about the processes that underlie production. A theory of performance (production or perception) will have to incorporate the theory of competence – the generative grammar of a language – as an essential part.

Thus, as Chomsky points out, the input and output ordering of structures in his grammar, as schematized in Fig. 4, does *not* match the ordering which is necessary for either of the performance processes of production or understanding. No real speaker performance process would begin with a *syntactic* structure from the Base, i.e. Deep Structure. Performance processes begin either with sound (Phonetic Representation) for understanding or with meaning (Semantic Representation) for production. The schema below shows how Chomsky's order in grammar differs from orders in performance production and understanding:

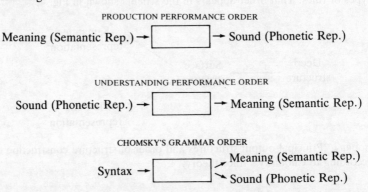

PRODUCTION PERFORMANCE ORDER

Meaning (Semantic Rep.) → [ ] → Sound (Phonetic Rep.)

UNDERSTANDING PERFORMANCE ORDER

Sound (Phonetic Rep.) → [ ] → Meaning (Semantic Rep.)

CHOMSKY'S GRAMMAR ORDER

Syntax → [ ] ⟨ Meaning (Semantic Rep.)
                 Sound (Phonetic Rep.)

Thus, if the ordering in his grammar were to be treated as successive steps in actual performance, the results would be entirely counter to whatever intuitions we may have about the performance process.[1] This being the case, Chomsky must reject the integral model for his grammar. It is for this reason that Chomsky developed the componential model of performance that he now champions.

Chomsky's 'generative-productive' distinction

Since Chomsky does not intend his grammar to be an operating integral model of performance, one may be puzzled when he says that the Base sub-component 'generates' Deep Structures or the Transformational sub-component 'generates' Surface Structures, etc. According to Chomsky, *generate* means 'define,' not 'produce.' Consequently, such objects as Deep Structure, Semantic Representation, etc., are not actually produced by the grammar in a psychological sense but rather they are defined, i.e. generated, by the grammar. Thus, for example, while the Base does not actually produce an infinite number of Deep Structures, it is said to 'define' an infinite number of them.

An analogy may be helpful here. Consider the multiplication example referred to earlier. According to the multiplication model, which consisted of a Multiplication Table and *Use* rules, it may be said that such a model generates or defines all possible multiplication solutions. For example, even though one may never have been given the following multiplication problem of 87 × 96, in a sense, its solution:

$$\begin{array}{r} 87 \\ 96 \\ \hline 522 \\ 783 \\ \hline 8352 \end{array}$$

is already defined by the knowledge involved in the multiplication model. It may be said, therefore, that a multiplication model generates or has the potential of defining an infinite number of solutions. Similarly, just as the multiplication model represents one's capacity with regard to possible multiplication solutions, so, too, does Chomsky regard his Base sub-component, for example, as representing a speaker's capacity with respect to possible Deep Structures. However, whether this analogy is actually a proper one and whether the 'generative–productive' distinction is valid are matters for concern in the succeeding sections of this chapter.

Knowledge and linguistic derivations

According to Chomsky, a grammar represents the knowledge that speakers have of their language, knowledge which consists of rules and lexical items. If the grammar which Chomsky postulates were a psychologically real one, then speakers would have acquired the knowledge represented in the schema shown in Fig. 5. The sets of rules and lexical entries appearing in the schema are intended to have a psychological

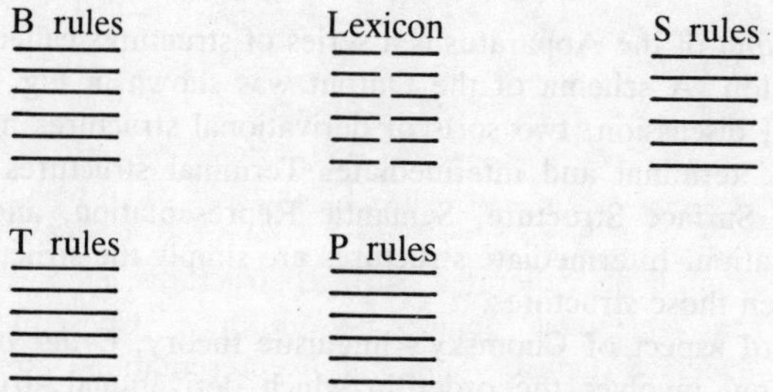

FIGURE 5. The apparatus: grammatical knowledge according to Chomsky

significance. That is, every aspect of every rule and lexical entry which is written in Chomsky's grammar is hypothesized to have some correspondence in the minds of speakers.

Now, what are not included in the schema shown in Fig. 5 are any of the output structures which the theory is said to generate, e.g. Deep Structure, Surface Structure, and Semantic Representation. Actually, these structures are only part of what the grammar generates. The entire output is what Chomsky calls a linguistic *derivation*.

More precisely, the linguistic derivation of a sentence for Chomsky involves all of the aspects shown in Fig. 6. The symbol $\triangle$ in that schema signifies a structure. Thus, starting from the left of the figure, the order of construction of a derivation begins with the symbol 'S' and is followed by the application of Base rules (X, Y, and Z). As each Base rule applies, an *Intermediate Structure* is formed. Thus, Intermediate Deep Structure *1* consists of one Base rule X, e.g. S $\rightarrow$ NP + VP, while Intermediate Deep Structure *2* consists of Intermediate Deep Structure *1* plus an additional rule, Base rule Y, e.g. NP $\rightarrow$ D + N, and so on, until finally, no other Base rules are applied. The resulting structure, which has lexical items inserted into it, is called Deep Structure.[2] The number of Intermediate Structures will depend on the number of rules applied. The symbol n indicates that there may be an unlimited number of such structures. Thus, we see that Intermediate Structures will be generated from not only the Base rules, but from the Transformational, Semantic, and Phonological rules as well. Chomsky's grammar will generate an unlimited number of linguistic derivations; one complete derivation for each of the unlimited number of possible grammatical sentences.

Chomsky's psychological claims

At this point, Chomsky's theory may be fruitfully described in terms of three major aspects: Apparatus, Output, and Order of Structure Construction. (These are my own names, and not Chomsky's.) The *Apparatus* consists of a lexicon and rules, essentially Base, Transformational, Semantic, and Phonological. A schema of the Apparatus was shown in Fig. 5.

The *Output* of the Apparatus is a series of structures called a linguistic derivation. A schema of the Output was shown in Fig. 6. For the purpose of discussion, two sorts of derivational structures may be distinguished, terminal and intermediate. Terminal structures are Deep Structure, Surface Structure, Semantic Representation, and Phonetic Representation. Intermediate structures are simply the structures which fall between those structures.

The third aspect of Chomsky's linguistic theory, *Order of Structure Construction*, involves the order in which derivational structures are constructed by the Apparatus. This order was shown in Fig. 4. Thus,

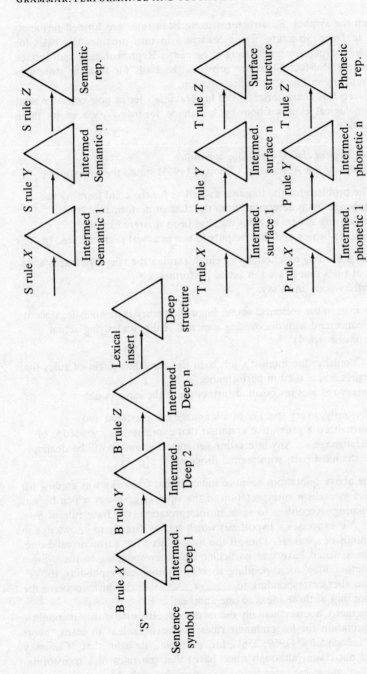

FIGURE 6. Simplified schema of Chomsky's derivation of a sentence

given the symbol 'S,' structures using Base rules are formed terminating in Deep Structure. Deep Structure in turn provides the basis for forming structures terminating in Semantic Representation and Surface Structure. Surface Structure provides the basis for forming structures terminating in Phonetic Representation.

Given this characterization of his grammar, let us now consider what psychological claims Chomsky has made regarding each of its three aspects.

Psychological claims regarding apparatus

Concerning the Apparatus, Chomsky (1965) stated the following:

> The problem for the linguist, as well as for the child learning the language, is to determine from the data of performance the underlying system of rules that has been mastered by the speaker-hearer and that he puts to use in actual performance. (p. 4)

Thus, according to Chomsky, a child learning the language learns a system of rules that is used in actual performance.
Chomsky goes on to say:

> Hence, in the technical sense, linguistic theory is mentalistic, since it is concerned with discovering a mental reality underlying actual behavior. (p. 4)

For Chomsky, the linguist's job is to describe the system of rules that underlies and is used in performance.
Chomsky restates his position further on in the same book:

> Obviously, every speaker of a language has mastered and internalized a generative grammar that expresses his knowledge of his language . . . Any interesting generative grammar will be dealing, for the most part, with mental processes . . . (p. 8)

The above quotations seem to indicate that Chomsky was arguing for a strict mentalistic interpretation of the rules of grammar which he was postulating. According to such an interpretation, the Base rule of S → NP + VP expresses a hypothesis which relates directly to knowledge in the minds of speakers. Thus, if the hypothesis were a true or valid one, speakers would have one particular idea corresponding to the symbol S, another idea corresponding to NP, another corresponding to VP, and another corresponding to ____ → ____ + ____ which concerns the relationship of those ideas to one another.

Whether Chomsky actually did or did not advocate such a mentalistic interpretation for his grammar rules has been unclear to many theorists. Lamendella (1969: 258), for example, thought that 'Chomsky would not claim (although some have) that the rules of a transformational grammar are intended to be isomorphic with the cognitive system of "rules" that people possess after having learned a language.' Because I thought the opposite was the case, I wrote to Chomsky asking what his position was. I remarked that I believed that he (Chomsky) did indeed intend to make the mentalistic ('isomorphic') claim. I enclosed a copy of the Lamendella article in the letter. Chomsky replied (November 1970) as follows: 'You have read my intentions correctly [regarding 'isomorphism']. I would (and repeatedly have) made the claim that a transformational grammar is a theory of the system of rules that a person possesses (internalizes, or whatever) after having acquired a language. Thus linguistics seems to me a sub-branch of theoretical psychology.' Thus, it is the mentalistic interpretation for rules which Chomsky intends. Lamendella was not entirely wrong, however, for, as will be shown later, Chomsky did not always assign such an interpretation to his theory.

Psychological claims regarding output

While, as far as I have been able to determine, Chomsky has not explicitly claimed psychological validity for intermediate structures, he clearly has made such a claim for the terminal structures of a derivation. With regard to Deep Structure, for example, Chomsky (1967b: 6) has said, '. . . this structure [Deep Structure] must be rediscovered by each child who learns a language.' Obviously, Deep Structure is posited to be psychologically valid, i.e. to psychologically exist, otherwise a child could not be expected to 'rediscover' it. Chomsky (1967a: 399) has also said, 'A central problem for psychology is to discover the characteristics of a system PM. . . .' The system PM is a sentence perception or understanding model whose output is Deep Structure, Surface Structure, Semantic Representation, and Phonetic Representation. Since a sentence perception model deals with psychological output, and since these terminal structures are identified as output for the PM system, clearly such structures are hypothesized to be psychologically real by Chomsky. Thus, there is little doubt that Chomsky claims that terminal structures appear in the minds of speakers.

Although Chomsky has not explicitly stated that intermediate structures are psychologically valid, by implication he is at least obliged to champion such a status for the rules and lexical items which comprise those structures. This follows since intermediate structures are entirely a function of the rules and lexical items of Chomsky's grammar – rules and lexical items which Chomsky claims are psychologically valid.

Psychological claims regarding order of structure construction

Concerning the psychological validity of the order in which structures of a derivation are constructed, Chomsky (1965) has said:

> When we say that a sentence has a certain derivation with respect to a particular generative grammar, we say nothing about how the

speaker or hearer might proceed, in some practical or efficient way, to construct such a derivation. These questions belong to the theory of language use – the theory of performance. (p. 9)

Does Chomsky imply here that an entire derivation, intermediate as well as terminal structures, is psychologically real by his saying that 'we say nothing about how the speaker or hearer might proceed, in some practical or efficient way, to construct such a derivation'? In any case, we see that Chomsky emphatically denies that the order in which a derivation is constructed in his grammar theory says anything about the way that a speaker might construct such a derivation.[3]

Chomsky actually goes further than just denying that the order in which structures are constructed specifies any sort of order in performance. He states that the order in grammar could not possibly be the order in performance. Consider again, the following from Chomsky (1967a):

It would be tempting but quite absurd, to regard it [Chomsky's grammar and its derivations] as a model of performance as well. Thus, we might propose that to produce a sentence, the speaker goes through the successive steps of constructing a base-derivation [Deep Structure], line by line from the initial symbol S, then inserting lexical items and applying transformations to form a surface structure, and finally applying the phonological rules in their given order . . . There is not the slightest justification for any such assumption. (p. 435–6)

The reason that Chomsky is obliged to deny any psychological claim as to the validity of the order involved in constructing derivations concerns performance processing on the part of speakers. Speakers, in actually producing a sentence, would not begin with syntax as is the case in constructing a derivation in his competence model. In producing a sentence, a speaker would begin with an idea, a meaning, a Semantic Representation. Similarly, neither would a speaker in perceiving or understanding a sentence begin with syntax. Rather, the speaker would begin with an input that is related to sound. It is because no language performance process begins with syntax that Chomsky is obliged to deny psychological validity to his grammar order of construction. As we have seen, he actually does make this denial.

Summary of Psychological Claims
The psychological claims that Chomsky has made from 1965 regarding the three major aspects of his grammar theory may be summarized as follows:

1. *Apparatus*. The rules and lexical items which Chomsky writes are hypothesized to have correspondences in the minds of speakers,

i.e. the rules and lexical items are claimed to have a psychological reality.

2. *Output.* The terminal structures of Deep Structure, Surface Structure, Phonetic Representation, and Semantic Representation are held to be psychologically valid. Chomsky's claim for intermediate structures is uncertain.

3. *Order of Structure Construction.* Chomsky claims the order of structure construction for a derivation would never occur in speakers, i.e. the order is a psychologically invalid one.

The psychological invalidity of Chomsky's grammar

Dependency of rules on order of construction

Consider some possible grammars which involve the same terminal structures as Chomsky's but which differ in terms of the order in which derivations are constructed. Three such orders and the order of Chomsky's grammar are shown below.

Let us consider what a grammar involving Possibility 1 above would be like. A set of rules will be necessary in order to derive Deep Structure from Semantic Representation. We can call these Semantic (S) rules. These rules would have to be different from Chomsky's Semantic rules, because Chomsky's Semantic rules are written to conform to an order based on a derivational construction that begins with Deep Structure and terminates in Semantic Representation. On the other hand, the Transformational (T) rules which would be necessary to derive Surface Structure from Deep Structure, and the ones which would be necessary to derive Phonetic Representation from Surface Structure would be the same as those Chomsky posits. This is so because the order of structure construction here is the same order as Chomsky postulates in his theory.

Now let us consider what a grammar incorporating Possibility 2 above would be like. The Phonological (P) rules which would be necessary to derive Phonetic Representation from Surface Structure would be the same as those which Chomsky postulates. For, he, too, derives Phonetic Representation from Surface Structure. The Semantic rules necessary to derive the Semantic Representation from the Deep Structure would also be the same as Chomsky's for Chomsky, too, postulates the same order of construction for these structures. However, the Transformational rules that would be necessary to derive Deep Structure from Surface Structure would not be the same as Chomsky's, for he postulates the reverse order of construction for these structures.

With regard to Possibility 3 we see that Phonological and Transformational rules different from Chomsky's would have to be posited. Only the Semantic rules would be the same.

In considering what rules would be necessary to postulate in just

POSSIBILITY 1

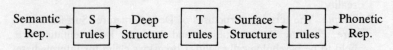

Semantic → S rules → Deep Structure   T rules → Surface Structure → P rules → Phonetic Rep.

POSSIBILITY 2

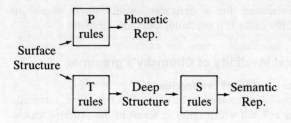

P rules → Phonetic Rep.

Surface Structure

T rules → Deep Structure → S rules → Semantic Rep.

POSSIBILITY 3

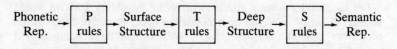

Phonetic Rep. → P rules → Surface Structure → T rules → Deep Structure → S rules → Semantic Rep.

Chomsky's standard theory

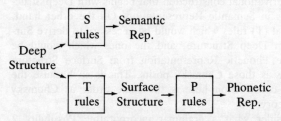

S rules → Semantic Rep.

Deep Structure

T rules → Surface Structure → P rules → Phonetic Rep.

these three orders (many other orders are also possible), we thus see that depending on the order, particular Semantic, Phonological, and Transformational rules which are different from Chomsky's are required. Clearly then, *the particular rules which are posited for a grammar are a function of the postulated order according to which structures are constructed.* That is to say, the specific rules of a grammar cannot be written independently. They are written to conform to the particular order of construction that is postulated.

The psychological contradiction in Chomsky's theorizing

Chomsky allows an order of structure construction which he himself characterizes as psychologically absurd to determine the character and composition of his rules of grammar. (Whether Deep Structure as in the Standard Theory or Surface Structure as in the Trace Theory provides the input to the Semantic Component does not change the basis for this characterization.) Since his grammatical rules have been formulated in accord with that psychologically absurd premise, one can only conclude that in general the rules of Chomsky's grammar must be as psychologically absurd as the premise on which they were based.

It should be noted that although as a whole Chomsky's grammatical rules are psychologically invalid, it does not follow that *all* are. Some of the Phonological rules, for example, might be valid as might be some of the Transformational rules. Similarly, some of Chomsky's terminal structures such as Surface Structure or Phonetic Representation might also be valid. Independent psychological evidence, however, is required before a determination can be made. Chomsky's claim that Surface Structures now contain traces which indicate which Transformational rules have been applied in its derivation thus would also require some supporting psychological evidence. I would like to emphasize that evidence which is based solely on formal criteria is not acceptable for this purpose. Since formal criteria of adequacy are so often presented in Chomsky's defense, some discussion of such criteria is in order here. Formal criteria such as simplicity or elegance, it should be recognized, are alone inadequate to provide psychological support for a theory. The principle of parsimony is one that is meaningful only if applied under certain conditions. It would make little sense, for example, to compare two theories which claim that the world is flat and decide that one or the other of them is true simply on the basis of some simplicity metric. The selection of the simpler of competing theories is hardly sufficient grounds for establishing validity. A criterion of simplicity is meaningful only if it is applied to theories not already considered invalid on other grounds. Then, too, there is a serious question as to whether one simplicity metric or another should apply. After all, what may be simple for a computer may not be simple for a person, or vice versa. And, if psychological validity is to be the criterion, it is the nature of people which must be considered.

It makes sense to apply a simplicity metric criterion only when two (or more) competing theories have equally met all other relevant criteria of adequacy. Thus, that Chomsky's grammar may be simpler than some other grammar does not by itself provide support for the psychological validity of his grammar. A criterion of simplicity can never override any independent conclusion concerning psychological validity. For, if psychological phenomena are being considered, it is psychological criteria which must take precedence over formal criteria (Steinberg, 1976).

The underlying reason for Chomsky's psychological contradiction
Chomsky was not always a mentalist. In fact, his psychological theorizing came some years after he established the basic outlines of his linguistic grammar. Prior to the 1960s, Chomsky did not hold that the rules

and lexical items of his grammar had counterparts in the minds of speakers. Nor did he hold that his grammar represented speaker knowledge. As I have detailed elsewhere (Steinberg, 1975b), Chomsky in the 1950s was anti-mentalistic, formalistic, and a Behaviorist supporter.

Consider, for example, a few quotations from Chomsky's (1955) work, *The Logical Structure of Linguistic Theory*, of which his famous 1957 work *Syntactic Structures* is but an excerpt.[4] (Emphasis in the quotation is mine, unless otherwise indicated.):

> The form of the theory that we have described [Chomsky's grammar], where every notion appearing in the theory is completely analyzed in terms of a set of operational primitives, is a very strong one. A weaker conception of scientific theory can be given. But it seems to me that this is a correct way to state the goal of that aspect of linguistic theory that we are here considering.
>
> 'Wells [(1954)] has pointed out recently that philosophers have, by and large, rejected as a general criterion of significance, the strong kind of reductionism that we are suggesting [i.e. where 'every notion appearing in the theory is completely analyzed in terms of a set of operational primitives'] as necessary for our particular purposes. *He offers this in criticism of Bloomfield's program of avoiding mentalistic foundations for linguistic theory.* It is true that many philosophers have given up a certain form of reductionism, of which Bloomfield's program (and our restatement of it) is an instance [Bloomfield advocated reducing psychological terms to physiological terms, according to Wells], as a *general* [Chomsky's emphasis] criterion for significance, and have held that such terms as 'soluble,' 'has such-and-such a molecular structure,' etc. (or the real number system), must be introduced into scientific theory even if not amenable to the kind of analysis once sought. However, I do not believe that this is relevant to Bloomfield's anti-mentalism. *The fact that a certain general criterion of significance has been abandoned does not mean that the bars are down, and that 'ideas' and 'meanings' become proper terms for linguistics, any more than it means that ghosts are proper concepts for physics.* If this rejection of an old criterion is not followed by construction of a new one, then it simply has no bearing on the selection of the legitimate terms for a scientific theory. Where it is followed by some new sense of 'significance,' then *if this new sense is at all adequate, it seems to me that it will rule out mentalism for what were essentially Bloomfield's reasons, i.e. its obscurity and general uselessness in linguistic theory.* Thus Quine rejects reductionism, suggests an alternative, and rejects mentalism.[13] (pp. I 19–20)
>
> ([13]Quine, *From a Logical Point of View*, p. 48 (The chapter titled The Problem of Meaning in Linguistics). Cf. Goodman, *Fact, Fiction, and Forecast* for a discussion of the problems touched on in

these remarks. As Goodman puts it, 'Lack of a general theory of goodness does not turn vice into virtue; and lack of a general theory of significance does not turn empty verbiage into illuminating discourse' (p. 58)).

Chomsky rejects mentalistic explanations, equating ideas and meanings with ghosts. The views of Behaviorist philosophers, Quine and Goodman, are quoted with approbation. Chomsky argues that mentalism is to be ruled out of linguistics for Bloomfield's reasons, which are that mentalism is obscure and useless in linguistic theory. Chomsky reiterates this anti-mentalistic point of view a number of times throughout the work. In one place, for example, he says: ·

Whatever the situation may be in other sciences, I think that there is hope of developing that aspect of linguistic theory being studied here on the basis of a small number of operational primitives, and that *introduction of dispositions (or mentalistic terms) is either irrelevant, or trivializes the theory.* (pp. I 20–1)

Thus, in the 1950s Chomsky rejected mentalistic explanations.
· For Chomsky, the primary goal of linguistic analysis at that time was not to represent the knowledge of speakers. It was to distinguish grammatical from ungrammatical sentences. In *Syntactic Structures* Chomsky (1957) states:

The fundamental aim in the linguistic analysis of a language L is to separate the *grammatical* sequences which are the sentences of L from the *ungrammatical* sequences which are not sentences of L and to study the structure of the grammatical sequences. (Chomsky's emphasis, p. 13)

He goes on to say:

Any grammar of a language will *project* the finite and somewhat accidental corpus of observed utterances to a set (presumably infinite) of grammatical utterances. In this respect, a grammar mirrors the behavior of the speaker who, on the basis of a finite and accidental experience with language, can produce or understand an indefinite number of new sentences. Indeed, any explication of the notion 'grammatical in L' (i.e. any characterization of 'grammatical in L' in terms of 'observed utterance of L') can be thought of as offering an explanation for this fundamental aspect of linguistic behavior. (p. 15)

Because a grammar can do what a speaker can do, i.e. provide as output an infinite number of grammatical sentences, therefore, the output of the grammar (not the grammar itself) can be said to correspond to a psychological reality. Nowhere in this and the previous work does Chomsky make any psychological claim for the rules of his grammar.

On the other hand, in a number of places, one finds Chomsky challeng-
ing the notion that the apparatus of a linguistic theory should describe
any sort of reality, such as when he downgrades a 'God's truth' or 'describes reality' approach to linguistics in contrast to a 'mathematical
games' approach (Chomsky, 1955: I 58–9).

It is unfortunate that Chomsky did not inform his readers of the
change in psychological claims regarding his grammar which he made
from 1955 to 1965. As a result, many readers, like Lamendella, who
had assumed that Chomsky's views were consistent on the matter became confused. Evidently, Chomsky's reversal during this same period,
of his position regarding the relevance of meaning for linguistic theory,
was more noticeable.

Be that as it may, what is important to note is that while Chomsky
changed his views on the psychologizing of grammar, he did not change
the essential organization of his grammar. Syntax had a primary role
while he was an anti-mentalist formalist, and syntax continued to have
this primary role even when he added semantics to the grammar and
became a mentalist. The assignment of a primary role to syntax and a
secondary role to semantics is essentially incompatible with any reasonable model of speaker performance.

Generative semantics, semantic case grammar, and psychological reality

As was detailed in the previous chapter, the rules of Generative
Semantics and Semantic Case Grammars are designed to flow from a
semantic to a phonetic structure. The order of construction of a derivation, therefore, conforms to the outline of a production process. As
such, such grammars *are* possible psychological theories of how people
produce sentences. Whether or not speakers actually do produce sentences in the way which those grammars specify is a matter which is
considered in Chapter 7. There it is proposed that speakers do not produce sentences on the basis of such a grammar but on some modification of it.

If regarded as hypotheses of the production process, these grammars
would fall into the category of integral type performance models. For,
in order to achieve the aim of producing sentences, no component
other than the grammar itself is essential. (Short-cut facilitating
strategies could, of course, be developed to work with the grammar,
but still the essential process would not be dependent on these
strategies as in the Chomskyan componential model.) On the other
hand, if these semantic based grammars are to be used in a model of
the process of understanding, where the flow goes from sound to meaning, such grammars alone are inadequate for the task. If they are to
serve such a function, then some sort of use rules of the type that

Chomsky postulates for his model of performance would be necessary. Such rules are discussed in Chapter 7.

In a sense, the problem of psychological validity is only a problem for those linguists who wish to make psychological claims about their theories. Generally, the Generative Semanticist and Semantic Case theorists have avoided making psychological claims. They pay lip-service to 'competence' and 'knowledge' but avoid discussion which would clarify the meanings they assign to such terms. Most theorists have yet to come to grips with the question of what the psychological goal of their linguistic theorizing should be. Only some realize that 'psychological reality is the *sine qua non* for any linguistic theory which aspires to achieve explanatory power' (Derwing, 1977: 16).

Notes

1. It might occur to some readers that if Chomsky's Phonological, Semantic, and Transformational rules could be used in reverse, the necessary perform-ance connections between Phonetic Representation and Semantic Representa-tion would be made. That is, a connection would be made from Phonetic Representation to Surface Structure, from Surface Structure to Deep Struc-ture, and from Semantic Representation to Surface Structure in the case of Trace Grammar Theory. (In the interest of brevity only the Trace Theory will be considered below.) Such rules, however, cannot meaningfully be used in reverse. The reason for this relates to the essential character of Phonolo-gical, Semantic, and Transformational rules. All specify a change, but only if certain environment or context conditions are present. It is because of the environmental or contextual conditions and the ordering of rules based on these conditions that rules cannot be meaningfully reversed.

   With respect to the reversibility of Phonological rules, let us consider the Chapter 2 example of a Phonetic Representation, that of [merziydhowts] for the sentence *Mares eat oats*. In this, as in most speech utterances involving sentences, pauses or junctures between individual words are generally deleted and various elisions occur. The problem with a sentence like *Mares eat oats* is that its phonetic form is similar to other different syntactic constructions, e.g. a noun + noun phrase of *Jersey goats* and a verb like *finalize*. Each of these phonetic strings has three syllables and the same stress pattern. That being the case, given [merziydhowts] as input and applying phonological rules in reverse, not only would the proper word segmentation for the intended sen-tence be a result, i.e. [merz + iydh + owts], but ungrammatical strings like *[merziy + dhowts] (on the pattern of *Jersey goats*) and *[merziydhowts] (a single non-word on the pattern of *finalize*) would also result. The grammar then would generate a variety of Surface Structures, some grammatical and some ungrammatical. Although this is a problem in itself for linguists like Chomsky who would want a grammar to filter out ungrammatical sequences, more basic and insurmountable problems remain. One of these concerns trace markers. Since the Phonological rules do not involve the selection of traces from the set of Transformational rules (each component operates inde-pendently of the other) the Surface Structures which would be generated by the reverse Phonological rules would not contain any traces. Hence, the proper Surface Structure could not be recovered by the reverse phonological process.

With respect to the reversal of Semantic rules, there are a number of reasons why the reversal of Semantic Rules will not work to recover Surface Structure. One principal one concerns the insertion of lexical items. Surface Structure requires the inclusion of lexical items as part of its structure. However, because, according to Chomsky, the insertion of lexical items occurs mainly with the generation of Deep Structure and does not involve Semantic rules, the reverse application of Semantic rules could not yield a Surface Structure with lexical items. (Some lexical items are inserted after a Transformational rule such as Affix Hopping applies.) For Semantic rules to do this, specific rules would have to be formulated that would search the lexicon to fit given meanings. This, of course, is the type of rule which Chomsky's rivals, the Generative Semantics and Semantic Case Grammar theorists have formulated.

Then, too, there is the problem of obligatory transformations in Chomsky's grammar. Surface Structures similar to *The boy who the girl likes laughed* (*whom* or *that* could also occur besides *who*) and *The boy the girl likes laughed* could not be provided by Semantic rules in reverse. Such structures, ordinarily derived from a Deep Structure similar to *The boy the girl likes the boy laughed*, must have had relevant Transformational rules applied to them. Unless certain Semantic rules are specially designed to search the set of Transformational rules to discover which rules might apply to its semantic structure, the proper Surface Structure cannot be recovered. Again, this is not something that Chomsky's grammar is designed to do.

The above problems which demonstrate the irreversibility of Semantic rules in Trace Theory are similar to those which involve Chomsky's Interpretive Semantics and Standard Theory grammars, as well. It is worth noting that if the reversal of Semantic rules really could work and Chomsky could link Semantic Representation to Surface Structure which in turn links to Phonetic Representation, then Chomsky would have achieved one of his fundamental theoretical aims, which is to connect meaning (Semantic Representation) with sound (Phonetic Representation). By doing so, however, he would have demonstrated that such a connection could be established without any need for Base rules, Transformational Rules, and Deep Structure. Parsimony would oblige him to drop these aspects of his theory. In effect, he would be left with a grammar that had the essential semantic-based organization of that of his opponents, the Generative Semantics and the Semantic Case theorists.

2. In Chomsky's grammar, lexical insertion takes place all at once, just after the last Base rule has applied.

3. It is interesting to note that some linguists, e.g. Lakoff (Lakoff & Thompson, 1975), disagree with this approach. Lakoff holds that every rule which a linguist writes must conform to a performance process and that no non-psychological formalisms should be included in a linguistic theory. What Lakoff advocates is a completely cognitive (mentalistic) theory.

4. It should be noted that Chomsky's 1975 version of his original dissertation (Chomsky, 1975c) has been edited. This editing tends to mitigate the force of statements which espouse principles that are later abandoned.

Chapter 5

Empiricism, rationalism, and behaviorism

In this chapter, Mentalist and Behaviorist views are considered, particularly as they relate to issues concerning the nature and acquisition of knowledge. The mentalist theories of Empiricists and Rationalists and the behaviorist theories of Radical and Neo-Behaviorists are discussed. Detailed consideration is given to Chomsky's theory of innate knowledge.

Mentalism and behaviorism

A mentalistic conception

The conception of the relationship of thought, language, and speech that was outlined in the preceding chapter is clearly a mentalistic one. According to that conception, a person is regarded as having a mind that is distinct from that person's body. (Brain is a physical entity having weight, size, color, etc. and thus is part of the body.) Body and mind are seen as interacting with one another such that one may cause or control events in the other. An example of body affecting mind would be the activation of a pain receptor in the body after being stuck with a pin, resulting in a feeling of pain being experienced in the mind. An example of mind affecting body would be when a person doing trimming in the garden decides, in the mind, to cut down a certain plant, and then does so using his or her body. According to this interactionist view, which is similar to the one proposed by Descartes (1641: Meditation VI), persons behave the way they do either as the result of body acting alone (as in breathing) or interacting with mind (one can hold one's breath or lift one's hand). The following schema illustrates the mind-body relationship with respect to environmental stimuli and behavioral responses in the world:

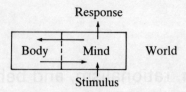

Schema 1. An Interactionist Conception of Mind, Body, and World

Thus, a response may be the result of the body acting alone in pure physiological functioning or in concert with the mind. Input stimuli may affect the mind through the body. This conception, it may be noted, is neutral with respect to the issue of Free Will; it does not specify whether the mind operates deterministically according to its own laws. Incidentally, the interactionist would argue that it is because of these two basic types of 'stuff' in the universe, the material and the mental, that sentences such as *The idea of square is purple* and *Happiness weighs 3 grams* are odd. For, in these sentences physical attributes (weight and color) are attributed to non-physical mental entities (idea and mental state).

Empiricism and rationalism as mentalism
It should be noted that the above conception also is neutral with regard to the question of innate ideas (knowledge). All mentalists will agree on the existence of mind and that humans have knowledge and ideas in the mind. What they do not agree on is how those ideas got there. Are the ideas derived entirely through experience (the Empiricist position) or are some ideas already in the mind at birth (the Rationalist position)? And, within their respective schools, Empiricists and Rationalists also disagree. The nature of the disagreements within these schools will be briefly mentioned here, since it will serve to provide a clearer understanding of them.

Before continuing, there is an important matter concerning terminology which must be cleared up. The words *Empiricist* and *Empiricism* have developed two distinct meanings. One, the more traditional, concerns the mentalistic philosophical school of which Aristotle (4th cent. B.C.) and John Locke (1690) were members. (It is this sense which this writer shall use for these words throughout this chapter and book.) The other meaning involves that of placing a high value on facts and subordinating theory and speculation in accord with those facts; nothing is implied about mentalism. This sense is the one that Behaviorist theorists, in particular, are considering when they use the word. (*Empiricalism*, perhaps, would be a better term to describe their outlook.)

Rationalists disagree as to what processing activates innate ideas and as to what kinds of ideas are innate in the mind. The classical theorists, Plato (4th cent. B.C.) and Descartes (1641), hypothesized that along with experience, the operation of reason was necessary to make innate knowledge functional (the term Rational derives from this interpretation). A modern day theorist, Chomsky (1967b), however, denies that any such operation as that of reason, logic, or intelligence is necessary. Rather he sees the mind as having relatively independent innate faculties of knowledge where only specific experiences relating to a specific faculty would activate the innate knowledge. (A detailed evaluation of Chomsky's views is presented in the latter half of this chapter.) Bever (1970), on the other hand, seems to prefer the positing of more general cognitive innate structures that are applicable to all fields of knowledge. All Rationalists agree, however, on the essential principle that some knowledge is innate in humans. Different Rationalists, for example, have posited that concepts such as justice, infinity, God, perfection, triangle, noun, and phonetic features are innate. They argue that such ideas cannot be intelligibly derived from the experience of the individual human, e.g. how can the idea of infinity be derived from finite experience? The Rationalists have the problem, however, of explaining how any such idea became innate in humans in the first place. Would not innate ideas somehow originally have had to be gained through experience? (For Descartes (1641), the answer was simple, God placed those ideas in the minds of human beings.)

While all Empiricists agree that no ideas constituting knowledge are innate (justice, infinity, God, etc.), they do not agree on whether any other sorts of ideas are innate. For Putnam (1967), a contemporary Empiricist, a general intelligence in the form of 'General Multi-Purpose Learning Strategies' is innate. One acquires knowledge through the use of this intelligence. For the more classical Locke (1690), however, intelligence or reason was not innate but acquired. (The question as to what constitutes knowledge, therefore, is at issue here.) The contemporary psychologist Piaget follows in the Lockean tradition, preferring to derive intelligence from action and experience (Piaget & Inhelder, 1969; Piaget, 1968).

Another issue which divides Empiricists is one which concerns the question of whether ideas in the mind which embody knowledge may be universal (general) as well as particular. One *Particularist*, e.g. James Mill (1829), holds that there are no universal ideas, only particulars. Thus, for him the meaning of the word *dog* in a generic or class sense consists of a set of particular dog ideas in the mind. The word *dog* is thus not the linguistic name of a unitary general idea, but of a set of particular dogs. A *Universalist*, e.g. John Locke (1690), on the other hand, argues that there are universal or general ideas in addition to particular ones. For him, the meaning of the generic *dog* consists of one general abstract, i.e. a universal idea that is applicable to all particular dogs. The particularist's objection to this doctrine is that any such concept is inconceivable. If, for example, a dog has a nose and eyes, what is the shape of a 'universal' nose which must cover all possible noses, and what is the color of a 'universal' eye which must cover all possible eye colors?

Related to this disagreement among *Empiricists* is another important one. It concerns the acquisition of abstract principles or propositions, such as those involving mathematical theorems or transformational rules. The issue involves whether sense data alone and their combinations are sufficient to account for all human intellectual knowledge. A grammatical transformational rule, such as the sort which Chomsky describes, for example, cannot be sensed directly from experience; rather, it is an abstract construction which underlies the sense experience. While some theorists like James Mill (1829) and Hume (1748) do not allow for the acquisition of principles which are not themselves sense data (sense data can combine to form complex ideas but these ideas contain only the original sense data), other theorists like Locke and John Stuart Mill (1843) and more recent ones like Putnam do posit that abstract principles may be acquired on the basis of sense data. They talk of such operations as reflection, induction, and types of intellectual functioning. As far as these latter theorists are concerned, Empiricist theory does have at its disposal a means for accounting for the type of abstract rules and operations which Chomsky and most modern theorists believe is necessary to account for the language abilities of speakers.

TABLE 1. Behaviorist and mentalist positions on body and mind

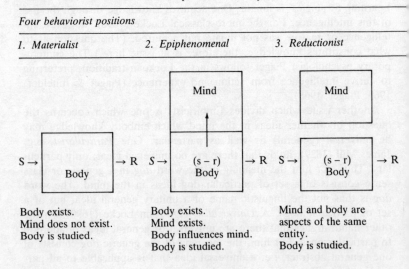

Four behaviorist positions

1. Materialist	*2. Epiphenomenal*	*3. Reductionist*
Body exists. Mind does not exist. Body is studied.	Body exists. Mind exists. Body influences mind. Body is studied.	Mind and body are aspects of the same entity. Body is studied.

Anti-mentalist views contrasted

In order to put more clearly into perspective the mentalistic conception that has been proposed, it would be instructive to contrast it with anti-mentalist conceptions. In my view, three basic issues distinguish mentalists from anti-mentalists. These may be expressed in terms of questions:

(1) Do humans have minds? (Consciousness, feelings, and ideas are considered to be some of the attributes of mind.)

(2) If humans have minds, do their minds influence the behavior of the body?

(3) Should the subject matter of psychology, including linguistics, include that which is subjective or private, i.e. involve entities which are not objective in nature?

Table 1 outlines some major positions in schema form which result from different combinations of answers to these questions.

Mentalists, such as Locke, Descartes, Putnam, Chomsky, and the Gestalt psychologists would answer each of these questions in the affirmative. Anti-mentalists, such as the Behaviorists, however, would give a negative answer to at least one of these questions. Let us consider some of the negative answers. However, before doing so, it might be noted that certain mentalists such as Berkeley (1710) might give a negative response to Question (2) if it was felt that it implied that mind was not the primary stuff of the universe. From this radical mentalist

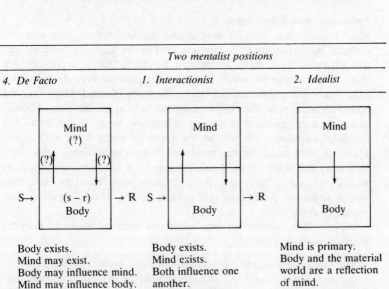

Two mentalist positions

4. De Facto   *1. Interactionist*   *2. Idealist*

Body exists.	Body exists.	Mind is primary.
Mind may exist.	Mind exists.	Body and the material
Body may influence mind.	Both influence one	world are a reflection
Mind may influence body.	another.	of mind.
Body is studied.	Both are studied.	Both are studied.

view, known as idealism, body and the rest of the physical world are mere constructions of the mind.

Materialist behaviorism

A 'no' to Question (1) would have been given by John B. Watson, the founder of Behaviorism. Watson regarded mind and consciousness as religious superstitions which were irrelevant to the study of psychology. Watson (1924) stated:

> . . . belief in the existence of consciousness goes back to the ancient days of superstition and magic . . . Magic lives forever. . . . These concepts – these heritages of a timid savage past – have made the emergence and growth of scientific psychology extremely difficult. (pp. 2, 3)

Watson's criterion for determining whether something did or did not exist was whether or not it was observable. Thus, he stated:

> No one has ever touched a soul (mind) or seen one in a test tube, or has in any way come into relationship with it as he has with other objects of his daily existence. (p. 3)

Psychology was regarded as indistinguishable from physiology. 'It is different from physiology only in the grouping of its problems, not in fundamentals or in central viewpoint.' (p. 11)

Epiphenomenal behaviorism

Most Behaviorists after Watson found his materialism (the essential doctrine being that there is only one stuff in the universe, the material) too extreme. They have formulated positions that generally do not deny the existence of mind. However, in practice they do not differ from Watson because none advocates the study of mind. Many take the epiphenomenal view that mind exists but only as a reflection of bodily processes with the mind in no way influencing events in the body. For example, one may feel pain as the result of being stuck with a pin. However, that feeling in the mind will in no way influence subsequent behavior. All behavior (and mental events) is entirely determined by bodily processes. Thus while these theorists allow mind to exist, they give it no power. And, since it is without power, there is no compelling reason to study it.

Skinner is evidently one who takes this point of view. In his later writings, he says:

> The fact of privacy (non-objective subjective events) cannot of course, be questioned. . . . Though two people may in some sense be said to see the same light or hear the same sound, they cannot feel the same distention of a bile duct or the same bruised muscle. (1964, p. 2)

The 'fact' of subjective events and feelings (presumably in a mind) are not at issue. However, such a fact is not to be interpreted as indicating that mental states and processes warrant study, for they do not influence behavior. Thus, Skinner (1971) says, 'It [Behaviorism] rejects explanations of human behavior in terms of feelings, states of mind, and mental processes, and seeks alternatives in genetic and environmental histories.' (p. 35)

With regard to clarifying this point of view let us consider the example of Hillary's conquest of Everest. Hillary has said:

> The battle really, in a sense, is with yourself. The – mountain is sort
> of – is really giving you an environment, and then what you're
> tackling, the – problems within yourself, your own internal fears and
> – even your doubts, perhaps, about your ability to persist and to
> meet the – the problems and all the rest of it.[1]

The epiphenomenalist would have us believe that what Hillary is talking about is entirely irrelevant to his behavior. That is, his state of mind contributed nothing to the endeavor but had merely reflected what the body had already achieved. The epiphenomenal Behaviorist philosopher Ryle (1949) thus scoffs at what he terms Descartes' 'ghost in the machine' concept where the 'ghost' (mind) manipulates the 'machine' (body). He and the other epiphenomenalist theorists would like us to think that it is more reasonable to believe that machines can manipulate ghosts!

Reductionist and de facto behaviorism

Other Behaviorists take a reductionist view. They may allow that mind exists as does body, but they believe that whatever happens in the mind also happens in the body. They hold a kind of Spinozan double-aspect position, believing that both mind and body are two aspects of a single reality. (This view contrasts with the epiphenomenal view which holds that body is the primary reality.) Since, by taking this position, one can learn all there is to know about mind by a thorough study of body, there is no need to study mind. Thus, in a sense, mind reduces to body. Such being the case, mind can be studied entirely through body in relative metaphysical comfort.

Most Behaviorists, I think, are vague and non-committal about their beliefs on the mind-body issue. They may believe that mind exists and even causally interacts with body, but they reject the study of mind because it is not objective and presents difficulties in conducting empirical investigations. Such theorists say that they are neutral with respect to metaphysical issues. However, because they do not engage in the study of mind, but study only body with relationship to the world, in practice they do not differ from materialists, epiphenomenalists, and reductionists. As such they are *de facto* behaviorists.

Essence of anti-mentalism

Not all anti-mentalist theory is as simple as Watson's or Skinner's. Some theories may be as complex as those posited by the Neo-Behaviorists, e.g. Osgood (1971) and Mowrer (1960). In these theories, internal stimuli and responses mediate between observable stimuli and responses. The character of the mediating entities is such that they are part of the body; no mental mediators are permitted. Such theories differ markedly, however, from those of the Radical Behaviorists, e.g. Watson and Skinner, according to which no hypothetical mediating stimuli and responses are posited. Then, too, anti-mentalist theory may be as subtle as the philosophical Behaviorist type theories of Ryle (1949: 199) and Quine (1960: 34–5) who hold that the object of psychological study should be bodily dispositions or inclinations for behaving. Despite the diversity, however, all anti-mentalist theorists hold one principle in common; they do *not* study mind. Rather, they study bodily (including brain) processes and events with relationship to the physical environment.

Three arguments for mentalism

In support of the mentalistic conception of the relationship of thought, language, and speech, I offer three arguments in favor of the mentalistic point of view.

Mentalist argument: Insincerity

Suppose that I tell someone, 'I will pay you tomorrow.' Suppose, too, that when the next day comes, I do not pay that person. Now, if while making the statement I never had any intention of paying the person, we would say that I had been insincere. However, if I did have the intention but simply forgot the next day to make the payment, we would not say that I had been insincere; I would have been forgetful or irresponsible. Thus, for exactly the same observable situation (I say that I will pay tomorrow but do not), two very different judgments may be made. Clearly the basis for the judgment depends on something besides the observable situation since that situation is identical in both cases. That basis is the intention, a state of mind, of the speaker at the time the statement was made. Without considering the intention, as do the Behaviorists, judgments of insincerity, lying, and the like, are not comprehensible. What we do in ordinary life, of course is to attempt to determine indirectly what intention the person had. Since we cannot observe a person's mind to discover an intention, we make judgments based on the person's previous behavior both with ourselves and others.

Mentalist argument 2: Behavior relating to dreams

Consider the following true case. My wife, who does flower arranging, had dreams in which she created unique and original arrangements. After she woke up, she would copy the arrangements of her dreams. Now, if mental states such as dreams are to have no role in the explanation of behavior, as the Behaviorists would have it, how can the behavior of my wife be accounted for? We may even obtain a verbal report of her dream before she makes her waking-life arrangement. What would explain the correspondence between the verbal report and the behavior which creates the waking-life arrangement?

Consider, too, the case of persons talking aloud in their sleep while having dreams. Suppose in the middle of the night I shout, 'I don't want to buy Nixon a skate-board,' and then I wake up. I tell my wife, who had been awakened by my shouting that I had a dream in which the Supreme Court rules that I must buy Nixon a skate-board despite my strong objections. To explain my behavior (my verbal report of the dream, what I shouted, and the close correspondence between the two) is relatively easy from a mentalistic point of view. My behavior is a response to the mental experience of a dream. If, as the Behaviorists maintain, mental events are not to be considered as determinants of behavior, then I cannot see how the behaviors in question are to be explained.

Mentalist argument 3: Toothache and dentist
Suppose that I tell you that I had a toothache and went to the dentist. Now, how is my behavior of going to the dentist to be explained? I would say that I went to the dentist because I felt a pain in my tooth and I wanted to get relief from that pain. In this mentalistic interpretation, a state of mind, that of experiencing pain, is the cause of my behavior of going to the dentist.

A Behaviorist account of going to the dentist will include talk of prior conditioning of objective stimuli and responses and perhaps of generalization of those stimuli and responses. The basic problem with any such explanation is the following: How did I know that I had a toothache, and why did I formulate sentences concerning that toothache, if I cannot use a criterion of experienced pain? Since I cannot observe the interior of my tooth, I cannot observe any impinging stimuli which might activate the pain receptors. How then did I know that I was in pain? Without the phenomenal experience of pain, I could not know, and would not have behaved as I did.

Just because phenomenal experiences such as pain cannot be directly observed, it does not follow that such experiences cannot be incorporated into scientific theory. Phenomenal experience may be inferred or corroborated by personal reports of the experiencer. Thus, one may infer that someone is experiencing pain based on reliable objective observations concerning the stimuli impinging on him or her and based on the person's behavioral responses to those stimuli.

The making of inferences regarding unobservables should not frighten Behaviorist psychologists. After all, this is done in Physics all the time. Consider the phenomenon of gravity, for example. This theoretical entity is similar in some important respects to mentalistic entities: gravity is inherently unobservable; only its effects can be observed; it controls the behavior of objects which *can* be observed. Mental phenomena, however, have an important advantage over physical theoretical entities such as gravity. For, while no one can directly experience gravity (only its postulated effects), one can directly experience certain mental events such as feelings and images. Thus, I might hypothesize that you have a pain, based on the stimuli and responses which I observe. I may attempt to corroborate that hypothesis by getting a report from you. Of course, the report may be a false one in that what you say may not correspond to what you experienced in your mind. (How else could a judgment of truth or falsity be made in such a case without reference to the contents of the mind!) Still, despite the possible unreliability of such data, is not the mentalist in a better position than the physicist who deals with theoretical physical entities concerning which no phenomenal data can be gathered?

Chomsky's rationalism

A discussion of the Rationalism-Empiricism issue would not be complete without a detailed consideration of the views of the brilliant contemporary Rationalist thinker, Noam Chomsky. In this section I shall outline Chomsky's theory of innate knowledge and language acquisition. I shall then evaluate the major arguments that he has offered in support of that theory.

Faculties of the mind and LAD
According to Chomsky, humans are born with minds that contain innate knowledge concerning a number of different areas. One such area or faculty of the mind concerns language. Chomsky has called that innate language knowledge LAD, language acquisition device. It is Chomsky's belief that such faculties of the mind are relatively independent of one another. For example, he believes that innate knowledge alone is sufficient for the acquisition of language and that mathematical or logical knowledge is not needed (MacIntyre, 1970). (Actually, this is one basis for Chomsky's oft-repeated assertion that language acquisition is independent of intelligence and logic.)

It is important to note that knowledge which is innate is not functional or operational and it may not become so unless certain experiences stemming from the world interact with it. Thus, experience is an essential element in the acquisition of knowledge. Its role, however, is not so much to form or shape knowledge as it is to activate the knowledge that is already innate but latent in the human being.

The function of LAD is to provide a person with a particular gram-mar (sets of rules and lexical items), given language data (sentences, in particular) of that language. Thus, for example, given English sen-tences as input, LAD constructs a grammar of English in the child's mind. Hence, LAD provides: (a) the basic ideas for forming the par-ticular rules and particular lexical items of any grammar; and (b) the operational means according to which, over time, such an outcome may be achieved. These contents and functions of LAD which Chomsky also refers to in his writings as Universal Grammar, will now be discus-sed in greater detail.

Content and operation of LAD

Chomsky incorporates three classes of innate ideas into LAD. These are: *substantive* ideas, *formal* ideas, and those which I shall call *con-structive* ideas. The substantive ideas are those ideas which appear in relations or are manipulated by operations, i.e. phonetic, syntactic, and semantic features. The *formal* ideas are those which express relations or manipulations, i.e. the Base rule and Transformation rule functions. For example, in Base rules, which have the form $A \rightarrow B + C$, e.g. $S \rightarrow NP + VP$, the elements A, B, and C are the substantive ideas, while the relationship of $\ldots \rightarrow \ldots + \ldots$ is the formal idea. In Transforma-tional rules, which have the form $X \Rightarrow Y/Z$, i.e. some structure X changes in some way to a different structure Y, under a certain condi-tion Z, the formal idea is $\ldots \Rightarrow \ldots / \ldots$, where $\Rightarrow$ can represent any of a number of changes (deletion, addition, substitution, permutation). The combination of substantive and formal ideas provide the basis for the construction of any grammar of a language.

The third class of innate ideas, the *constructive*, are those ideas which enable the mind to construct a particular grammar using the sub-stantive and formal innate ideas, given particular language data as in-put. According to Chomsky (1967b), the constructive ideas will func-tion to select and evaluate particular linguistic hypotheses. Thus, for example, the simplest rules will be selected for inclusion in the particu-lar grammar while those rules which are faulty or more complex will be rejected. Such a process is a function of the innate constructive ideas. Thus, Chomsky not only indicates in LAD the basic stuff out of which a particular grammar is to be constructed, he also indicates how and by what means such an operation is to be carried out.

Unfortunately, Chomsky is hardly more detailed about the contents of LAD than what is presented above. While Chomsky has written a great deal concerning arguments in favor of his LAD, he has written almost nothing concerning its content and operation. Thus, for exam-ple, the crucial question of how any innate particular language idea, e.g. that of Noun, might be activated by experience is not discussed. Hence, we do not know if the experience of the speech sound of any noun of a language or the experience of an object, say, is necessary for its activation. Neither do we know whether one or more experiences of the same or of a different type are believed to be necessary in this regard. Chomsky presents his LAD theory in the most general of terms.

Chomsky's arguments for LAD

Let us now consider some of the major arguments which Chomsky presents in support of his LAD theory. The four which will be considered are: (1) the peculiarity of grammar; (2) imperfect input data; (3) the irrelevance of intelligence; and (4) the ease and speed of child language acquisition.

1. PECULIARITY OF GRAMMAR.   According to Chomsky (1967b: 6);

> Deep structures seem to be very similar from language to language, and the rules that manipulate and interpret them also seem to be drawn from a very narrow class of conceivable formal operations. There is no *a priori* necessity for a language to be organized in this highly specific and most peculiar way. There is no sense of 'simplicity' in which this design for language can be intelligibly described as 'most simple.' Nor is there any content to the claim that this design is somehow 'logical.'

Because the grammar of every language is so peculiar, so un-simple, so un-logical, and yet so similar in the same aspects, Chomsky believes that it is necessary to postulate innate language knowledge in order to account for these facts.

One may question, as have many linguists, whether it is indeed the case that the nature of language is as Chomsky describes. Certainly, the Generative Semanticists and Case Grammarians would not agree that language is as un-logical as Chomsky believed. If, with such linguists, one does not believe that such a peculiar structure as Chomsky's 'Deep Structure' exists, nor does one believe that grammars are organized in the peculiar manner as Chomsky contends (with syntax 'primary', etc.), then one does not have peculiar phenomena that especially require explanation in terms of innate language knowledge. Of course, even if grammars were not as peculiar as Chomsky contends, the learning of grammar must still be accounted for, and, in this regard, a theory of innate knowledge may be postulated. Such a theory, however, would have to be posited for reasons other than peculiarity. Given the doubts of other linguists concerning Chomsky's grammar, and given the dubious psychological validity of that grammar (see Chapter 4), Chomsky's 'peculiarity' argument is hardly a compelling one.

And, if grammar is not as peculiar as Chomsky contends, it may not be as independent of other knowledge (mathematics, logic, music, etc.) as Chomsky holds. Structure dependent transformations and other general linguistic phenomena may occur in other domains of knowledge with the result that a more general cognitive capacity (rather than a specific knowledge capacity) may be hypothesized. Whether such a general cognitive capacity has at its base innate knowledge or not would still be an open question. The issue then shifts from how *peculiar* language knowledge is to be accounted for to how *general cognitive* knowledge is to be accounted for. It may then be argued whether the universality of this general cognitive knowledge is to be explained in Empiricist or Rationalist terms. The Empiricist might argue, as does Putnam (1967), that language originally was not the product of innate knowledge but the product of an invention of the mind, and that the reason why languages have so much in common is that the originally invented language spread (like the invention of the alphabet did) and that its most useful features and structures were retained by the borrowers. The Rationalist might object that 'invention' appears to be a magical explanation where something comes from nothing. On the other hand, the Empiricist might retort that if innate knowledge is attributed to humans, how is that knowledge to be accounted for in evolutionary terms? Would not the innate knowledge have to be experienced at some time in the human past? And, if so, would it not have to be said that such knowledge 'comes from nothing'? Such issues are clearly far from resolution.

2. IMPERFECT INPUT DATA. Chomsky (1967b) notes that children learn the grammar of their language despite having received language data that are 'meager in scope' and 'degenerate in quality' and despite those data being a 'minute sample of the linguistic material that has been thoroughly mastered.' He concludes that 'Thus the child learns the principles of sentence formation and sentence interpretation on the basis of a corpus of data that consists, *in large measure*, of sentences that deviate in form from the idealized structures defined by the grammar that he develops.' (p. 6, emphasis added) He then argues that children could not learn the grammar that they do, i.e. a system composed of rules that do not reflect those imperfections, unless they had the assistance of innate knowledge. Chomsky believes that Empiricists cannot explain such a phenomenon for they must hold that since defective language experience serves as input then the resulting grammar must be similarly defective.

Labov (1970a), however, has argued that 'The ungrammaticality of every-day speech appears to be a myth with no basis in actual fact. In the various empirical studies which we have conducted ... the proportion of truly ungrammatical and ill-formed sentences falls to less than two percent.' (p. 42) Other research since then has also supported Labov's view. Newport (1975), for example, in a long term study with 15 mothers reports an incidence of only 1 ungrammatical utterance in

1500. While Chomsky might revise his original claim regarding the incidence of ungrammatical speech, he nonetheless insists that any degree of ungrammaticality poses a serious problem. Chomsky (1975a: fn. 6) has argued:

> ... suppose that a scientist were presented with data, 2 per cent of which are wrong (but he doesn't know which 2 per cent). Then, he faces some serious difficulties, which would be incomparably more serious if the data were simply uncontrolled experience, rather than the result of controlled experiment devised for its relevance to theoretical hypotheses. The fact that these difficulties do not seem to arise for the language learner, who is, of course, faced with degenerate data of experience, requires explanation.

I myself doubt that if only 2 per cent of data were degenerate that learners would have much difficulty. Learners tend to simply discard that which they do not understand. And, unless the 2 per cent of the data in question always involved the same linguistic problems (which is quite unlikely), then we would expect correct instances of the data to appear in the future for the learner to process.

As to Chomsky's claim that only a 'minute sample' of language is experienced, one may ask whether there is reason to believe that the 'minute sample' does not actually contain all of the linguistic *structures* in question, i.e. is the 'minute sample' an adequate sample of linguistic *structures* although it represents only a small proportion of the total number of sentences? One wonders what particular linguistic structures Chomsky has in mind such that they may be learned even though no instances of them are reflected in the sentences which have been experienced.

3 THE IRRELEVANCE OF INTELLIGENCE.   Related to Chomsky's peculiarity of grammar argument is his contention that language learning is essentially independent of intelligence. In support of this thesis, he argues that grammar is peculiar not logical, hence, he implies, since it is not a direct function of rational operating intelligence, it must be a function of innate language knowledge. He further argues that '... vast differences in intelligence have only a small effect on resulting competence (knowledge of grammar)' (Chomsky, 1967b: 3). Since the issue of peculiarity which concerns the first argument has already been discussed in a previous section, let us consider this further argument regarding vast differences and small effect. The basis of that argument evidently is as follows: If intelligence is relevant to language acquisition, then more intelligent people should acquire a greater competence. However, greater and lesser intelligent persons acquire nearly the same competence. Since different degrees of intelligence do not affect competence, the variable of intelligence is irrelevant to the acquisition of

competence. (What Chomsky goes on then to argue is that since the uniformity of competence is not due to intelligence, it must be due to some other agency, which, for him, is innate language knowledge.)

This argument of Chomsky has one major weakness. It is that Chomsky supposes that increases in intelligence beyond that of low intelligence should result in greater or improved competence. In other words, he assumes that an optimum competence cannot be acquired through low intelligence. This assumption is entirely unwarranted since it may well be the case that low intelligence is all that is necessary for the acquisition of competence. After all, both high and low (but not defective) intelligence people learn to drive cars, to do arithmetic, etc. Yet, we do not generally consider such observations as evidence that intelligence is irrelevant to the learning of those tasks. Lenneberg (1967) made observations which directly support this interpretation. Concerning the relationship of intelligence to language acquisition, he said,

> The study of the mongoloid population, as well as that of additional cases of mental retardation, indicates that there is a certain 'IQ threshold value' that varies with age and that must be attained for language to be acquired. Individuals below this threshold have varying degrees of [language] primitivity... It is noteworthy that *this threshold is relatively low*. (pp. 310–11)

Incidentally, it might be noted that it is not necessary for Chomsky to deny a role to intelligence in order that he posit the existence of innate knowledge. After all, for many eminent innatists, the operation of some sort of intelligence in terms of reasoning or logic is essential for bringing out and making functional ideas which were innate. (See Descartes, 1641, for example.) They would not agree with Chomsky that intelligence is irrelevant to language acquisition.

4. EASE AND SPEED OF CHILD LANGUAGE ACQUISITION. According to Chomsky (1962: 529):

> A young child is able to gain perfect mastery of a language with incomparably greater ease [than an adult] and without any explicit instruction. Mere exposure to the language, for a remarkably short period, seems to be all that the normal child requires to develop the competence of the native speaker.

And further, Chomsky (1967: 4) says:

> We observe further that the tremendous intellectual accomplishment is carried out at a period of life when the child is capable of little else, and that this task is entirely beyond the capacities of an otherwise intelligent ape.

Since the child's remarkable accomplishment could not have been acquired through a simple accumulation of learning acquired through experience along Empiricist principles, then, Chomsky suggests, the child must have had the assistance of innate language knowledge.

One basic underlying premise on which this argument rests is that four or five years (or whatever length of time it takes the child to acquire a grammar) is not a long time. Putnam (1967) challenges that assumption directly with the view that a child of four or five will have had more than enough experience with which to learn a language. Perhaps five years would be a long time if the child had to learn the peculiar grammar that Chomsky has in mind. Perhaps not. However, unless one knows precisely what it is that the child learns, one cannot seriously begin to evaluate the plausibility of this premise.

Chomsky's contention that the child intellectually accomplishes little else other than to acquire language during the early years is undoubtedly extreme. By the age of five years children learn a great deal intellectually that is of a non-linguistic nature. Deaf children who are denied language, for example, acquire a perceptual and social knowledge of the world that allows them to be identified as rational human beings.

As to Chomsky's comment that an 'otherwise intelligent ape' fails to learn language, it would seem that research has since shown (Premack & Premack, 1972, for example) that apes can to some degree learn language. Whether this indicates that apes, too, have innate knowledge or that they have learned what they have learned through intelligence remains an open question.

It should be kept in mind that if arguments are placed in support of a theory and those arguments are found faulty, it does not necessarily follow that the theory is false. Chomsky's LAD theory may indeed be true; however, the arguments which he presents in its favor do not persuade me that this is so.

Note

1. Hillary's remarks were broadcast on 5 June, 1978 on the CBS Radio *Newsbreak* program directed by Charles Osgood.

Chapter 6

Language and thought

> The Comfort and Advantage of Society, not being to be had without
> Communication of Thoughts, it was necessary, that Man should find
> out some external visible Signs, whereof those invisible *Ideas*, which
> his Thoughts are made up of, might be made known to others
>
>   John Locke (1690)
>   *An Essay Concerning Human Understanding*,
>   Book III, Chap. ii, sec. 1

There is an ancient belief which many people uncritically hold today.
It is that thought is somehow dependent on language. The principal
formulations concerning the relationship of language and thought have
been expressed in recent times as follows: (1) Speech production or
other behavior is fundamental for thought; (2) Language is a fundamental basis of thought; (3) The language system *per se* provides
specifics of one's view of nature; and (4) The language system *per se*
provides specifics of one's culture. These notions will be critically examined in this chapter, as will some faulty assumptions that underlie
these notions. Following this discussion, instances where language does
influence thought are detailed. Finally, a conceptual framework which
integrates language, speech, and thought is proposed.

Given the nature of the topic under discussion, most objections which
are offered cannot be expected to be definitive. The essential purpose
of the objections proposed in this chapter, therefore, is to raise reasonable doubts concerning the notions under scrutiny. This will be attempted without any serious attempt at defining the nature of one of the
fundamentals in the discussion, that of thought. Such a concept, rather,
is treated as a theoretical primitive whose definition awaits the results
of future inquiry. The general notion of thought which shall be sub-
scribed to in this chapter is one whose essentials have been shared with

mentalist philosophers throughout the centuries, e.g. Plato, Aristotle, Descartes, Locke, and Kant. For while these philosophers have disagreed on such issues as the nature of thought and the origin of ideas, they all have agreed on the existence of mind and thought, and its influence on behavior.

Four inadequate notions concerning thought, language, and speech

Notion 1: Speech production or other behavior is the basis of thought

Contemporary proponents of this view hold that thought is a kind of behavior, mainly speech. Typically, such theories are held by behaviorists who wish to reduce the notion of thought or cognition to that which is observable or potentially observable. They reject any notion that affirms the existence of mental process and its relevance to the causation of behavior. The psychologists Watson, Skinner, and Staats, the linguist Bloomfield and the philosopher Ryle are but a few who propose such a conception. Advocates of the motor theory of speech perception – the theory that the understanding of speech requires a prior motor act of some sort, e.g. sub-vocal speech or internal articulation – are also generally involved in a similar conception, e.g. Liberman.

The following quotations characterize the view in question:
John B. Watson (1924):

> The behaviorist advances the view that *what the psychologists have hitherto called thought is in short nothing but talking to ourselves* . . . My theory does hold that the muscular habits learned in overt speech are responsible for implicit or internal speech (thought). (p. 238–9) Speaking overtly or to ourselves (thinking) is just as objective [physical] a type of behavior as baseball. (p. 6) (emphasis is Watson's)

B. F. Skinner (1957):

> The simplest and most satisfactory view is that thought is simply *behavior* – verbal or nonverbal, covert or overt. It is not some mysterious process responsible for behavior but the very behavior itself in all the complexity of its controlling relations, with respect to both man the behaver and the environment in which he lives. (p. 449)

Leonard Bloomfield (1961) from a 1942 paper:

> The fully literate person has succeeded in reducing these speech movements to the point where they are not even visible. That is, he has developed a system of internal substitute movements which serve

him for private purpose, such as thinking and silent reading, in place
of audible speech sounds. (p. 31)

Gilbert Ryle (1949):

> Much of our ordinary thinking is conducted in internal monologue of
> silent soliloquy, usually accompanied by an internal
> cinematograph-show of visual imagery. This trick of talking to
> oneself in silence is acquired neither quickly nor without effort; and
> *it is a necessary condition of our acquiring it that we should have*
> *previously learned to talk intelligently aloud and have heard and*
> *understood other people doing so.* (p. 27) (emphasis mine)

Thus, Ryle regards thinking, which for him is talking to oneself in silence, as an accomplishment that has a speech base.

Alvin Liberman (1957):

> . . . articulatory movements and their sensory effects mediate between
> the acoustic stimulus and the event we call perception. (p. 122)

Let us consider some objections which may be raised with regard to
the position of these theories. Not all objections, however, will apply
to all theorists. Then, too, some of the objections placed under succeeding notions may also be applicable to these theorists. And, as was
noted before, given the abstract and intangible nature of the subject
matter, no objection can be expected to be definitive. The principle
aim, rather, is to provide a number of objections whose combined
effect is to raise reasonable doubts about the notion in question.

Objections to Notion 1

1. Speech understanding precedes speech production in normal children
Normal infants learning a language come to understand speech prior to
producing it themselves. For example, a one-year-old child may be able
to understand a sentence like *Put the banana on the table* yet still may
be only at a one-word (or even no-word) stage of speech production.
The research that has been done in this area confirms this common
observation of parents. For example, Huttenlocher (1974) studied four
children and found that their speech understanding was well in advance
of their production ability. Similarly, Sachs and Truswell (1976) found
that children who could say only single words could understand speech
structures composed of more than one word, e.g. *Kiss ball* and *Smell
truck*. Then, too, Steinberg and Steinberg (1975) report the case of a
normal child who from one to two years of age was taught to read and
understand a number of written words, phrases, and sentences before he
had developed the ability to utter them. Thus, the fact that children
have the ability to understand speech indicates that they must have the
thought that is involved in the comprehension of speech. And, the fact

that children learn to understand speech prior to producing it indicates that speech production is not necessary for the development of thought. That children are able to construct and utter words and sentences which provide a meaningful communication only after they gain an understanding of language items first is not surprising. The sound forms of the words of a particular language, the meanings of those words, the syntactic relations in a sentence, etc. cannot be known by a child without prior exposure and some analysis of that language.

2. *Speech understanding without speech production in handicapped children*

Persons who are congenitally mute or have congenital spastic paralysis and are otherwise normal acquire a normal understanding of speech even though they cannot produce it or can only produce it laboriously and faultily. For example, Steinberg and Chen (1980) report the case of a three-year-old Japanese girl who was congenitally mute but hearing. Although she could utter only a few sounds, that child could understand what was spoken to her. (Appropriate behavioral responses to a variety of complex instructions provided empirical evidence for this.) She was even taught to read complex Japanese writing, through matching cards with objects. Clearly, that she was able to understand language indicates that she was able to think. The existence of thought could not have been dependent on the acquisition of the ability to speak because she had no such ability.

If it is then to be argued, as Skinner does, that behavioral responses other than speech may be the basis of thought, it then remains to be demonstrated what particular behavioral responses, e.g. muscular or glandular activities, are involved. In this regard, it might be noted that about 50 years ago, behaviorist psychologists were delighted to discover that changes in electrical potential occurred in parts of the bodies of subjects who were instructed to think of certain motor activities. For example, changes in electrical potential in the musculature of the right arm occurred in response to instructions to think about lifting that arm. Many psychologists then believed that they had begun to localize thought and meaning in the body. The problem with this theory is that it incorrectly predicts that a loss of thought or meaning will occur with damage or removal of body parts. It also fails to explain how persons with congenital paralysis or muscular deficiencies of various sorts can acquire an understanding of language. (See Osgood (1953: 648) for a critical review of such research attempts.)

The fact that persons with various speech and behavioral deficiencies acquire the ability to understand language, and that such an ability must include thought, however one defines such a term, shows that the development of thought does not depend on speech production and other behavior.

3. Simultaneous speaking and thinking

Consider a situation where a person is talking to someone but is thinking of something else at the same time. That person might be talking to someone about a movie and also be thinking about how the other person looks, etc. One might even be telling a lie. Clearly, two distinct processes with different content are occurring at the same time. However, if thought were merely some kind of internalized speech, serious problems would arise from this behaviorist conception. For, according to this conception, the variables which control the content and construction of sentences are the same for overt and covert speech. They do not postulate one set of variables which would determine sentences for overt speech and another set of variables which would determine sentences for covert speech. Rather, the principal model holds that one set of variables determines the content and construction of sentences. (Other types of variables, e.g. reward contingencies, will then determine whether the sentence will be uttered.)

The issue of lying particularly places such a view in a difficult position. For, given a single stimulus situation, how could two different and opposing sentences (one expressing a true or actual state of affairs and one expressing a false or non-existent state of affairs) be constructed as responses? Such a problem places behaviorists in a dilemma, for, if they accept the necessity of having two different processes for overt and covert sentence construction, they would subvert the essential intent of the original theory. That intent was to eliminate (because it was associated with mentalism) the need for an independent cognitive level called thought by equating it with speech or deriving it from speech.

Notion 2: Language is a fundamental basis of thought

Many theorists, such as Vygotsky, Sapir, and Whorf hold that the language system, with its rules or vocabulary, forms thought or is necessary for thought. For example:

Vygotsky (1934)

> Thought is not merely expressed in words; it comes into existence through them. . . . The relation between thought and word is a living process: thought is born through words. (pp. 125, 153)

Edward Sapir (1921):

> The writer, for one, is strongly of the opinion that the feeling entertained by so many that they can think, or even reason, without language is an illusion. (p. 15)

Benjamin Whorf, from his 1940 paper (Carroll, 1956):

> The background linguistic system (in other words, the grammar) of each language is not merely a reproducing instrument for voicing

ideas but rather is itself the shaper of ideas, the program and guide for the individual's mental activity, for his analysis of impressions, for his synthesis of his mental stock in trade. *Formulation of ideas* is not an independent process, strictly rational in the old sense, but *is part of a particular grammar*, and differs, from slightly to greatly between different grammars. We dissect nature along lines laid down by our native language. (p. 212–13. emphasis mine)

It might be noted that Vygotsky differs from Whorf in that he does not make language the ultimate source of meaning. Rather, Vygotsky sees meaning (thought) as arising from an interaction between language and environment. The environment is not considered to be an independent source of meaning, however.

Objections to Notion 2

1. Deaf persons without language think

There are many deaf children who do not begin to acquire language until a rather late age, often after five years, when they begin to attend special schools. These are typically children who have a congenital hearing loss of over 90 decibels and are unable to receive speech, and whose parents (usually hearing) do not know sign language. These children, when at play and when participating in activities around the home, appear to behave just as intelligently and rationally with respect to their environment as do hearing children. If one holds that language is the basis for thought, one would have to argue that these children do not think. And, if one holds that grammar determines how we 'dissect nature,' then it must be argued that either the non-language deaf children cannot dissect nature or that they do it differently from children who do have grammars. No such difference has ever been noted, nor has it ever been observed that deaf children who acquire language late undergo a radical change of perception. Rather, research evidence points to the opposite conclusion. Furth (1966; 1971), for example, provides research data which shows no difference in intelligence between normal and deaf persons, even though the language knowledge of the deaf persons is generally far below that of hearing persons. The case of Helen Keller whose language knowledge was minimal until she was eight years old also is relevant to this issue. It would be insupportable to maintain that she could not think nor sensibly perceive the world prior to that age.

2. Multilinguals as unitary persons

Consider persons who are proficient in more than one language. If the language system forms thought, and if different languages form different thought systems, then such persons would have formed more than one system of thought. (It would not have been possible under the theory to form a single system because opposing concepts derived from the different languages would be involved.) Persons knowing three languages would have formed three systems of thought, for example. If multilingual persons have many different thought processes, such persons would not have coherent intelligence or personalities. Different guiding ideas would be involved with the different languages. Then, too, such persons would have difficulty in using the knowledge gained through one language when operating in the other languages, since thought is supposed to be language-specific and not universal according to this theory. No evidence of the malfunctioning and other sorts of problems for multilingual persons which the theory predicts has ever been offered in support of the theory. Casual observation of multilingual-multicultural persons might sometimes seem to provide such support, e.g. a person might be aggressive in one culture but passive in another, or polite in one and impolite in another. However, such observations, it must be realized, cannot be taken at face value as indicating true differences in thought or personality. In life, even in a monolingual cultural environment, a person plays a variety of roles some of which involve such different demands and relations that it appears that a different person is involved. It is not uncommon, for example, for a subordinate to be surprised at how the boss behaves when the subordinate visits the boss' home. Deference, manner, etc. may change from situation to situation. It would be erroneous, however, to interpret such changes as indicating different systems of thought.

Cases of persons who live in only one environment but have learned a number of languages simultaneously in that environment perhaps provide the best test of the theory in question. For there are a multitude of variables involving multilinguals who have lived in different cultures and they must be controlled if proper conclusions are to be drawn. In this regard, I would like to offer the case of a family whom I know well. Two sons grew up in that family speaking English, Japanese, and Russian. The father speaks English, the mother Japanese, and the grandmother, who lives with them, Russian. The two boys, four years apart in age, each learned all of these languages simultaneously from birth. As far as can be observed, the children are no different from monolingual English children of their age in terms of beliefs, values, personality, and their perceptions of the world and nature. One would not expect such an outcome from a theory which predicts that significant differences will occur due to the effects of learning such disparate languages as English, Japanese, and Russian.

3. Intelligent animal behavior and perception

Animals do not ordinarily have language. Yet it may be observed that many species, e.g. chimpanzees, porpoises, whales, elephants, and dogs, do behave creatively and intelligently and that they respond to the physical world as if they perceived it in much the same way as we do (Ardrey, 1970). Such thought, however minimal, could not have been acquired by the animals through grammar. This indicates that thought and perception must have some basis other than language. Then, too, consider the cases where chimpanzees and a gorilla have learned some language (Gardner & Gardner, 1969, 1975; Premack & Premack, 1972; Patterson, 1978). Language has even been used creatively by them. For example, one chimp who knew the signs for *rock, berry, water,* and *bird* combined those signs to express new concepts when coming into contact with a Brazil nut and a duck; the chimp signed *rock-berry* and *water-bird.* It would be hard to claim that these animals are able to think but that their brothers and sisters cannot.

Notion 3: The language system per se provides specifics of one's view of nature

Whorf, Sapir, Korzybski, and others are of the view that one's knowledge of vocabulary or syntax influences one's perception and understanding of nature. Benjamin Whorf, from Carroll (1956):

> Concepts of 'time' and 'matter' are not given in substantially the same form by experience to all men but depend upon the nature of the language or languages through the use of which they have been developed. (p. 158) Newtonian space, time, and matter are not intuitions. They are recepts from culture and language. That is where Newton got them. (p. 153) We are thus introduced to a new principle of relativity, which holds that all observers are not led by the same physical evidence to the same picture of the universe, unless their linguistic backgrounds are similar, or can in some way be calibrated. (p. 214)

Philipp Frank (1953):

> Einstein's *relativity of time* is a reform in semantics, not in metaphysics. (p. 218)

Objections to Notion 3
1. Vocabulary and perception
Psychologists have tried experimentally to determine what effects, if any, knowledge of the vocabulary of language has on perception or behavior. (See Niyekawa-Howard, 1972, for a comprehensive survey of such research.) The principal problem in doing research on the question is this: since in an experiment only a few of the multitude of the language, cultural, and behavioral variables can be controlled, one can never be reasonably sure that an observed effect is not due to some uncontrolled variable. Suppose, for example, that we compare English

speakers to Japanese speakers with respect to their counting and mathematical ability because we have a hypothesis about the effects of their language; we expect English speakers to be better than Japanese speakers in quantification because in English, nouns must be marked for number and verbs must agree in number while such is not the case in Japanese. Let us further suppose that English speakers performed better in counting and mathematics than the Japanese speakers. Can we conclude that language difference was the cause of the observed differences in performance? Clearly not, since other variables such as kind of schooling and cultural interest in mathematics could just as reasonably have caused the effect in question. Then, too, there are many other aspects of a language that involve quantification. If valid conclusions are to be drawn, these too must be taken into account.[1]

Some substantive results, however have been provided by experimental research. The work of Brown and Lenneberg (1954) and Lantz (1963) indicates that knowing words does not influence perception of the world. They find, rather, that knowing word forms (spoken or written) may aid memory. Thus, with regard to color words, speakers who must remember a color but do not have a word form for it have more trouble remembering it than speakers who do have such a form. (The sound of a word evidently provides an additional memory clue for association.) More recently, Kay and McDaniel (1978) in a large cross-cultural investigation found no difference in perception of colors for different language speakers. They conclude that '... rather than language determining perception, it is perception that determines language.' (p. 610) Similarly, there is no reason to suppose that Eskimos learn to perceive varieties of snow through their language rather than through their life experience. After all, English-speaking skiers are able to distinguish a variety of types of snow despite the lack of vocabulary in English. What they do to describe the physical condition of snow is to create phrases, e.g. *powder snow, wet snow*, etc. Then, too, life experience does not always lead us to coin vocabulary items. For example, English speakers are surely quite aware of the idea of 'male dog' (we have the superordinate *dog* and the female *bitch*); 'back of hand' (we have *palm* for the front or underside); and of a singular superordinate idea for 'cow' and 'bull' (*cattle* is plural) even though they do not have individual words for those ideas. After considering his own and other research, Lenneberg (1967) concluded:

> The empirical research discussed in previous sections (partly stimulated by Whorf's own imaginative ideas) indicates that the cognitive processes studied so far are largely independent from peculiarities of any natural language and, in fact, that cognition can develop to a certain extent even in the absence of knowledge of any language. The reverse does not hold true; the growth and

development of language does appear to require a certain minimum
state of maturity and specificity of cognition. (p. 364)

2. Same language forms, changing meanings

Consider such items as: *The sun rises, sunset, red hair, time flies*, and
kick the bucket. As the result of our hearing and using such items, the
theories under consideration imply that we would come to believe that
the sun actually rises of its own accord, that a person's hair is actually
red, and that kicking buckets is what death is all about. The fact of the
matter is that we can believe something quite different from what the
language literally specifies and that the continual use of a language
form may not change an underlying thought. This situation necessarily
implies that the meanings of these language forms had their origins in
other than the language forms themselves, e.g. by perceiving the world
we learn that a person who is said to have red hair actually may have
orange-brown colored hair. We do not perceive the color as red no
matter how often we use the word red. Such a result runs counter to
the implications of the theories being assessed here.

3. Multilinguals' view of nature

If the language system forms or guides thought in the way we perceive
nature, then multilinguals must be said to have a variety of ways of
viewing the physical world. The multilingual would have as many different conceptual-perceptual systems of the physical world as he or she
has languages. If it is true that different languages have distinctive and
important effects on the way we view nature, then the multilingual
must similarly have distinctive and important ways of viewing nature.
As was noted in a previous section, no such differences have ever been
noted.

Notion 4: The language system per se provides specifics of one's culture

Many theorists believe that even if language is somewhat distinct from
thought, nevertheless, knowing a language will itself condition one's
cultural or social beliefs or views of the world. In the 19th century,
Wilhelm von Humboldt (1836), for example, held that language embodies the spirit and national character of a people. The views of the following theorists are similar, although of a more recent vintage:
Edward Sapir (1929):

> Language is a guide to 'social reality.' Though language is not
> ordinarily thought of as of essential interest to the students of social
> science, it powerfully conditions all our thinking about social
> problems and processes. Human beings do not live in the objective
> world alone, nor alone in the world of social activity as ordinarily
> understood, but are very much at the mercy of the particular

language which has become the medium of expression for society. It is quite an illusion to imagine that one adjusts to reality essentially without the use of language and the language is merely an incidental means of solving specific problems of communication or reflection. The fact of the matter is that the 'real world' is to a large extent unconsciously built up on the language habits of the group. No two languages are sufficiently similar to be considered as representing the same social reality. The worlds in which different societies live are distinct worlds not merely the same world with different labels attached. . . . We see and hear and otherwise experience very largely as we do because the language habits of our community predispose certain choices of interpretation. (p. 209)

Alfred Korzybski (1933):

. . . a language, any language, has at its bottom certain metaphysics which ascribe, consciously or unconsciously, some sort of structure to this world. Our old mythologies ascribed anthropomorphic structure to the world, and of course, under such a delusion, the primitives built up a language to picture such a world and gave it a subject-predicate form. (p. 89) . . . the aristotelian type of education (through language and its subject-predicate form of representation) leads to the humanly harmful, gross, macroscopic, brutalizing, biological, animalistic types of orientations which are shown today to be *humanly adequate*. These breed such 'führers' as different Hitlers, Mussolinis, Stalins, etc., whether in political, financial, industrial, scientific, medical, educational, or even publishing, etc., fields, fancying that they represent 'all' of the *human* world. (p. xxxi)

Objections to Notion 4
If it is indeed the case that the language system does provide a view of culture and society and our outlook on the world, we would expect to find differences and similarities in such essentials as philosophy, religion, politics, or societal structure to be a function of language. In this regard, the following objections may be raised.

1. Same language, different world views
Consider, for example, the contemporary United States where native speakers of the same English language vary in terms of their philosophical, religious, and political ideology. Variation may be observed among speakers in the same neighborhood and even in the same family, e.g. the mother may be an atheist, the father a Christian, the daughter a Hare Krishna, and the son a Zen Buddhist. If it is true that language influences or determines one's world view, then we should expect greater uniformity since only one language system is involved. (While there are dialect differences in the United States, they are

generally minor with respect to syntax and vocabulary, although sometimes major with respect to pronunciation. Unless one would want to
make the dubious claim that pronunciation *per se* is a determinant of
world view, dialect differences cannot be regarded as being a significant
factor.) Since the uniformity that the theory in question implies has not
been demonstrated, there is reason to doubt the validity of the theory.
Then, too, if factors other than the language system can account for
cultural change and variation, then there is no special need to assign
such an explanatory role to the language system.

2. Same language over time and world view change
We may observe that a society may change its world view even though
its language remains relatively unchanged. For example, in less than
100 years, China has changed from Feudalism (under the Manchus) to
Capitalism (under Chiang) to Communism (under Mao). Yet, the language has changed relatively little over that period in terms of its syntax or what may be called its basic grammar. Similar changes may be
noted in the history of many countries. (Minor but highly observable
changes in forms of address and titles do occur, e.g. *comrade* and
citizen, but even these language changes cannot be said to be determined
by the prior language situation.) If we observe that changes in world
view occur without changes in language, then what can be said to be
the world view of any language at any point in time? Those who would
argue for the world view thesis are obliged to show what world view is
inherent in what features of language. Then, too, if changes in world
view can occur due to causes other than the language system, it remains to be proved that language is the cause of any change at all.

3. Different language, similar world views
Consider that many countries having widely different languages may
share similar political, social, religious, scientific, and philosophical
views. If a language system influences or determines world view, then
we should expect that different languages or language families should
hold different world views. Such is not the case. On the contrary, we
find, for example, that Buddhist, Christian, Communist, Capitalist, authoritarian, democratic, militaristic, royalist, and vegetarian doctrines
are shared by speakers of many very different languages.

4. One language can describe many different world views
A language system is said to embody a particular world view and guide
one's thinking with respect to that world view. However, if this were
true in any significant respect, then it would be difficult or even impossible for a language to express different world views. Yet, the Bible
of the ancient Hebrew people and the Communist Manifesto of the
Europeans have had their essential ideas translated into most of the

world's languages. The theories being assessed are unable to account for such a phenomenon.

That a perfect translation between languages is difficult to attain is insufficient of itself as evidence that each language has its own thought or system of thought. A perfect translation may be difficult or impossible to obtain not because thought is not universal but because the words which compose sentences are often associated with different implications, presuppositions, attitudes, feeling, and politeness in the languages. Thus, while it is not difficult to match sentences of different languages in terms of their primary essential meaning, it is very difficult to match them in terms of all their secondary meanings and implications.[2] Consequently, the lack of exact correspondence may not indicate any difference in thought but only a difference in the way ideas have been assigned to the words and structures of a language.

5. Multilinguals and world view

If a person is a multilingual, this theory predicts that such a person will have as many distinct world views as language systems. Thus, a multilingual would have to hold competing views as being true. No support has ever been found for such a prediction.

Some faulty assumptions underlying the inadequate notions

What might be the basis for theorists advocating the four notions just discussed? Aside from the anti-mentalist position of some of the behaviorist theorists who would treat thought as some sort of speech or behavior that is potentially observable, there are certain faulty assumptions which might have been made that led to the invalid conclusions. I will consider three such assumptions. The first involves regarding the surface elements of a sentence as the only meaning elements of that sentence. The second concerns how the meaning of words is acquired. The third and final assumption concerns so-called primitive language and primitive intellect.

Surface structure does not directly represent semantic structure

The most serious deficiency in the theorizing of Whorf, Sapir, Korzybski, Skinner, Von Humboldt, and others concerns the assumption that the directly observable words or the structure of a sentence represent all of the semantic or thought elements of that sentence. These theorists drew conclusions largely based on what linguists today would consider a superficial surface structure analysis. Whorf (Carroll, 1956), for example, states that 'Our Indian languages show that with a suitable grammar we may have intelligent sentences that cannot be broken into subjects and predicates' (p. 242), and that '... the Hopi language contains no reference to "time" either explicit or implicit' (p. 58). Such statements (since rejected by subsequent linguists) are made essentially because it is assumed that surface structure represents all of the structure of a sentence. However, if Chomsky and contemporary linguistics have demonstrated anything, it is that surface structure often does not directly exhibit basic relations and meanings. Consider, for example, a sentence like *The needle hurt* which has a simple surface structure. Such a sentence does not overtly express a cause-effect relation, yet in our understanding of the sentence such a relation is involved. We understand that the needle has been the cause of someone's being in pain, the effect. Making inferences about the thought of speakers solely on the basis of a surface structure analysis is hardly a valid procedure. Actually, considering only the surface structure of languages makes it appear that languages are more different than they really are. It is not surprising, therefore, that relatively few language universals were noted by such theorists.

Meaning is not linguistic in origin

Let us consider the meanings of words. Except for the minor case of onomatopoeia, the relationship between a word and its meaning is conventional. Thus, when one hears a word for the first time, e.g. the English word *tantivy*, its meaning (if it is not composed of known morphemes) is not apprehended. The meaning that is to be associated with a particular sound sequence must be acquired. It is not possible to know from the sound sequence alone that the meaning of *tantivy* is 'a gallop or rapid movement.'

Meaning for words is acquired in four main ways: (1) a sound form is associated with an object, situation, or event in the world, e.g. the sound [dawg] with the object 'dog'; (2) a sound form is associated with an idea or experience in the mind, e.g. [peyn] with the feeling of pain; (3) an inference may be made in linguistic context, an idea may be suggested, e.g. in reading a paragraph one word may not be known but because everything else is understood, its meaning may be guessed by inference; and (4) an analysis of known component morphemes may suggest a meaning for the sound form, e.g. the meaning of *unprimitive* can be gained through knowledge of *un* and *primitive*.

In considering these four ways of acquiring word meaning, we may note that the first two involve non-linguistic sources. In (1), the experiencing of objects, situation, and events in the world provides a basis for meaning, and in (2), experiences in the mind itself provide a basis. Language is not involved except to provide empty sound forms for association. While (3) and (4) provide meaning through the medium of language, it must be recognized that the meaning of the language that is used as a basis for determining the meaning of the unknown word had non-linguistic origins itself (in (1) or (2)). Thus, the ultimate source of all meaning is based on non-linguistic experiences of the world or mind. This view, it is worth noting, does not conflict with the view that all essential ideas may be innate in the mind (Chomsky, 1967b). It would conflict, however, with a view that all innate ideas were part of language, for that would allow language to be the ultimate source of all essential ideas. Such a view has never been proposed, to my knowledge, and it certainly conflicts with the position of Chomsky who has argued in his 'faculty of the mind theory' that different groups of ideas are innate in the mind, e.g. language ideas, mathematical, and logical ideas, and these groups of ideas function and develop relatively independently of one another (MacIntyre, 1970).

The mistake of Vygotsky, Whorf, and others is to assume that hearing the sound form of a word (an unknown one) itself provides some sort of meaning. A language sound form itself, however, does not provide meaning.

The myths of primitive language and intellect
One often hears observers of other cultures say that such-and-such a people are not logical or rational or that they are somehow deficient in intellect. Such supposed deficiencies are frequently attributed to their having a primitive language. Yet, as far as primitive language is concerned, modern linguistic research has never found a single language that could be called primitive. Thus it is that Chomsky (1967b) can with some assurance assert that all languages are of similar complexity, with each having similar basic forms and operations. And, while other linguists such as the Generative Semanticists disagree with Chomsky on what the basic form and operations might be, they do not disagree that all languages are constructed and operate with essentially the same principles. Lenneberg (1967) summed up the current view on the issue of primitive language quite nicely when he said, 'Could it be that some languages require "less mature cognition" than others, perhaps because they are ... primitive? In recent years, this notion has been thoroughly discredited by virtually all students of language.' (p. 364)

Persons who classify other persons as illogical or irrational are typically unaware of the premises which the other persons are using to draw conclusions. Observers have a natural tendency to attribute their own values and beliefs to unfamiliar peoples. That is true, too, for non-standard speakers of such dialects as Black English. Labov (1970b), however, clearly demonstrated that logic does underlie the utterances of those speakers. Once one learns the premises that a people hold, their behavior and statements which were previously thought to be strange or illogical immediately become rational. Then, too, because most logical arguments are only presented in fragments in ordinary

conversation, an unsophisticated observer could easily miss what is
essential. For example, one child might say to another, *You have more
candy*. Implied here is the following argument: Premise 1: We should
have an equal amount. Premise 2: You have more than me. Conclusion: You should give me some to make it equal. It is well to keep in
mind that anthropologists have never found a group of humans who
were not rational or logical. Until evidence to the contrary is produced,
there is no basis, therefore, for believing that any people are inferior in
thought or language.

Where the use of language influences aspects of thought

In considering the objections raised concerning the four notions regarding the relationship between thought and language, it must be concluded that language, speech, or behavior, is not the basis of thought
and that the language system *per se* does not provide the specifics of
one's view of nature or culture. Nevertheless, although knowing a language does not affect the nature of thought with respect to its basic
categories, systems, and operations, there are important cases where
the use of language could be said to affect the content and direction of
particular thoughts. Three particularly important instances are:
(1) language may be used to provide new ideas; (2) language may be
used to bring about a change in beliefs and values; and (3) language
may be used to assist memory. Each of these is now briefly discussed.

Providing new ideas through language

Suppose that I say, *Every July 4, Stalin drank Coke and sang the Star-
Spangled Banner*. In all likelihood, this sentence and the idea it expresses would be novel for you. If so, then the idea formed in your
mind must be the result of hearing the sentence which I uttered. Concerning that novel idea or thought conveyed by the sentence, it is important to note that it is not the component ideas and relations which
are new but their unique arrangement. The vocabulary and structure
were already known. Thus, novel sentences are created and understood
on the basis of what a speaker already knows about the language in
terms of its syntax and vocabulary. And, if new words are to be introduced, they are explained in terms of old ones. Thus, while, for example, Freud's psychoanalytic doctrine is unique in terms of the ideas it
represents, it is not unique from the point of view of language. No new
syntax and only a small number of vocabulary items were introduced.
The effect on people's minds, however, has been profound. Thus, we
see that while knowing a language by itself does not influence thought,
the *use* of that language may indeed affect the content and direction of
particular thoughts.

Changing beliefs and values through language

As a result of reading the Communist Manifesto, one's values, beliefs, and world view could be radically changed. Persons who are so changed politically, religiously, etc., are often said to 'think' different-ly. However, it should be recognized that what occurred were mainly changes in the truth and attractiveness values which were assigned to propositions. Because a person's behavior may have changed radically as a result, an uncritical observer might erroneously infer that commen-surately great changes must have occurred in basic thought categories and operations. The more satisfactory explanation is that changes in truth values, goals, and purpose account for the changes in observed behavior. This, of course, is the essence of persuasion through lan-guage.

Language may be used to assist memory

The fact that we have language and can write language enables us to preserve ideas and to build on those preserved ideas. Our thinking is undoubtedly stimulated by ideas we hear and read. Without language, no human group could have developed much of a culture of any sort. It is language that allowed for the development of modern science, tech-nology, and industry. However, just as the research with color words shows that having a word can assist memory but does not, in and of itself, affect perception, neither is there any basis for assuming that any of our fundamental categories and operations of thought have been affected by this development. The thought processes of non-technological peoples, for example, have not been shown to differ in fundamentals from peoples of technological societies.

Summary of effect of language use

The mere fact that a person knows a language does not affect the na-ture, content, and direction of that person's thought. The language sys-tem is neutral with respect to the thoughts it conveys. However, the content and direction of the particular thoughts of a person can be affected by other persons' use of language. Receiving sentences which others have constructed and communicated can influence a person but not with regard to that person's basic categories, or operations of thought.

Language, the instrument of thought

Relationship and development of thought and language

The relationship between language and thought which shall be pro-posed here is essentially one which was advocated by Locke (1690) some three centuries ago. It is that thought is independent of language, that language is dependent on thought, and that the function of language is to provide a means for the expression or communication of thought. The following schemas outline this view of the development of thought and language and their relationship:

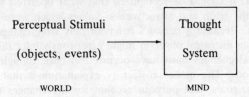

Schema 1. Development of thought in the child

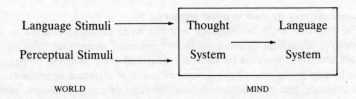

Schema 2. Development of language in the child

Thus, the thought system in the mind of the child develops over time as input stimuli of the world, e.g. visual, auditory, and tactile stimuli representing objects, events, and situations in the environment are experienced by the child.[3] Until thought is sufficiently developed (ideas of objects, relations of objects, states and actions of objects), words uttered in the presence of the child are not meaningfully processed. (This view is similar to that of the Piagetian school, e.g. Sinclair-De-Zwart, 1969.) When that happens and when language input is experienced in coordination with objects, events, and situations, then language can begin to be learned. Over a period of time, the language system, with its vocabulary and grammatical rules, is formed.

Part of the language system is actually part of the thought system, for the meaning and semantics of the language system are those ideas that are part of the content of thought. There is not one idea for *dog* in language and another in thought. Such a view would be unparsimonious in the extreme. Rather, the thought and language systems are joined through meaning and ideas.

Function and nature of the language system
There are two basic functions of the language system that have been constructed by the thought system. The first is to provide physical speech sounds as output, given a particular thought as input. This is the process of speech production and it may be illustrated as follows:

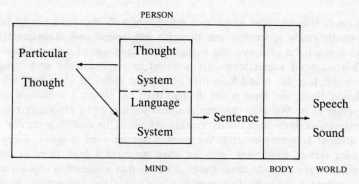

Schema 3. Expressing a Thought in Speech

The second basic function is to provide a particular thought as output (in the mind), given speech sounds as input. This is the process of speech understanding and it may be illustrated as follows:

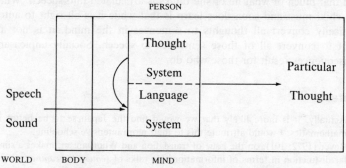

Schema 4. Recovering a thought from speech

According to the above conception, language is a system in the mind which relates mental thoughts to acoustic (physical) speech. Thus, two different kinds of stuff, mental and physical, are brought into a relationship through the language system. It is the phonological and phonetic aspects of the language system (the sound aspect) that operate through the body for the purpose of causing speech to be produced through the mouth and causing speech to be understood through the ear.

Supposed thinking in a language by this conception

It is often observed that sound forms of words come to one's awareness while one is thinking. It is a mistake, however, to conclude from this that the sound forms themselves are thought. Such word forms are merely reflections of some underlying ideas. Thus, it is thought which determines the selection of word forms. As children, we learn to encode thoughts into language and then into acoustic speech. Because we discover that in order to interact effectively with people, we must be instantly ready to express our thoughts into speech, we consequently develop a habit of converting thoughts into language at a mental level. That is, word sound forms are selected to represent the underlying thought. It is this sound form that we become aware of when we think. Hence, the sound form is not thought itself but simply a secondary reflection of it. Whether the mental sound form is to be physically realized as speech through the motor skill system of the body is generally a matter of voluntary control. We speak when we want to speak, except under certain conditions, such as when we have a high fever or are under great stress. At those times, it seems that whatever is thought of is realized as speech. This would indicate that the connections from particular thought to mental language and then physical speech are automatic and that it is only with conscious effort (our normal condition) that we do not say everything that we think. When a child first learns to speak, it seems that the child does not have complete control and that much of what he or she thinks is articulated into speech. What the child must and soon does learn is that while it is all right to automatically convert all thoughts to sentences in the mind, it is not all right to convert all of those sentences to speech. Socially unpleasant consequences result for those who do.

Notes

1. Actually, it is more likely that we would find the Japanese to be better in mathematics. I would attribute this to their more intensive schooling.
2. Bever (1972: 101), on the issue of translation and Whorfianism, makes a similar distinction in terms of information. He talks of *semantic meaning* (critical concepts) as opposed to *linguistic idea* (non-critical cultural overlays).
3. This view is neutral with respect to the issue of innate ideas since all rationalist theorists, e.g. Chomsky, require relevant environmental experience to activate innate ideas.

Chapter 7

Sentence production and understanding

The production process

Relevance of syntactic and semantic based grammars

It was established in Chapter 4 that the syntactic based grammars of Chomsky are psychologically invalid since their rules are formulated on the basis of a premise that Chomsky himself admits is psychologically 'absurd.' That premise is that the order of the construction of a structure in the derivation of sentences begins with syntax and ends with semantics and phonetics. The reason such an order cannot reasonably he held to be psychologically valid is that it does not conform to either of the essential language processes which speakers use. It does not conform to the process of sentence production, which takes meaning and converts it to speech sounds, nor does it conform to the process of sentence understanding (comprehension, recognition, interpretation) which takes speech sounds and converts them to meaning. Rules of a grammar which are written to describe a process that speakers would not use (no one would begin to produce or understand sentence by first generating an abstract syntactic structure) cannot be regarded as psychologically valid. Such being the case, syntactically based grammars cannot be considered in any serious way as contributing to the development of theory which concerns the production and understanding of sentences by speakers.

The situation for semantic based grammars, however, is quite different. As was noted in Chapter 4, since the rules of semantic based grammars are written to conform in outline to a psychologically real process, that of sentence production (where given meaning a sound form is derived), such grammars may be considered as possible psychological theories of how speakers produce sentences. However, while such grammars contribute very greatly to our understanding of the essentials of the production process, one principal consideration precludes our accepting such grammars as theories of the production process. That consideration involves the requirement that the Surface Structure as a whole be provided as input to the phonological component.

Linearity and efficiency considerations

It is the belief of many psycholinguists, e.g. Schlesinger (1977) and Watt (1970), as well as myself, that in producing (and understanding) sentences no distinct sequencing between semantic, syntactic, and phonetic levels need be maintained. That is, an entire level of structure need not be entirely formed before other levels can begin formation. For example, in production, while a part of Surface Structure could be receiving a phonetic interpretation, other parts of Surface Structure could be just becoming formed. Then, too, because the production of a sentence involves the output of words in a linear order, i.e. words are uttered one at a time in sequence, it is possible for the Phonetic Representation of some words to be uttered while other syntactic structures and phonetic representations are in the process of incipient formation. The number of words which may be uttered while other processing continues depends on the nature of the complexity of the sentence. The faster that words of a sentence can be uttered (in their proper order), the less is the burden on memory. The same is true in sentence understanding where words may be understood before all have been received. Our capacity to process lengthy and complex sentences is increased to the extent that our short-term memory, which is limited, is relieved of unnecessary storage. The speed at which we may process a sentence also is increased by a model which permits more than one type of processing to occur in time. For what must also be accounted for in both the production and understanding of sentences is the fantastic speed at which processing is accomplished. Thus, there is good reason to suppose that a complete Surface Structure need not be formed before Phonological rules can be applied. If semantic based grammars are to be regarded as psychologically valid, they must be modified in accord with the actual psychological processing of speakers.

There is one special set of operations that must be incorporated into any production model, a set that involves the exploitation of frequently occurring structures. Familiar phrases like *the little boy* or *bread and butter*, and familiar sentences like *Mary had a little lamb* or *Where is it?* undoubtedly are stored in memory in their entirety as is a lexical item like *dog* or *eclipse*. There is no reason to suppose that such sentences need to be created in the way that novel sentences must be. Rather, given that one wishes to express the meaning of one of these stock items, no grammar rules need be applied. In memory, the appropriate phonetic representation will be stored directly with the meaning just as it is for morphemes and idioms. Thus, frequency of occurrence will establish permanent entries for phrases and sentences the same way as it does for lexical items. Such storage could help to explain how it is that familiar sentences are easier to produce and understand than unfamiliar sentences.

This view on familiar phrases and sentences is not in accord with theorists such as Chomsky who has asserted that 'The sentences used in everyday discourse are not "familiar sentences"' and that 'In fact, even to speak of "familiar sentences" is an absurdity' (Chomsky, 1967b: 4). While he is quite right in arguing that habit or conditioning alone cannot account for novel sentence use, it does not follow that habit or conditioning must play no important role in language learning and performance. The fact that speakers are able to produce and understand sentences at the fantastic rate that they do could never be explained, if we supposed that every sentence had to be constructed through the application of all related rules. (It is ironic that Chomsky should argue against familiar sentences when he himself has made certain sentences such as *John is easy to please* and *Colorless green ideas sleep furiously* familiar to his readers.)

Aside from providing a direct meaning-sound association for rapid processing of production and understanding, familiar phrases and sentences may provide a basis for the processing of novel phrases and sentences which are similar to them. If we have stored a familiar phrase and sentence, e.g. *the little boy* and *The dog ran*, we should not need to reprocess everything when structurally similar phrases and sentences that we have never dealt with before such as *the little girl* and *The cat ran* are to be produced or understood. It is likely that through simple substitution (*girl* for *boy* and *cat* for *dog*) we have entire ready-made semantic or phonetic sequences at our disposal. Undoubtedly, the amount of time that it takes to search through a myriad of stored data is less than that which is needed to produce or understand the sentence through the regular rule-use channel. Direct access to phrases and sentences should be nearly as rapid as it is for individual words. Our quick access to the sound or meaning of idioms provides some evidence in this regard. Since idioms, e.g. *kick the bucket* and *leaves a bad taste in the mouth*, by their nature are the sort of items whose sound and meaning connection cannot be determined through ordinary analysis but ultimately must rely on an arbitrary association, such items must be stored in memory and indexed somehow on the basis of sound and meaning.

Some aspects of the production process
The aim of the production process is to provide a set of sounds for a thought that a speaker wishes to convey. This may be done through the use of elaborate syntactic and phonological rules or, when the situation warrants, directly through a meaning-sound association. The thought

which a speaker intends to express (also to be referred to as the meaning of a sentence or Semantic Representation) consists of two basic components, *purpose* and *proposition*.

The purpose component of the Semantic Representation involves the speaker's aim or intention in communicating a proposition to a listener. In the philosophical and linguistic literature this topic appears under such names as *speech acts* and *illocutionary acts*. Most of the work in this area originated with Austin (1962) and has been developed by many theorists, most notably Searle (1969; 1975). For example, with regard to the proposition of ['happy,' 'John'] a speaker may assert that the proposition is true by means of the sentence *John is happy*. Or, a speaker may make a denial (*John is not happy*), a question (*Is John happy?*), an order (*Be happy John*), a promise (*I promise that you will be happy John*), a warning (*You may not be happy John*), or a prediction (*You will not be happy John*). All of these different purposes involve the same proposition of ['happy,' 'John']. Incidentally, sentences with the same form can be used to express different purposes, e.g. *John is not happy* can be used to provide a simple description as well as a denial.[1]

The proposition aspect is essentially that formulation which philosophers, linguists, and others refer to as consisting of arguments, predicates, and certain basic modifiers such as those concerning quantification and time. (Chapter 3 presents the fundamentals of this notion in the discussion dealing with semantic based grammars.) Thus, for example, the sentence *John pushed Jim* consists of a proposition with the following conceptual (non-linguistic) elements: two arguments ('John,' 'Jim') and one predicate ('push'). The arguments fit the requirements of the predicate idea 'push' such that a complete thought is formed. Whether all or some of a predicate idea's argument requirements are expressed in a sentence varies from language to language. For example, while all three arguments of the English verb *send* may be specified in a sentence (*John sent the parcel to Mary*), specifying only one or two arguments may also be sufficient (*The parcel was sent, John sent the parcel*) although which particular arguments can appear is restricted (**John sent, *John sent to Mary*). Modification can be made to arguments and predicates or to propositions as a whole. For example, an argument can be quantified as represented by the noun phrases *a boy, some boys*, and *three boys*; a predicate can be modified in terms of aspect, e.g. *ran* (action completed) and *is running* (action continuing); and a proposition can be modified in terms of time, e.g. *John came* (event described by a proposition which occurred in the past), *John came in the morning* (event occurred at a specific time in the past), or in terms of probability, e.g. *I expect John to come* and *John will probably come*.

While the form of a sentence is mainly determined by purpose and proposition, other variables, too, may significantly affect its form. Some of these are focus, politeness, and reference.

Focus: Arguments may be given prominence or emphasis by being assigned different orders in a sentence, e.g. *John gave the ball to Mary, The ball was given to Mary by John*, and *Mary was given the ball by John*.

Politeness: Different words may be substituted depending on the level of politeness and formality, e.g. *I hear his old man croaked* as opposed to *I hear his father died*.

Reference: Arguments involved may be expressed as noun phrases in a number of ways: (1) as a proper name, e.g. *John, Mary, Santa Claus*; (2) as a pronoun, e.g. *she, it, we, they*; or (3) as a noun with modification. Modification may appear in the form of determiners (e.g. *a pen, these pens*), quantifiers (e.g. *two pens, the pens*), adjectives (e.g. *green cheese, the happy boy*), phrases (e.g. *the gloves on the dresser, the meat in the tin*), and clauses (e.g. *the cheese which is green, the meat which is in the tin, the girl who sells matches*). All such noun modification, it is worth noting, involves one common basic semantic function and that is to single out or bring to prominence one or more objects that are members of a class of objects.

The basis according to which a speaker selects a proper name, a pronoun, or a noun with modification to represent an argument in a proposition depends not only on such a consideration as whether one or more objects is being referred to but also on what the speaker estimates the listener's knowledge of the argument to be. A proper name is used by a speaker if the speaker estimates that the listener knows the name and has sufficient knowledge about the object referred to so that what is said about it can be properly interpreted, e.g. *Joe English wants you to phone him*. If the speaker estimates that the listener does not know the name, the speaker may decide to introduce it by using a non-restrictive relative clause to provide a description, e.g. *Joe English [who is] from the State government, wants you to phone him*. Otherwise, the speaker will use some sort of complex noun phrase, e.g. *Someone [who is] from the State government wants you to phone him*.

Whether or not *a* or *the* will be used in a noun phrase depends on referent awareness and quantity considerations. Awareness of a referent can be established either through linguistic or environmental means. With respect to linguistic means, consider a case where a speaker says *When dealing with a child, always treat the child with respect*. In the phrase following *treat*, the word *the* is appropriate because an awareness of the referent has been established. If the phrase had *a*, the result (*When dealing with a child, always treat a child with respect.*) would be inappropriate since the speaker is referring to the same entity or class. My own use of *a speaker* and *the speaker* in the previous sentences illustrates the same point.) With respect to reference being established through environmental means, consider where one salesclerk says to another *The customer wants to know if we sell clocks.* This may be said if the customer is in view and is identifiable by the listener. It would be inappropriate to use *A customer* . . . in such a situation.

It might be well here to note the use of pronouns since their use, too, is governed by prior linguistic and environmental reference. For example, *A boy came for you, but he didn't wait* is appropriate since prior reference is provided by the noun phrase *a boy.* It would not be appropriate to say *He came for you* . . . without any prior reference. Such reference can be provided through the environment, which is, of course, the ultimate basis for all reference. For example, one salesclerk might say to another *She wants to know if we sell clocks* if the person referred to as *she* is present for the salesclerk who is being addressed to identify.

Concerning number, a variety of considerations are involved with respect to the use of *a* and *the.* A few will be noted here. A speaker must consider whether one or more of a class of objects are involved (*a dog* and *the dog* for one or the generic, and *the dogs* for more than one) and whether the object being referred to is the only member in the class. Regarding this latter point, we say *the present president of the U.S.* and not *a present president of the U.S.* because there is only one present president of the U.S., and we would say *the man who sells magazines downstairs* and not *a man who sells magazines downstairs* if there is only one man who sells magazines downstairs.

The essentials of the sentence production process are shown in Fig. 7. The following remarks are intended to help explain the operations and components of the process.

Thought process. This universal thinking process uses knowledge and a stock of concepts to produce thoughts. It is stimulated by various mental and physical influences.

Knowledge. A basic stock of conceptual elements and relations out of which knowledge of the world (excluding language) is constructed and stored. The conceptual basic stock is universal to all human beings.

Purpose + Proposition. This is the essential thought which a person wishes to communicate to someone. It is conceptual (non-linguistic) in nature. Communication of the thought may be realized through linguistic or behavioral means. Purpose involves such intentions as questioning, denying, asserting, and warning with respect to a proposition. The proposition itself consists of three types of non-linguistic concepts: arguments, predicates, and qualifiers.

Information required by language. This consists of language independent concepts such as certain referential and politeness data. What is to be included varies from language to language. English, for example, re-

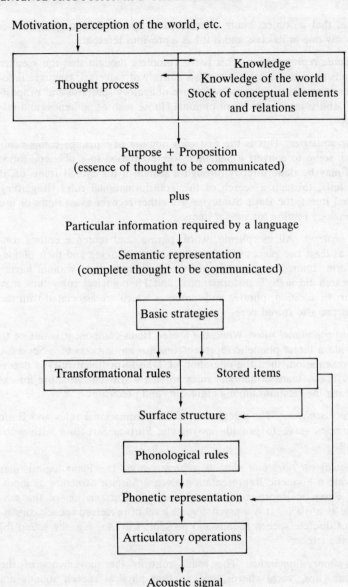

Motivation, perception of the world, etc.

Thought process ⟷ Knowledge
Knowledge of the world
Stock of conceptual elements
and relations

Purpose + Proposition
(essence of thought to be communicated)

plus

Particular information required by a language

Semantic representation
(complete thought to be communicated)

Basic strategies

Transformational rules   Stored items

Surface structure

Phonological rules

Phonetic representation

Articulatory operations

Acoustic signal

FIGURE 7. Essentials of the sentence production process

quires that an object being referred to be specified as to whether it is the only one in its class and if it has a previous referent.

Semantic representation. This is the complete thought that the speaker intends to communicate. It consists entirely of universal, language independent concepts, some of which are obligatory (purpose and proposition) and some of which are optional (those such as politeness and reference).

Basic strategies. This is the first of a number of language components which serve to convert a Semantic Representation to a phonetic form. This may be done directly through a search of the Stored Items or, if this fails, through a search of the Transformational rules. Regarding Stored Items, the Basic Strategies will either recover exact items or use an analogy routine for similar items.

Stored items. All morpheme, word, phrase, and sentence entries contain at least two pieces of information, their meaning and their phonetic form. Immediate direct recovery of a phonetic form without having to search through Transformational and Phonological rules thus may occur. In addition, phrases and sentences which are associated with the items are also stored here.

Transformational rules. When the Stored Items component is unable to provide a direct phonetic representation for any aspects of a Semantic Representation, then the operation of Transformational rules is necessary. These Transformational rules provide a syntactic structure for expressing the relations among arguments and predicates.

Surface structure. The operations of Transformational rules and Basic Strategies serve to provide a syntactic Surface Structure with word forms.

Phonological rules and phonetic representation. The Phonological rules provide a Phonetic Representation given a Surface Structure as input. The Phonetic Representation provides the pronunciation of the sentence as a whole. It is a psychological level of perceived speech consisting of discrete speech sounds and prosodic features, e.g. the sound [b] and the stress

Articulatory apparatus. The brain controls the movements of the tongue, lips, vocal chords, etc. so that physical speech sounds are produced.

Acoustic signal. This consists of sound waves which are describable in terms of frequency, amplitude, and change over time. Speech sounds are not identifiable as discrete units. Rather, a complex continuous blending of waves constitutes the speech sound signal.

The understanding process

Semantic orientation required

Given speech sounds as input, the problem is to explain how we recover ideas, more specifically, Semantic Representations. The view that shall be offered here, it should be noted, does not regard such a process as being principally oriented to the recovery of syntactic structure as is the view of Fodor, Bever, and Garrett (1974) and Foss and Hakes (1978), among others. Such theorists as these attempt to work within a Chomskyan syntactic based grammar framework. They see the immediate goal of the sentence understanding process as the determination of a syntactic Deep Structure where the rules of Chomsky's semantic component then would provide a Semantic Representation for the Deep Structure. (Presumably, these theorists would now, with the advent of Chomsky's Trace Grammar, aim to recover a trace 'enriched' Surface Structure since it is such a structure that Chomsky now uses as input to the semantic component. – See Chapter 2 for some details of Chomsky's Trace Grammar.) In accord with this view, such theorists advocate strategies that are principally formulated in syntactic terms. For example, Bever (1970) and Fodor, Bever, and Garrett (1974) postulate that a string of incoming words which is identified in terms of their grammatical class (determiner, noun, verb, etc.) will have applied to them a syntactic strategy for English such as NP + V + NP, where the NP prior to the verb is identified as the subject and the NP following the verb is identified as the object. Such a view of the process of sentence understanding is mistaken in the extreme. A more parsimonious and intuitively satisfying approach to the process is one that is geared to the immediate recovery of the meaning aspects of a sentence. Basic strategies, therefore, should be specified in terms of semantic elements. Thus, rather than NP + V + NP as a strategy, the strategy would be something like Agent + Action + Object. How a semantically oriented understanding process might operate is outlined below. (For a more detailed treatment of many other aspects of semantically oriented processing, the reader is referred to Schlesinger, 1977.)

Anticipating propositional structures

In ordinary conversation, the interchange of sentences is often fantastically rapid. Listeners do not wait until an entire sentence is uttered before they begin to interpret what has been said and to formulate a response. What happens is that as words are being received, the listener projects a possible semantic interpretation. Additional words serve to confirm or not confirm that interpretation. In the case of the latter, a new interpretation will be projected. Listeners are able to project possible semantic interpretations based on what they know about language and the world, and on what they might expect given the relative frequency of previously occurring linguistic and world events and situations.

I would like to demonstrate how, on the basis of limited word input, we project propositional structures. By way of illustration, permit me to ask you to complete the sentences which follow. Complete each in order and do not read ahead to minimize the effect of the later appearing sentences.

(1) *The* . . .
(2) *The girl* . . .
(3) *The girl who* . . .
(4) *The girl whom* . . .
(5) *The girl to whom* . . .
(6) *The girl who pushed* . . .
(7) *The girl who the* . . .
(8) *The girl the boy* . . .

Based on my own knowledge and intuitions, I will make the following predictions.

Sentence (1) (The . . .*)*. You probably created a sentence with an agent-action-(object) sequence of semantic elements, e.g. *The man threw the ball* or *The dog barked*, or one with an attribuant-attribute sequence, e.g. *The man is tall*. (The term *attribuant* represents the object which possesses the attribute and was originally coined by Sidney Greenbaum according to Schlesinger, 1977: 10)

Sentence (2) (The girl . . .*)*. You treated it similarly to Sentence (1). However, you selected content to fit the idea of 'girl.'

Sentence (3) (The girl who . . .*)*. You completed a sentence (clause) with *who* in it such that *who* represented *the girl*. The sentence functions to restrict the meaning of *girl*. Following that sentence, you placed a predicate to complete the argument represented by *the girl*. Thus, you might have produced a sentence like *The girl [who lost the dog] called the police* or *The girl [who the boy chased] took the bus*. In the embedded sentence or clause (enclosed in square brackets) *who* probably served as agent (as in *who lost the dog*) or object (as in *who the boy chased*). It is possible, but not likely, that *who* was treated as a receiver of the action as in *The girl [who Jerry gave the book to] took the bus*.

Sentence (4) (The girl whom . . .*)*. You completed a sentence with *whom* such that *whom* served as the object, e.g. *The girl [whom the boy chased]* . . . or, less likely, the receiver, e.g. *The girl [whom the boy gave the flowers to]* . . . . It is not possible for *whom* to be agent or attribuant of the embedded sentence.

Sentence (5) (The girl to whom . . .*)*. You made *whom* the receiver in the embedded sentence, e.g. *The girl [to whom Tommy gave the flow-*

ers] . . . . It is not possible for *to whom* to be the agent, attribuant, or object of the sentence.

Sentence (6) (The girl who pushed . . .). You made *who* the agent in the embedded sentence and added an argument to complete *pushed*, e.g. *The girl [who pushed Tommy]* . . . . It is not possible for *who* to serve as object or receiver.

Sentence (7) (The girl who the . . .). You created an embedded sentence such that *who* is the object (*The girl [who the boy likes]* . . .) or, less likely, the receiver (*The girl [who the boy gave the flowers to]* . . .). It is not possible for *who* to serve as the agent or attribuant of the embedded sentence.

Sentence (8) (The girl the boy . . .). You probably created an embedded sentence which serves to describe the object in question (girl) such that *the boy* is the subject and *the girl* is the understood direct object, e.g. *The girl [the boy likes]* . . . . Certain other structures are possible but not as likely, e.g. *The girl [the boy gave the flowers to]* . . . and *The girl the boy and the dog* . . . . It is not possible for *the girl* (understood) to be the agent or attribuant of the sentence.

The above data shows what our knowledge and expectations regarding language can enable us to do in recovering propositional structure in sentence understanding processing. Our knowledge of the world (including the people in it) and the expectations we have regarding that world similarly play a role in the anticipation of semantic interpretations. Evidence that we can and do anticipate in this way may be demonstrated in a number of regards as shown in the following.

Semantic and situational convergence
Given knowledge of a certain topic, we may anticipate what will follow as words of a sentence are progressively received. For example,

   In the election, Jimmy . . .
   In the election, Jimmy Carter . . .
   In the election, Jimmy Carter was defeated . . .
   In the election, Jimmy Carter was defeated for the presidency by . . .

Our knowledge of a topic comes to bear on what a speaker says such that we are led to expect what the speaker will further say. While individuals other than Ronald Reagan could be named by the speaker, the chances are that they would not.

We think ahead of the conceptual content of what speakers are saying and formulate thoughts and responses based on those suppositions. Conversations, discourse, and text involve a mixture of familiar and unfamiliar content, with the bulk of it familiar. A philosophical treatise may be heavier with the unfamiliar than a conversation between a husband and wife. In the latter case, often a word or two will suffice when among strangers full sentences and elaborate discourse may be necessary to convey the same information.

Even when structural cues are lacking, we are always ready with an interpretation. The interpretation of headlines and telegrams provides a case in point. Suppose you were asked to form a thought, based on a sequence of words like (after Schlesinger, 1977):

girl-threatened-flames-helped-firemen-escape

The following sentence would likely represent that thought:

A girl was threatened by flames but was helped by firemen to escape.

On the other hand, such a sequence of words could equally represent the thought in the sentence:

A girl although threatened by flames helped firemen to escape.

Given our knowledge of the world, where firemen usually help people to escape and not the other way around, we would expect the former and not the latter interpretation to be the correct one. Of course, we may be wrong, and it may be that it was indeed the girl who helped the firemen. Still, more often than not, our intuition is right.

A similar situation obtains with our interpretation of pronouns. Consider, for example, the following passage (after Charniak, 1972): *Mother took out a plate and placed a cookie on it. 'I'm sure Janet will like it,' thought Mother.* Most of us would assume that the *it* following *like* in the second sentence refers to the *cookie* although it need not. The *plate* could be the item referred to. Most likely we would assume that Janet is a child and as such is more interested in cookies than plates. Yet, this need not be so.

Our interest in the meaning of what we are hearing or interpreting often overrides the language form which we receive. Proofreading, for example, is such a difficult task because we must suspend our natural inclination to seek meaning in favor of judging form. Such an inclination is a primary one and appears quite early with children learning language. For example, Strohner and Nelson (1974) found that children aged two and three interpreted the following sentences in the same way despite the differing constructions, *The cat chased the mouse* and *The mouse chased the cat*, even though ordinarily the children could respond appropriately to the syntactic subject and object relations. It is only with age, and the experience that goes with it, that children realized that things may occur counter to their strongest expectations. Nevertheless, research shows that mature listeners also depend quite strongly on their semantic expectations. Fillenbaum (1971: 1974a; 1974b), for example, found that when asked to provide paraphrases for unusual sentences like *John dressed and had a bath* and *John finished and wrote the article on the weekend*, both of which have unusual sequences of events (*bathing* is expected before *dressing* and *writing* is expected before *finishing*), over 60 per cent of the subjects provided paraphrases which changed the sequence in accord with expectation. And even after they were asked to compare their work with the original, 53 per cent still provided the incorrect paraphrase. And even when unusual sentences are perfectly understood, subjects comprehend such sentences much more slowly than more usual ones. For example, Forster and Ryder (1971) found that a sentence like *Mary chewed spears throughout the corrupt talk* to be less readily understood than *John smoked cigars throughout the dreary play*. Such findings clearly demonstrate the role of conceptual expectation, for it is the sentences which are in accord with it that are processed more easily than those which are counter to it.

Sentence understanding processing: an illustration

An outline of how a particular sentence might be understood according to a semantically oriented process is now presented. Analysis will proceed linearly, on a word to word basis.[2] It is assumed that words may be retained in some sort of short term memory bank after they are processed. It should be recalled that the Semantic Representation, the recovery of which is the goal of the process, consists of two basic components, purpose and proposition. Various other information, quantification, reference, time, location, modality, etc., is included in the propositional structure.

To better illustrate the sentence understanding process, the reader is invited to join me in analyzing and thinking about each word as it is received. As in real life, only after all words have been received will the reader learn what the sentence is.

LISTENER PROCESS IN RECOVERING A SEMANTIC REPRESENTATION

INPUT: *Did*

OPERATION:	*Search*	Basic Strategies (see Fig. 7). Find one which receives a sound form.
	Obtain	Strategy 1: (a) *Search* Stored Items (with sound form).
		(b) *Search* Knowledge (with ideas stored with sound form).
	Apply	Strategy 1.
	Obtain	(i) *Did* consists of *do* and 'past.'
		(ii) *Did* is involved in sentences, hence Semantic Representations (not a greeting or interjection).
		(iii) When the first word in a sentence, *did* signals a question.
		(iv) *Did* is likely associated with an Action Predicate.

134

Search	Basic Strategies. Find one(s) which relates obtained information (i, ii, iii, iv) to a Semantic Representation.
Apply	Appropriate Strategies.
Obtain	(1) The essential form of a Semantic Representation (from *ii* above). This is shown in Fig 8.

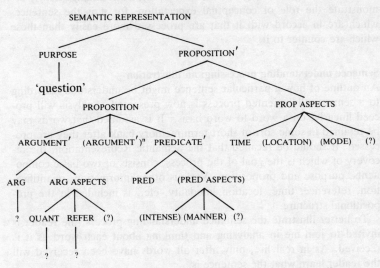

FIGURE 8. Essential form of a semantic representation which a listener expects to receive

(2) To that Semantic Representation, 'question' has been added to Purpose (from *iii* above), i.e.:

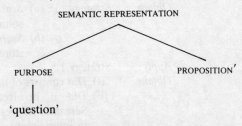

(3) To that Semantic Representation, 'past' has been added to Time in Proposition Aspect (from *i* above), i.e.:

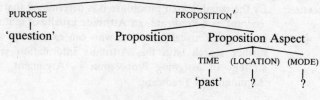

SEMANTIC REPRESENTATION

PURPOSE — PROPOSITION'

'question'   Proposition   Proposition Aspect

TIME (LOCATION) (MODE)

'past'   ?   ?

Search	Basic Strategies. Find one(s) which integrates information on current Semantic Representation.
Obtain	Strategy 2: Assign

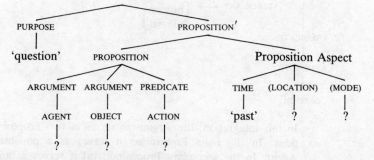

Proposition ——— Argument + Argument + Predicate

Agent   Object   Action

This is a highly frequent propositional form.

Apply	Strategy 2.
Obtain	

SEMANTIC REPRESENTATION

PURPOSE — PROPOSITION'

'question'   PROPOSITION   Proposition Aspect

ARGUMENT ARGUMENT PREDICATE   TIME (LOCATION) (MODE)

AGENT OBJECT ACTION   'past'   ?   ?

?   ?   ?

INPUT: *the* (Words thus far: *Did the*)

OPERATION:

Search	Basic Strategies. Find one which receives a sound form.
Obtain	Strategy 1: (a) *Search* Stored Items.
	(b) *Search* Knowledge.
Apply	Strategy 1.
Obtain	(i) *the* relates to an Argument
	(ii) The Argument is likely a member of a class of objects rather than a proper name
Search	Basic Strategies. Find one(s) which relates obtained information to a Semantic Representation.
Apply	Appropriate Strategies

INPUT: *corrupt* (Words thus far: *Did the corrupt*)

OPERATION: By the usual Search procedure it is determined that:
                'corrupt' is a Predicate, an Attribute usually of mature hu-
                man beings, usually persons who can exercise power. A
                further search with this Attribute information yields a
                strategy of assigning Proposition → Argument

                Argument   + Predicate
                    | |
                Attribuant   Attribute

                Integrating all of this information directly into the Pro-
                position portion of the Semantic Representation, the fol-
                lowing structure obtains:

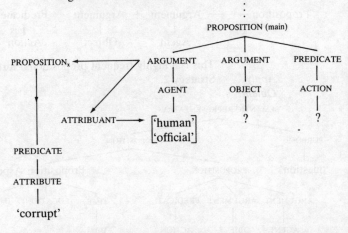

In this integration, the Argument serves in two Propositions. In the main Proposition it serves as a possible
Agent. In the secondary Proposition (x) it serves as an
Attribuant to which the Predicate Attribute 'corrupt' is
attributed. With regard to this complex dual propositional
relation, an important point must be raised. Why would a
listener continue to expect the main proposition to be
filled out? Why does a listener not consider the Semantic
Representation complete as a simple question about
whether someone is corrupt? The reason for this relates
to our knowledge of the form of sentences. We know that
a sequence such as *Did the corrupt man* is incomplete,
even though semantically we might be able to make complete sense of it. Based on our knowledge of English, we
know that *do* is not used in questions involving a direct
Attribuant-Attribute relationship. We can say *Is the man
corrupt?* but not *Did the man corrupt* where *corrupt* is to

be interpreted as an Attribute. Then, too, the positioning of an Attribute prior to an Attribuant Argument (*corrupt man*) indicates in English that a secondary modification is being made to the Argument and that the Argument has a role to play in a more primary proposition. An important processing principle is made manifest through this situation. It is that the recovery of Semantic Representations is made in conformity with the surface input elements. Surface elements must be stored in short term memory and monitored even as semantic integrations are being formed.

It should be noted that the original Semantic Representation outline shown in Fig. 8 only provided the essentials of a simple representation. As was later shown, that representation can be expanded and made more complex. A Proposition can be integrated with an Argument as in the case of *corrupt*. Entire propositions can be conceptually linked, e.g. *If* Proposition 1, *then* Proposition 2, or *Either* Proposition 1 *or* Proposition 2. Basic Predicates, too, can be modified such as by an intensifier as in *talk loudly* or by manner as in *run quickly*. The conceptual ability to construct such structures is another aspect of the operations and composition of our thinking capacity.

INPUT: *congressman* (Words thus far: *Did the corrupt congressman*)

OPERATION: The appearance of this item confirms the expectation of an Agent Argument that is human and corruptible, such as a politician. The congressman concept is integrated into the Semantic Representation.

INPUT *who* (Words thus far: *Did the corrupt congressman who*)

OPERATION: This item indicates that a secondary proposition of which the directly preceding Argument (in this case, 'congressman') is a component will follow directly. Linguistic knowledge informs the Listener of this and further provides the information that (i) *who* represents the Argument of 'congressman,' and (ii) the Argument may serve in any of a variety of semantic roles, e.g.:

The corrupt congressman:
(a) *who hid the money* . . .
    who represents an Agent role
(b) *who the woman accused* . . .
    who represents an Object role
(c) *who the cooks gave the money to* . . .
    who represents a Receiver role

Situations such as (a) and (b) are probably more likely than (c). Since both (a) and (b) seem to be equally probable, the listener may not make an assignment at this point but wait until further word input resolves the ambiguity.

INPUT: *the*

OPERATION: This provides the information that an Argument and not a Predicate will follow. It strongly rules out the likelihood of (a) above where *who* plays a semantic role such as Agent (... *who hid the money* ...). Possibility (b) in which *who* serves as semantic object (... *who the woman accused* ...) is more likely. As a semantic object it is likely to be involved in some Action and by a human Agent. However, a listener could be misled by assuming that *who* represents a semantic object since it is possible but not so likely that an embedded sentence like ... *who the police were fooled by* ... might follow in which case *who* would be the Agent in a passive sentence. On the basis of probability, a Listener would then posit the following complex argument structure on the basis of the input string *Did the corrupt congressman who the*:

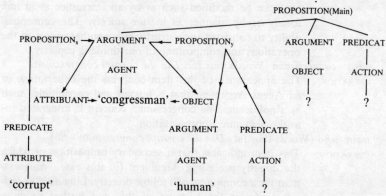

INPUT: *police*

OPERATION: *This* item confirms that a human Agent serves as Argument in Proposition Y. 'Police' is added to Agent in Proposition Y. On the basis of life experience one could suppose a number of actions which the police could take with respect to a corrupt politician such as search and arrest.

INPUT: *arrested*

OPERATION: This item specifies the Action which the police took, and that such an event occurred in the past. This completes Proposition Y. The fact that there is a gap after *arrested* in the sequence *the police arrested* is not of concern because our knowledge of grammar indicates that it is acceptable in the given context, that of a relative clause.

INPUT: *telephone*

OPERATION: This Action Predicate is directly assigned to the main Proposition since no Predicate is outstanding for any other Proposition. It requires an Object Argument for completion. Who the congressman that the police arrested might telephone is a matter of conjecture – wife, children, friends, a lawyer?

INPUT: *a*

OPERATION: Object Argument on its way. It is one in number.

INPUT: *lawyer*

OPERATION: The Object Argument is identified and the main Proposition is completed.

INPUT: *from*

OPERATION: An Argument Location will follow which will indicate the source of some Proposition or Argument.

INPUT: *the*

OPERATION: Argument on its way.

INPUT: *jail*

OPERATION: The Argument Location is specified. Given the previous information contained in the sentence and expectations regarding the world, the listener would posit that the event of the congressman telephoning the lawyer took place in jail. The Listener could be wrong, however, since it is possible, but less likely, that *from the jail* is a modification of *lawyer* such as in *The lawyer from the jail laughed.*

INPUT: Ø

All uncertainties and problems have been dealt with. A Semantic Representation for the sentence *Did the corrupt congressman who the police arrested telephone a lawyer from the jail?* has been recovered. That Semantic Representation with most essentials is shown in Fig. 9

The above description of the recovery of a Semantic Representation for a sentence is meant to provide the reader with an intuitive grasp of how the sentence understanding process might proceed. What has been provided is not an explicit model but some ideas from which an explicit model can be constructed. The construction of an explicit model of sentence understanding is probably the greatest challenge facing psycholinguists today. Its importance should not be underestimated. For the sentence understanding process forms the basis on which the process of sentence production develops and without knowledge of those processes, attempts to understand the process of language ac-

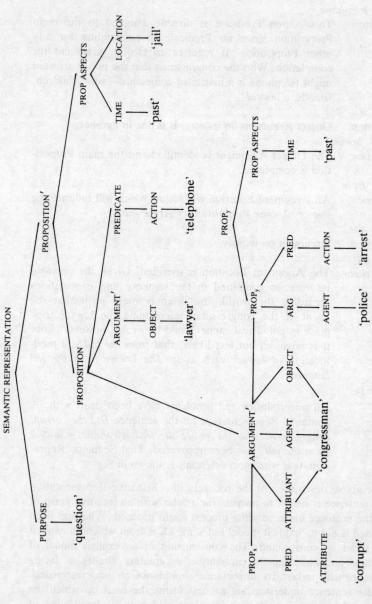

FIGURE 9. Some essentials of recovered semantic representation for the sentence. *Did the corrupt congressman who the police arrested telephone a lawyer from the jail?*

quisition will be severely limited. However, with the insights provided by such theorists as Schlesinger (1977), Wanner (1980; with Kaplan & Shiner, 1975), Frazier and Janet Dean Fodor (1978) it is hoped that a comprehensive workable model will be provided in the not too distant future.

Notes

1. In the production model which I envisage, different sentences which overtly express different propositions and different purposes are produced from different Semantic Representations. Therefore, sentences like *Pick up your things, It's messy in here*, and *Would you like to clean up your room*? would have different Semantic Representations even though all have the same ultimate purpose. Thus, the Semantic Representation which a speaker expresses in a sentence may not reflect the speaker's true purpose since it is only the overt purpose which a sentence represents. What a speaker does is to think over alternative means for conveying an idea and then decide on a Semantic Representation to be conveyed. See Searle (1975) for insights into how a speaker and listener communicate purpose using sentences which only indirectly express one's intentions.
2. In actuality, speakers may often wait for entire phrases or sentences to be received before initiating detailed processing since the larger unit may already be stored as a whole.

Chapter 8

Child language acquisition

Speech production, speech understanding, and thought

Speech understanding as the basis of speech production

In learning language, we understand speech before we produce it. With the exception of the odd word or phrase, children are not able to utter words and sentences meaningfully until after they have had the opportunity to hear and understand the words, phrases, and sentences which others speak. Consider such typical children's utterances as 'Want gum,' 'No wash,' 'Why it's not working?' and 'Where I can put them?' Since children are not born with the knowledge of any particular language, e.g. English, it is necessary that they be exposed to a language in order to learn it.[1] It is further necessary that the speech to which children are exposed be related to objects, events, and situations in the environment. Children will not learn language, if all that they are exposed to is speech, no matter how many times it is uttered. Thus, for example, even if one heard the speech sound 'neko' a dozen times, one would have no way of knowing that it means *cat* (in Japanese) without some environmental clue. The sound form of a word must be associated with something that gives a clue as to meaning. Without a sound-meaning association, the mere utterance of the sound form is of little communicative significance. Only when speech sounds are used appropriately in situations is there a basis for imputing language knowledge to the utterer. The parrot is a classic case in this regard.

Interestingly, while the ability to utter speech sounds in appropriate situations is a good indicator of language knowledge, the absence of that ability to produce speech may not indicate a lack of language knowledge. For example, there are hearing persons who cannot speak or who speak with great difficulty, such as those with cerebral palsy. Yet such persons may understand all that is spoken to them. I personally know of such a case, a three-year-old mute but hearing girl in Japan. She could understand what was said to her and was normal in all other respects, except for the ability to produce speech.[2] Such a case serves to illustrate the primacy of speech understanding. Clearly, language learning may occur without speech production but not without speech understanding. Speech understanding forms the basis for speech production.[3] That children are unable to utter words or sentences for the purpose of communication without gaining an understanding of sentences first, could hardly be otherwise. If a child did not first learn to understand the meaning of words and sentences, the child would not be able to use words or sentences in a meaningful way, except by chance. Aside from these considerations, there is empirical evidence that speech comprehension develops in advance of speech production. Parents have always noted that children are able to respond appropriately to speech more complex than what the children are able to say. (My son was no exception. He even learned to read many words, phrases, and sentences before he was able to say them (Steinberg & Steinberg, 1975).)[4] Aside from anecdotal evidence, there exist findings from research studies which were especially designed to compare understanding and production capabilities. These studies, too, demonstrate the primacy of understanding. Huttenlocher (1974), for example, studied four young children and found that they were able to understand speech at a level beyond that to which they had progressed in production. The children selected objects which were named and were able to respond appropriately to commands even though they did not use such words and structures in their own speech. One boy, for example, responded appropriately to such distinctions as *baby's diaper* and *your diaper*, and *baby's bottle* and *your bottle* (*baby* referred to the boy's younger sister). Similarly, in another study, Sachs and Truswell (1976) found that children who could say only single words could understand speech structures composed of more than one word. The children responded with appropriate behaviors when given novel word combinations such as *Kiss ball* and *Smell truck*.

Unfortunately, although speech understanding plays a crucial role in language acquisition, relatively few research studies have been devoted to its investigation. Most of the language acquisition studies have been concerned with the development of speech production. The reason for this is simple; production studies are easier to do. The product of the speech production process (the child's utterance) is something that can be directly observed while the product of the understanding process cannot. Understanding can only be inferred on the basis of relevant behavior. Consequently, those testing comprehension have had to rely on indirect methods, such as asking children to perform in response to requests or to answer questions. The difficulty involved in attempting to gather relevant data from young children in these regards should not be underestimated. Consider the experience of some researchers (Brown & Bellugi, 1964: 135) with a two-year-old:

> *Interviewer*: Adam, which is right, 'two shoes' or 'two shoe'?
> *Adam*:   Pop goes the weasel!

Thought as the basis of speech understanding

As was noted earlier, merely hearing the speech sounds of a word does not provide a child with its meaning. An object, event or situation must occur along with it. For 'neko,' an association with the object 'cat' (or its picture) is necessary. Of course, for those who already know some language, the meaning of a word may be conveyed through the descriptive use of other words. The source of the meaning of those descriptive words, however, it ultimately based on an association with speech sound and object. One cannot begin to learn such abstract words as *thought, clever, interesting*, and *hungry*, without first learning words for items which are directly observable in the world. The basic language principle that a combination of speech sounds represents something other than itself, i.e. a meaning symbol, might never be acquired otherwise.

Thus, in learning language the child must hear speech sounds in conjunction with the perception of objects, events, and situations. Both types of experience are independent of one another in the sense that the perception (seeing, hearing, feeling, etc.) of objects, events, and situations in the world is not dependent on the hearing of the speech sounds and vice-versa. Seeing a cat and hearing 'neko,' for example, are independent perceptions. Hearing the sound 'neko' does not provide us with an experience which will be the basis for the ultimate meaning of the word. The same is true in learning the meaning of sentence structures. Simply hearing the speech sounds 'John chased Bill,' and knowing the meanings of the individual words *John, chased*, and *Bill* is insufficient information for determining who is doing the chasing and who is being chased. One must hear sentences in conjunction with related events in order to learn that English has an Agent-Action-Object sequence. Thus, by hearing the sentence *John chased Bill* along with an experience of the event of 'John chasing Bill,' the child is provided a basis for learning that it is 'John' who is doing the chasing and that it is 'Bill' who is being chased. Language is a system which allows for the labelling of thoughts in terms of physical sound so that the thoughts may be communicated to others. Thought, however, is independent of language, including as it does ideas, feelings, percepts, emotions, etc. (For details concerning this view of the relation of language and thought, see Chapter 6.) As such, thought provides the basis for speech understanding which in turn provides the basis for speech production.

The development of brain, thought, and language
The contention of the eminent theorist Lenneberg (1969) that the development of language is dependent on the biological maturation of the brain is not in itself in conflict with the above interpretation of relationships. It could be held that the maturation of the brain permits the development of ideas which in turn allows for the development of language. Lenneberg, by the way, does *not* favor the innate ideas view of Chomsky, e.g. 'Syntax does not have a genetic basis any more than do arithmetic or algebra' (Lenneberg, 1969: 642). Whether or not biological maturation of the brain is or is not necessary for the development of ideas and thought is an issue which is unresolved. One could reasonably argue that at birth the child is completely endowed with all of the basic brain materials and functions which are necessary for the development of thought and that the growth of the brain (which is indeed a fact) is actually due to the accumulation of new learning. Thus, a correlation between brain growth and intellectual growth could be the result of intellectual growth stimulating brain growth (and vice-versa) such that new neural connections are formed, cell bodies increase, etc. Such an interactionist view differs sharply from that of Lenneberg's in which biological maturation is regarded essentially as an independent primary cause of events.

Incidentally, the evidence which Lenneberg offered to provide support for his theory that language development is restricted by the biological maturation of the brain has never been confirmed and it can have opposing interpretations. For example, Lenneberg's hypothesis that the development of motor skills such as reaching, sitting, standing, walking, etc. is highly correlated with the production of syllables, one word utterances, two word utterances, etc. has not been supported by research. Undoubtedly, there is some correlation between ordinary motor skills and speech production because an essential part of speech production itself involves motor skills. In learning to form sounds, articulations with the mouth, tongue, lips, vocal chords, etc., must be practiced and brought under intentional control. Brain maturation may well be a primary independent determinant in such a case. However, it must be kept in mind that with respect to children's acquiring the ability to produce meaningful and complex one word, two word, and multi-word utterances, brain maturation may or may not be a primary determinant. An explanation is still required for why it is that children, who, at a one word stage, can easily say and meaningfully use words like *Joy* and *see*, do not also formulate a two word utterance like *Joy see*, even though they understand similar utterances and can utter individual words which combine similar sound forms, e.g. *Joicey*. There is usually such a lag between the production of one and two word utterances and such a lag cannot be explained by any need for more articulatory motor skill development. My own view is that the lag is due not to brain maturation but what the child conceives to be necessary in order to express a thought. A child who has the thought of wanting juice is not aware that more than the word 'juice' is required. Children do not realize that others cannot read their minds and only with experience do they come to understand that longer and more complex utterances are necessary to convey their thoughts precisely.

Innate ideas, intelligence, or undifferentiated schema as the basis of thought

Given that thought is independent of language, one may wonder what is the origin of thought. (Although this issue was discussed in detail in Chapter 5, additional comment will be made here with reference to child language acquisition.) As early as the first and second years, children's speech exhibits a variety of complex ideas. For example, as shall be detailed later, children say such things as 'big truck' (semantically, the *object* 'truck' is assigned the *attribute* 'big'), 'Daddy chair' (the *object* 'Daddy' *possesses* another *object* 'chair'), and 'Mommy give' (the *object* 'Mommy' is the *cause* of an *action* of 'giving'). Since language itself does not provide the child with such ideas as *object, attribute, possesses, cause*, and *action* the question arises as to how the child acquired them. Obviously, interaction with the world is necessary. But, were the basic ideas already in the mind in some form even before the physical stimuli of the world were sensed, i.e. the innate ideas view of the Rationalists? Or, were the ideas derived entirely through experience with none being in the mind (latent or otherwise) prior to experiencing of the world, i.e. the experiential view of the Empiricists. (The word Empiricist here is used only in the sense of the mentalist philosophical school of Aristotle (4th cent. B.C.) , Locke (1690), John Stuart Mill (1843), etc., and not in the sense which Behaviorists use it, i.e. to give primacy to observation and facts.)

While Rationalists and Empiricists disagree with one another as to the origin of knowledge in the mind, each group disagrees within itself as to what exactly is or is not innate. The Rationalists disagree with one another on whether or not there are specific ideas for language and other areas of knowledge such as mathematics. Chomsky (1965; 1966), for example, argues that there are ideas inherent in the mind which pertain only to language, and are separate from those involved in mathematics. On the other hand, others such as Bever (1970) argue that the innate ideas are of a more general nature, so that, for example, mathematics and language would essentially have the same basic underlying ideas. All Rationalists do agree, though, that innate ideas alone are not sufficient for the learning of language or anything else. Some degree of experience is necessary to activate those ideas which are otherwise latent in the mind. The important question of to what degree experience is necessary has never been seriously addressed, however.

As for Empiricists, although they agree that no specific knowledge is inherent in the mind, they disagree as to what else may be there prior to birth. John Locke (1690) argued hundreds of years ago that there was nothing in the mind at birth, no knowledge, no principles for acquiring knowledge, nothing. Even the will (intention) had to be derived from experience. Other Empiricists have taken a less radical position. Putnam (1967), for example, argues that the mind inherently contains 'general multipurpose learning strategies' (a notion similar to the concept of general intelligence) by means of which knowledge is derived from experience. (For Putnam, while intelligence consists of ideas, such ideas do not constitute knowledge but are only a means for acquiring knowledge.) Piaget, on the other hand, has argued that intelligence, which is the basis for the acquisition of such knowledge as language, is derived from experience after birth. What humans are born with are 'undifferentiated schemas' from which intelligence develops (Piaget & Inhelder, 1969; Piaget, 1968). Thus, while Empiricists all agree that no ideas which constitute knowledge are innate in the mind, they do not agree on whether there are, innate in the mind, types of ideas which would assist in the acquisition of knowledge. As far as language acquisition data is concerned, I do not believe that any will serve to settle any of these controversies. Both the Rationalist and Empiricist theories are sufficiently vague so that any observational datum can be given an explanation. Be that as it may, aside from such ultimates, there is still a great deal that can be discovered about how human beings acquire language. The following sections will attempt to provide support for that claim. Because of the paucity of studies regarding the development of speech understanding, discussion will be concerned with how the child's speech production ability develops.

Development of speech production

Vocalization: babbling to speech

Prior to uttering speech sounds, infants make a variety of sounds, crying, cooing, gurgling. Infants everywhere seem to make the same variety of sounds, even children who are born deaf (Lenneberg, Rebelsky & Nichols, 1965). The ability and propensity to utter such sounds thus appear to be unlearned in humans. Later, children ordinarily begin to babble, to repeat what may be described as consonant-vowel combinations, e.g. 'ma-ma,' 'pa-pa.' The sounds which infants make involve many but not all of the speech sounds which occur in languages of the world. For example, English sounds like the 'th' in *though* and the 'th' in *thin* are rare as are the click sounds common in such African languages such as Zulu. In time, however, such vocalizations take on the character of speech. From as early as six months of age, and before they utter words in the language, it seems that infants from different language communities begin to babble somewhat distinctively and with some of the intonation of their language (Tonkova-Yampol'skaya, 1969; Nakazima, 1962; Lieberman, 1967). However, this has not been firmly established (Moskowitz, 1971: 37–44). This is a learned phenomenon and is obviously based on hearing; deaf infants as might be expected, do not progress to this distinctive stage of babbling. It is from this advanced stage of babbling that infants move into uttering their first word. Often this occurs at one year of age.

When children begin to utter words, somewhat surprisingly, only some of the sounds which they have heretofore been babbling appear in speech. The other sounds, therefore, must be re-acquired, in a sense. There may be some order to the acquisition of speech sounds. For example, sounds like /x/ (Bach), /ʌ/ (bud), /k/, /g/, and /i/ (seem) which commonly occurred in vocalization prior to speech may now tend to occur only after the acquisition of such sounds as /p/, /t/, /m/, /a/, and /o/. Thus, there may be a discontinuity between babbling and speech in that the kinds of vocalizations which occur in babbling are not direct precursors of speech. In the speech phase, it may be that consonants are acquired in a front to back order (where 'front' and 'back' refer to the origin of the articulation of the sound) with /m/, /p/, /b/, /t/, and /d/ preceding /k/, /g/, and /x/, while vowels are acquired in a back to front order with /a/ (ball) and /o/ (low) preceding /i/ (meet) and /ʌ/ (mud). Jakobson (1968) devised a theory based on his distinctive features theory of phonological opposition which attempts to predict the order of the acquisitions of speech sounds. In the main, however, empirical studies have not supported his predictions (Velten, 1943; Braine, 1971; Leopold, 1947; Ferguson & Garnica, 1975). There is much more variation in the order of acquisition than the theory predicted.

Two issues thus remain to be explained: the discontinuity between babbling and actual speech in the production of speech sounds, and the order of acquisition of speech sounds. In my view, the discontinuity issue involves, as the eminent linguist Jespersen noted many years ago, the distinction between intentional and non-intentional vocalization. Babbling is non-intentional in the sense that particular sounds are not under central cognitive control. The child does not set a prior intention for the making of the particular sounds which occur. The case of speech is quite different, however. Here sounds cannot be uttered at random but must match previously heard sounds which are conventionally associated with certain objects, needs, etc. In order to accomplish this feat, it is necessary that the child discover what sound is created by what speech articulators (mouth, tongue, vocal chords, etc.). It is this knowledge that the child must acquire in order to speak meaningfully. While vocalization for babbling is different from vocalization for speech with respect to intentionality, the vocalization of speech is dependent on that of babbling. In babbling, the child will chance on many of the various articulatory mechanisms for producing speech. The connections established by such exercise of the articulatory mechanisms undoubtedly will aid the child later in acquiring speech when intentional connections to the articulators for the purpose of activating speech must be established.

As far as the establishment of intentional connections is concerned, my opinion is that two variables dominate this process, *visibility of articulators* and *ease of articulation*. When the child becomes motivated to produce meaningful speech (this occurs after the child has learned to comprehend some words which other people say), the child begins to seek ways to produce desired sounds. The child then becomes alert to clues that relate to the articulation of speech sounds. The child watches where speech sounds come from and notes correlations between sounds and the position of noticeable speech articulators, the mouth and lips. It is mainly movements which the child observes and imitates. Since noticeable mouth and lip movements are primarily involved in the articulation of certain consonants, it is not surprising, therefore, that children tend to produce sounds like /m/, /p/, and /b/ before the others. Consonant sounds like the stops /k/ and /g/ and the fricatives /f/ and /s/, which involve the movement of unseen articulators, are generally learned later.

As for vowels, since all involve the use of many unseen articulators, children get little aid from direct observation. Rather, they must indulge in a lot of trial and error in order to secure the proper positions for articulators. It seems that those sounds which are closest to the resting position of the articulators, e.g. back vowels such as /a/, are easier to create and are learned first while those sounds which require more articulator control to create, e.g., tensed front vowels such as /i/, are learned later. However, over and above the operation of these variables of ease and visibility, there is the important one of *chance*. It seems that children may by chance discover and retain any sound-articulator connection, e.g. the daughter of Leopold (1953) was able to pronounce the word *pretty* with precision while being unable to pronounce other words composed of similar sounds.

Three early meaningful speech stages: naming and holophrastic, telegraphic, and morphemic-transformational

The naming and holophrastic stage: one-word utterances
The mere utterance of appropriate speech sounds, e.g. 'mama,' may or may not indicate word knowledge. Children can be said to have learned to say their first word when they are able to utter a recognizable speech form in conjunction with some object or event in the environment. The speech form may be imperfect, e.g. 'da' for *daddy*, and the associated meaning may be incorrect, e.g. all people are called 'da,'

but as long as the child uses the speech form reliably (the sound-meaning association does not occur by chance), it may be concluded that the child has acquired some sort of word knowledge.

The naming of objects is one of the first uses to which children put words, e.g. 'mama' names a person, although it may be preceded by words which accompany actions such as 'bye bye' in leave-taking (Greenfield & Smith, 1976). It appears that children first use nouns as proper names to refer to specific objects (Moskowitz, 1978), after which they may or may not extend the meaning correctly for common nouns (Clark, 1973). For example, while 'dada' may be used initially to identify one particular person, it may or may not be extended to include all men or all people. Or, 'wowwow' may be used to refer to one dog, and then be extended to refer to all animals, soft slippers, or people in furs. In time, of course, the proper extensions are learned.

However, children do not only use single words to refer to objects; they also use those same words to express complex thoughts which involve those objects. A young child who has lost its mother may cry 'mama,' meaning *I want mama*. Or a child may point to a shoe and say 'mama,' meaning *The shoe belongs to mama*. Research has shown that the young child expresses a variety of semantic functions by the single word (Greenfield & Smith, 1976). In such cases, the child uses a single word to express a thought for which mature speakers will use a whole sentence. It is because of this whole thought function that the one word speech stage is often referred to as the *holophrastic* stage. Actually, it is quite amazing how inventive children can be in the use of single words. Researchers have noted that children may describe a complex situation by using a series of holophrases. For example, 'peach, Daddy, spoon' was used to describe a situation where Daddy had cut a piece of peach that was in a spoon (Bloom, 1973), and 'car, go, bus' was used to describe a situation in which hearing the sounds of a car reminded the child that she had gone on a bus the day before (Scollon, 1976).

It is often not easy, of course, to interpret what a child is intending to convey by the single word. And, while knowing the child, the child's previous experiences, and elements of the present situation will serve to aid in the interpretation of an utterance, even the most attentive parents are frequently unable to interpret utterances which their children produce. Such failures in communication may provide children with an impetus for improving their communicative language ability. They will discover that longer, more elaborate constructions will better serve their communicative needs, needs which become more varied and complex as they grow older.

The telegraphic stage: two- and three-word utterances
Children do not proceed as rapidly from the one-word to two-word

utterances as one might expect. Why this should be the case is a matter of conjecture, although it is my view, as was discussed earlier, that children have to become aware that adding more words improves communication. In any case, around two years of age or so children begin to produce two- and three-word utterances.

The following table lists a number of typical two-word utterances along with what a mature speaker might say in the same circumstances. The possible purpose of each utterance is indicated as are some of the semantic relations involved.

The most striking features about the dozen and a half or so very ordinary utterances shown here are the variety of purposes and the complexity of semantic relations which they exhibit. The child uses language to request, warn, name, refuse, brag, question, answer (in response to questions), and inform. In order to gain these ends, the utterances involve such semantic relations and concepts as agent, action, experiencer, receiver, state, object, possession, location, attribution, equation, negation, and quantification.[5]

A second feature of the child's utterances is the low incidence of function words such as articles, prepositions, and conjunctions. Rather, it is nouns, verbs, and adjectives which mainly appear in the utterances. This is not surprising when one considers that these are the most informative classes of words and would be the first that children would learn to understand. The meanings of function words, *to John*, *with Mary*, *the car*, *candy and cake*, could never be determined if the meanings of nouns, verbs, and adjectives were not known. A child could guess what function a preposition like *on* might signify when hearing the sentence *The toy is on the table* in environmental context and with knowledge of the words *toy* and *table*. Without the knowledge of the meaning of the nouns, the child could never be certain, even in environmental context, which one of numerous possible functions is being expressed. From a listener's point of view, a similar situation obtains. A child's utterance which consisted of *The is on the* would have less communicative impact than *toy table*. It is because children's utterances at this stage appear to have the character of a telegram message, i.e. short and with content words, that this phase of speech development is often referred to as the *telegraphic* stage.

A final feature of the child's utterances which might be noted is the closeness of the child's word order to that of the speech of the mature speaker. The child learning English tends to say *My cup.* rather than *Cup my*, *Not tired* rather than *Tired not*, and *Mommy chair* rather than *Chair mommy*. Thus, even with only two word utterances the child exhibits some learning of the word order of the language. This is not to say that the child does not produce significant deviations (but more on this later). Nor is this a sufficient basis for claiming that the child real-

TABLE 2. Two word child utterances and their semantic analysis

Child utterance	Possible equivalent mature speaker utterance	Possible purpose	Semantic relations (expressed or implied)
Want cookie.	I want a cookie.	Request	(Experiencer)–State–Object
More milk.	I want some more milk.	Request	(Experiencer)–(State)–Object; Quantification
Joe see.	I (Joe) see you.	Informing	Experiencer–State–(Object)
My cup.	This is my cup.	Warning	Possession
Mommy chair.	This chair belongs to Mommy.	Warning	Possession
Mommy chair.	This chair belongs to Mommy.	Answer to Question	Possession
Mommy chair.	Mommy is sitting in the chair.	Answer to Question	Location
Big boy.	I am a big boy.	Bragging	Attribution
Red car.	That car is red.	Naming	Attribution
That car.	That is a car.	Naming	Equation
No sleep.	I don't want to go to sleep.	Refusal	Experience–State–Object; Negation
Not tired.	I am not tired.	Refusal	Experiencer–Negation; State
Where doll?	Where is the doll?	Question	Location
Truck table.	The truck is on the table.	Informing	Location
Daddy run.	Daddy is running.	Informing	Agent–Action
Joe push.	I (Joe) pushed the cat.	Informing	Agent–Action–(Object)
Push cat.	I pushed the cat.	Informing	(Agent)–Action–Object
Give candy.	Give me the candy.	Request	(Agent)–Action–Receiver–Object

izes that different word orders signal different semantic relations. Yet, it does show that the child has acquired a significant aspect of the ability to produce appropriate utterances.

While the child's production of language is minimal at the two and three word stage, this production is sufficient to reflect a great deal of the conceptualization and thinking on the part of the child. Such an advanced level of conceptual development surprised many theorists, including Piagetians whose age estimates had to be revised downward. (Actually, the true intellectual achievement of the child must even be greater since the present estimate is based on speech production data and not on speech understanding data which would reflect a more advanced conceptual level.) It is worth observing here that the speech production evidence for the conceptual development of young children has appeared relatively recently, mainly in the 1970s. For, in the 1960s, when child language acquisition research was first seriously begun, the focus was on syntax, not semantics. Chomsky's syntactic based theory of grammar was looked to as a source of ideas for analysis. Theorists, during that period, sought to characterize children's utterances wholly in terms of syntactic form. For children at the two- and three-word stage, there was little to do but classify utterances in terms of sequences of grammatical classes, e.g. *Mommy chair* = Noun + Noun and *Truck table* = Noun + Noun, e.g. Braine (1963), Roger Brown and Bellugi (1964), and McNeill (1970). Because children in using two- and three-word utterances tend to use only a few grammatical classes (nouns, verbs, adjectives) with the result that relatively few unique sequences of word classes are to be found, little was revealed by such analyses. (See de Villiers & de Villiers, (1978: 70) for a detailed criticism of these so-called Pivot-Open grammars.) Characterizing utterances wholly in terms of syntactic form fails to distinguish important semantic characteristics. For example, while *Mommy chair* and *Truck table* are both Noun + Noun sequences, the first may involve the concept of possession but the second only involves that of location. An increasing awareness of semantic aspects of language arose in the late 1960s with the proposal of semantically based grammars by linguists, the Generative Semanticists and Fillmore (Semantic Case Grammar). Child language analysts have given serious consideration to semantics ever since that time.

The morphemic and transformational stage
Morpheme Acquisition. When the child begins to produce longer utterances, then function words, inflections on nouns and verbs, and complex syntactic structures begin to make their appearance. Let us first consider the acquisition of some function words and inflectional morphemes. Table 3 shows the order of acquisition of 13 different morphemes from data gathered from three children (Roger Brown, 1973: 274).

TABLE 3. Order of acquisition of some morphemes by three children

| | | | Learning variables | |
| | | | Referent | Sound Change |
Order	Morpheme	Examples		
1	Present progressive	*Girl playing*	+	+
2	prepositions (*in* and *on* only)	*Truck in water* *Boy on horse*	+	+
3	Plural	*cats, boys, fishes*	+	−
4	Past irregular	*came, fell, went*	+	+
5	Possessive	*Jack's, Bob's, Chris'*	+	−
6	Uncontracted copula *be*	*I am happy* *He is happy* *You are happy*	−	+
7	Articles	*a dog, the dog*	−	+
8	Past regular	*jumped, jogged, wanted*	+	−
9	Third person reg.	*talks, sings, watches*	−	+
10	Third person irreg.	*He does* *She has*	−	+
11	Uncontracted aux. *be*	*I am playing* *She is playing* *You are playing*	−	+
12	Contracted copula *be*	*I'm happy* *Pat's happy* *Joe's happy* *You're happy*	−	−
13	Contracted aux. *be*	*I'm playing* *Pat's playing* *Joe's playing* *You're playing*	−	−

Based on data from Roger Brown (1973: 281).

Why these morphemes should have been acquired in the order that they have has been the topic of much speculation. As I see it, two principal variables, both of a universal nature, will serve to explain most of the obtained order. They are: *referentiality* and *sound change noticeability*. (See Peters, 1980, 1981 for a consideration of other pertinent variables.) *Referentiality* concerns the degree to which it is obvious that the language item refers to an object, event, or situation in the world. For example, having to distinguish one or more dogs (pluralization) in the world is easier than having to distinguish one person who is neither the speaker nor the listener (the third person singular marker). Then, too, in some cases such as the copula and auxiliary *be* (and their contracted forms) there is no referential distinction to be made at all. *Sound change noticeability* concerns how easy it is for a sound change to be perceived. For example, adding or changing vowel sounds is more noticeable than adding or changing consonant sounds. Adding vowels creates syllables which then must receive some degree of stress. Thus, a change from 'play' to 'playing' is more noticeable than a change from 'jump' to 'jumped' (/j∧mpt/). Vowel changes like 'come' to 'came' are also more noticeable than consonant changes.

If a value is assigned to each variable such that + indicates a high degree, and − indicates a low degree, one might obtain the pattern of pluses and minuses which I assigned and is shown in Table 3. In interpreting the patterns of pluses and minuses, it will be observed that items which were learned faster tend to receive a + on both variables, e.g. the present progressive tense and prepositions, while those which were learned slower tended to receive a − on both, e.g. the contracted copula and auxiliary *be*. Items with a mixture of + and − tended to be learned at a medium rate. It is worth noting that the variable of frequency would not serve to explain much of the order of learning. For, while highly frequent items like the article and the contracted and uncontracted forms of *be* as auxiliary and copula probably occur more frequently in adult speech than do the present progressive or the prepositions *in* and *on*, these highly frequent items were learned at a slower rate than the less frequent ones. Undoubtedly, frequency is a factor in learning, as are many other factors. Such a variable will come into play, however, only when other more potent variables have provided their effects.

Transformation Acquisition. With the production of longer utterances, simple structures are manipulated to produce more complex ones. *Pronominalization, question*, and *negation* are just a few of the many complex rules, i.e. transformations, which children acquire in their first five years. As an example, the acquisition of one transformation, that of negation, will be considered in detail.

Before presenting some of the acquisition data concerning negation, it may be useful to review some of the features of the negation process. Suppose we consider the sentences *Joe wants some candy* and *Joe is hungry*. Their negations may be *Joe does not want any candy* and *Joe is not hungry*. The child must learn a number of different things here: (1) when and where to insert the auxiliary *do*; (2) where to insert the negative marker (*not* occurs before the verb *want* but after the copula *am*); (3) tense assignment from verb to auxiliary (*Joe wants . . .* and *Joe does not want . . .*, *Joe wanted . . .* and *Joe did not want . . .*); and (4) what agreements must be made (*does* for third person singular present, and *some* changes to *any*).

According to the research of Klima and Bellugi (1966), there is a consistent pattern in the acquisition of negation, with negation being acquired in three main periods. Sample sentences and their analysis follow below for each period. Incidentally, these data are those taken from the same three children whose morpheme acquisition development was described above:

PERIOD 1

No money   No the sun shining.
Not a teddy bear.   No play that.
No singing song.   No fall!

In this, the earliest period, a negation marker (*Neg*), *no* or *not*, is placed at the front of an affirmative utterance (*S*), i.e. *Neg + S*. Children everywhere seem to do something similar. French children place *non* or *pas* before *S* (Gregoire, 1937), as do English children, while Japanese children follow *S* with *nai* (McNeill & McNeill, 1968), i.e. *S + Neg*, in accord with the surface structure of their language.

PERIOD 2

I don't want it.   That no Mommy
I don't know his name.   There no squirrels.
We can't talk.   He no bite you.
You can't dance.   I no want envelope.
Book say no.
Touch the snow no.

In the second period, the negative marker tends to appear internally within the utterance rather than outside of it as in the previous period. and the auxiliaries *do* and *can* appear with the negation marker. Klima and Bellugi believe that the children consider *don't* and *can't* as single words and do not analyze them as *Aux + Neg*. That the uncontracted forms of *do* and *can* do not appear is one argument which they present in support of their views.

PERIOD 3

Paul can't have one.   I am not a doctor.
This can't stick.   This not ice cream.
I didn't did it.   Paul not tired.
You didn't caught me.   I not hurt him.
'Cause he won't talk.   I not see you anymore.
Donna won't let go.   Don't touch the fish.
                                              Don't kick my box.

The copula *be* and the modal *will* appear with negation and imperative negatives are formed with *do* rather than the simple negative (*Don't touch the fish* as opposed to *No touch the fish* in earlier periods.) The children's mastery of negation at this period is nearly complete. Only a number of relatively minor problems, such as assignment of tense only to auxiliary (*You didn't caught me*) remain to be resolved.

With regard to progress through the periods, it was found that one of the three children reached Period 3 by two years of age, while the others reached that same period by around three and a half years. Such a difference dramatically demonstrates how vast individual differences may be in the acquisition of speech. One child may be uttering only single word utterances at 24 months while another may be producing elaborate sentences. On the other hand, all passed through a similar qualitative sequential pattern of development.

By five years of age, children are able to produce most of the essential structures of their language. Passives and other complex transformations, however, have yet to be acquired (Carol Chomsky, 1969; Palermo & Molfese, 1972). Although research has yet to demonstrate approximately when such structures are completely acquired, a rough estimate of 10 years of age may not be too far wrong.

Essentials in learning and processing

Nature of speech and environmental input

During the 1960s, Chomsky's theorizing about innate language knowledge had a dampening effect on the study of input, both language and environmental, with respect to the acquisition of language. A sort of mystical aura dominated the field. Language was not 'learned' but somehow mysteriously 'acquired.' (Actually, no clear distinction between the use of these terms *learned* and *acquired* has ever been drawn.) Typical of views at the time was that of the eminent language philosopher, Fodor. At a talk at the University of Hawaii in 1965, he suggested that a child could learn language simply by being exposed to sentences, with little necessity for relevant environmental stimuli (objects, events, situations). The speech of parents and others was not thought to be special, i.e. was not simplified, shortened or emphasized concrete referents, so as to assist the child in learning language. A similar view was voiced by McNeill (1966):

> It is as if he [the child who is learning a language] were equipped [innately] with a set of 'templates' against which he can compare the speech he happens to hear from his parents. This speech is a haphazard sample (at least initially), not at all contrived to instruct a child in basic grammatical structure. (p. 36)

Research has since shown, however that the nature of the speech and environmental input which ·children receive *is* especially contrived to assist language learning and that unfortunate children who have been exposed to language mainly through television or by overhearing adults' conversations do not acquire significant language knowledge

(Todd, 1972; Snow et al. 1976)[6]. Parents generally talk to their children about what is happening in the immediate environment and not about abstract or remote objects and events (Slobin, 1975; Phillips, 1973), and the speech they use is highly grammatical and simplified. Ungrammatical sentences ·are found to occur but rarely. Newport (1975), for example, in a long term study with 15 mothers reports an incidence of only 1 ungrammatical utterance in 1500 in their speech. Such findings are not perhaps surprising, but they would be if one were aware of the widespread acceptance of Chomsky's claim that children learn language despite being exposed to a high proportion of 'degenerate' sentences (Chomsky, 1967b). (Chomsky used this claim to support his theory of innate language knowledge arguing that a perfect grammar could not be learned from imperfect data, unless innate language ideas were available to assist acquisition. See Chapter 5 for more details.)

With regard to simplification, it has been found that in talking to children, adults generally use short simple sentences (Snow, 1972; Garnica, 1977; Seitz & Stewart, 1975), simple and restricted vocabulary (Phillips, 1973; Seitz & Stewart, 1975) e.g. *mama* instead of *mother, see* instead of *notice*, and simplified phonology and structure (Ferguson, 1964, 1977; DePaulo & Bonvillian, 1975), e.g. consonant plus vowel word patterns such as *wawa* and *byebye* are used rather than the more complex sound patterns of *water* and *goodbye*. Furthermore, they exaggerate intonation (Garnica, 1977; Drach, 1969; Cross, 1977), and frequently repeat or rephrase what they or their children say (Snow, 1972; Brown & Bellugi, 1964; Newport, 1975; Kobashigawa, 1969), e.g. adults tend to use higher pitch, slower speech, and more pauses, and they place more distinctive stress on words than they do ordinarily. Such exaggerations undoubtedly serve to highlight and to focus the child's attention on important constituents of sentences thus allowing the child to remember them more easily. Repetition and expansion also assist the child in this same regard. Expansions such as Child: *Mommy lunch.* Mother: *Yes. Mommy is making lunch*, or, Child: *Give Daddy.* Mother: *Give it to Daddy*, undoubtedly serve to promote learning.

It is interesting that not only adults, but children, too, tend to use simplified speech in talking with younger children. For example, four-year-old children produced simplified speech to two-year-olds but not to adults, even though some of the four-year-olds did not have younger siblings (Shatz & Gelman, 1973). It seems, too, non-parents also simplify speech (Sachs, Brown & Salerno, 1972), so much so that in adjusting themselves to the level of children (Snow, 1972) women with children do only slightly better than women who are not mothers. The simplification of speech may well be a universal phenomenon (Blount, 1972; Snow et al. 1976).

However, while there seems little doubt that simplification may facilitate the acquisition of language, the question remains as to whether simplification is essential for language learning to occur. It may not be, providing there is a close correspondence between what is said with what is happening in the environment. While unsimplified utterances are more difficult than simplified ones, still the child may be able to learn language. Although one sometimes hears of cases where it is said that the parents never used any sort of simplified speech, such cases have not been documented.

Imitation, rule learning, and correction

In learning language, children acquire much through imitation, i.e. by copying the language item that is modelled for them. They learn to say such words as *mama, dog, run, happy*, and *no*, such phrases and sentences as *Why not?*, *bread and butter*, and *Hold it!*, and, as was noted earlier, they tend to approximate the proper order of words in sentences. On the other hand, while much of language learning does involve imitation, this principle is inadequate to explain the more advanced and critical aspects of language learning. The child's production of certain novel single but morphologically complex words and sentences cannot be explained through imitation. Children commonly produce words like *sheeps, mouses, gooses, goed, comed, falled*, and *breaked* which they have never heard anyone say, as well as sentences like *No heavy, No the sun shine, When we can go?*, and *He is doing what?*. Clearly, children have formulated rules in their minds according to which they construct novel utterances. (This phenomenon relates to the discussion of the basic abilities of speakers in Chapter 1, where it was noted that speakers are able to produce and understand sentences which they have never experienced before.) While exceptions to rules must be learned, such as in pluralizing nouns (*sheeps) and in adding tense to verbs (*goed), and while rules such as those of negation and question must be further developed before mature speaker competence is achieved, it is evident that rule learning is taking place.

Unfortunately, some theorists have become so enamored with the fact of rule learning and the deviant forms which it frequently may produce, they lose sight of the whole of language learning. Moskowitz (1978: 95), for example, makes the claim that 'imitation seems to have little role in the acquisition process.' Such a view fails to consider three important points: (1) The child actually does imitate a multitude of words and phrases, and even a number of sentences. If this were not so, it is inconceivable how children would begin to develop a speech production capability. (2) Deviant forms, e.g. *sheeps and *comed, are derived on the basis of previously learned (imitated) regular forms, e.g. *dogs* and *walked*. (3) Word order in phrases and sentences tends to approximate the order of mature speakers. The fact that the child will produce deviant utterances according to some improperly conceived rule, e.g. *When we can go?*, is not to be denied. However, the fact that the child eventually will produce properly formed sentences surely is indicative of the child's desire to imitate the speech it hears. The child will seek to revise a previously formulated rule so that the output will match that of the mature speaker's output. Imitation thus can be said to promote the acquisition of speech with respect to two types of functions, through the direct copying of speech forms and through motivating the child to make rule adjustments so that imitations of the speech of others can be made. Clearly imitation plays a crucial role in the acquisition of the ability to produce speech.

While it used to be thought by many that correcting children's speech is essential to improvement, research has now shown that such is not the case. Parents pay little attention to the grammatical correctness of their children's speech (Roger Brown, 1973; Roger Brown, Cazden & Bellugi, 1969). Rather, they are more interested in the truth value, appropriateness, or cleverness of what their children say. When parents do attempt to correct their children's speech, the results are often fruitless and frustrating. Consider the anecdote cited by McNeill (1966: 69) in this regard:

> Son: Nobody don't like me.
> Mother: Nobody likes me.
> Above sequence repeated 8 times.
> Mother (in desperation): Now, listen carefully. Nobody likes me.
> Son: Oh! Nobody don't likes me.

While some progress was achieved (the s on like), the major concern of the mother, the extraneous occurrence of the auxiliary do, was not perceived by the child as needing correction.

Undoubtedly, there are cases where parents' corrections, particularly with older children, may directly result in improvement. However, because corrections are relatively rare with respect to the number of deviant utterances that a child actually produces, it is reasonable to conclude that correction does not play an important role in grammar learning. The desire of children to approximate mature speakers' utterances along with their remarkable intellectual ability for analysis and hypothesis formation is a sufficient basis for explaining children's progress in speech development.

The child's language learning problem

Given that the child has thoughts involving ideas, feelings, and needs which exist in the child's mind independently of and prior to language (see Chapter 6 for details of this position), the problem for the child in learning language is to determine how thought in the mind is related to speech in the physical world. The child must acquire a system of language, a system which provides a means whereby thought can be expressed in speech, and speech can be interpreted as thought.

The child begins to learn the language system by hearing speech which is coordinated with environmental objects, events, and situations. The (non-speech) environmental stimuli are what provide the child with clues as to what speech sounds represent what ideas in thought. For example, on hearing the speech sound of 'dog' in association with the appearance of the object 'dog,' the child can learn that the idea of dog is signalled by the speech sound 'dog.' Once the child learns the essential principle that speech sounds relate to objects and ideas, the child then seeks to identify ideas for the speech sounds which he or she hears. For example, language for physical objects (persons, animals, things) along with their physical attributes (*The dog is big*), states or conditions (*The toy is broken*), actions (*The dog is barking*), and relations (*John pushed James*) must be learned as must language for abstract or mental notions, e.g. *I am happy* and *I want candy* where self ('I') and mental states ('happy,' 'want') are involved.

The easiest learning for the child will involve the acquisition of speech for the physical class of items. Such items are readily observed and while the more complex ones do require the exercise of some degree of inference (in *John pushed James*, for example, the child must infer that the noun phrase prior to the verb is the agent of the action), nonetheless, that extent of inference-making is substantially less demanding than that for abstract and mental notions. Words like *happy, idea, likes, wishes, might*, etc. require a great amount of intellectual processing to determine their meanings. Observations in the physical world must be correlated with subjective experiences and analyzed. Such an accomplishment on the part of the young child is truly a great intellectual feat.

Underlying this remarkable accomplishment, and all of the others which the child achieves in language acquisition, is that of memory. For, in the course of learning to identify the words of the language, devising rules for syntactic constructions, and relating speech to environmental context and mind, the child utilizes a phenomenal memory capacity. The child must remember a multitude of particular words, phrases, and sentences along with the contexts (physical and mental) in which they occurred. For such data provide the basis for analysis. If, for example, children did not remember many of the words, phrases, and sentences which they heard, they would have little basis for abstracting rules and meanings. In effect, each phrase or sentence which they heard would be novel and the child would have no data to search for underlying patterns and principles. Language learning would not be possible. Aside from the common observation that children often remember, word for word, stories which they are told, there is some research evidence which gives some indication of how formidable the language memory of children may be. Studies on single word vocabulary knowledge have estimated that a six-year-old knows about

24,000 single words (Smith, 1941) and a seven-year-old knows about 54,000 words (Diller, 1978). (Unfortunately, estimates are not available on younger children.) Because so many individual words have been learned and because it is known that children also learn a host of idioms in phrase and sentence form, there.is no reason to believe that children do not also learn and store in memory a multitude of ordinary phrases and sentences as well. (A similar view has been proposed by Clark, 1977.) Such a prodigious use of memory capacity, it is worth noting, is not unique to language. For, in many other areas of life – in remembering faces, objects, music, past events, and vast quantities of knowledge in a variety of fields – the extent of human memory is similarly remarkable.

Relevance of linguistic and psychological theories in explaining language acquisition

As for the grammatical theories which contemporary linguists have proposed, child language researchers have exhibited a decided preference for those which are semantically based (Generative Semantics, Semantic Case Grammar) over those which are syntactically based (Chomsky's Standard, Interpretive Semantics, and Trace Grammar theories). Such is not surprising, for syntactic based grammars have developed least what child language researchers require most, and that is some specification of the meaning of sentences and its relationship to syntax. The focus of syntactic based theories on the relationship of one syntactic structure to another (Deep or Surface Structures) has offered only limited insight to child language theorists.

On the other hand, while semantic based theories have provided some basis for understanding what the process of sentence production might involve (a speaker beginning with the meaning of a sentence converts it through syntax to sound), such grammars do not provide an understanding of what might be involved in the reverse process, that of sentence understanding. Semantic based grammars (and all other linguistic grammars, as well) do not begin a sentence analysis with speech sounds as input. However, while linguists have not been working on this problem, psycholinguists have. As Chapter 7 shows, psycholinguists, particularly Schlesinger (1977) who has worked with a semantic based model, have provided important insights with respect to the construction of a model of speech understanding.

The inadequacy of behaviorist theorizing is demonstrated by the fact that children do not learn language simply by imitation but by acquiring abstract rules as well. Consider such items as *No play that, *No the sun shine, and *We go when? which children regularly produce. These items, when they appear for the first time, could not have been produced on the basis of imitation or reinforcement, or even simple generalization, because children are not exposed to such utterances.

Mature speakers do not speak like that. On the other hand, such data support the position of Gestalt learning theorists (Hilgard & Bower, 1966) who have long held that human (and higher animal) learning includes the hypothesizing of abstract principles to account for phenomena which are observed in the world. Such theorists devoted much attention to the problem of learning principles through induction. Still, there are certain aspects of language learning, particularly non-abstract vocabulary, where behaviorist theory is valuable. For example, the connection between speech sounds and objects, or between speech sounds and behavioral responses, must be learned on the basis of behaviorist principles such as exposure to stimuli, contiguity of stimuli, or contiguity of stimulus and response. Such principles are relevant because the essential relationship between a speech sound ('dog') and its meaning or referent ('dog') is an arbitrary one. There is no principle or rule which underlies the relationship as there may be with sentences such as those involving negation or questions.

The acquisition of abstract transformational rules presents a challenge to Piagetian theorists, not because the existence of such rules in any way invalidates the theory but because the theory provides no explanation for its development. Piaget devoted his efforts to describing the growth of a deductive (syllogistic) type of logic in children (Piaget, 1957; Phillips, 1969). His theory does not account for the induction of principles such as transformational rules. As Piagetian research shows, the deductive process begins its most active and advanced development after the age of five, by which time the child has already acquired through *inductive* logic the abstract basics of the language system. For the most part, only the very early stages of conceptual development in Piaget's theory have been employed by child language researchers. The development of the idea of an object with its attributes and relations, for example, has been related to noun and predicate acquisition, e.g. Sinclair (1970). On the whole, though, I would say that current Piagetian theory is much too vague and insufficient in certain respects to provide an adequate cognitive foundation for the acquisition of language. Rather than have such theory guide child language acquisition research. I would rather see such a theory revitalized on the findings of that research. It seems to me that child language research itself is the best guide that is available for investigating the intellectual development of children for in the past two decades, more has been learned about that development than in all time past.

Notes

1. A discussion of the innateness question is dealt with in an upcoming section in this chapter. It is enough to note here that concerning English, for example, since the English languge itself is less than 2,000 years old, it could not

have become innate through evolution. Furthermore, children whose ancestors come from areas with vastly different language backgrounds, e.g. China, Africa, and Polynesia, learn English no differently than do children whose ancestors come from Anglo-Saxon backgrounds.

2. This girl was a research subject in an early reading study. In less than a year with about 10 minutes per day of instruction, she learned to read over 75 words, most of them complex Chinese type characters (Steinberg & Chen, 1980). She would point to objects when shown written words, or select appropriate written words when objects were shown.

3. Exceptions to this formulation may occur with deaf children who are taught to pronounce words which they cannot hear. For example, they may learn to name an object like 'dog' by being trained to control such speech articulators as the mouth, vocal chords, lips, and tongue. However, while individual words may be learned in this way, syntactic constructions are not. If a deaf person has some residual hearing, there may be gains in this regard. If not, some type of sign language may be taught. In the learning of sign language in ordinary situations, it is interesting to note that the understanding of signs precedes their production thus paralleling the situation with speech for ordinary children.

4. At 12 months of age, he was able to identify the written words *boy*, *girl*, *baby*, and *car* by picking out the correct word card when the word was spoken, even though he could not say any of them. At 24 months he could identify 48 written words and some phrases and sentences, although he could say only about 15 of them.

5. The term *experiencer* is used differently from Fillmore here. I use it as a sentient being which experiences states or ideas. A *receiver* is an experiencer who is affected by an action.

6. It might be noted here that Lenneberg's claim that language can be learned under language deprived conditions was based on an inadequate analysis. His own observation, that retarded children who are 'attended by only one person, often an older retardate who herself lacks a perfect command of language' (Lenneberg, 1969: 637) learn language, actually indicates that the children may well have received sufficient speech input which was suitable for the acquisition of language.

Chapter 9

Second language acquisition and teaching

Second language processing and learning

Performance models

After two (or more) languages have been acquired, how do the speech understanding and speech production processes function? Does lexical, syntactic, semantic, and phonological knowledge become integrated? Is second language knowledge and processing entirely independent of the first? Or, is there an interaction? Does first language processing change with the acquisition of a second? Is there an integration of processes? Unfortunately, no theories are available which address these basic questions. Such a lack of theory is not surprising, however, given that an understanding of a prerequisite and relatively simpler problem, that of first language performance, is similarly not available. (See Chapters 4 and 7 for some discussion of the problem of performance models for first language processing.) Without a prior understanding of first language functioning, the possibility that second language functioning interacts or becomes integrated in some way with the first cannot be explored. However, it would seem that certain basic operations involved in sentence understanding or production would be similar for a first or second language. In understanding a sentence, for example, regardless of whether a first or second language were involved, one would first listen to the incoming speech sounds and then attempt some morpheme or other constituent identification through a search of stored items.

Actually, only one serious model of second language functioning has been proposed to date, Osgood's *Compound-Coordinate Bilingual* theory (Osgood & Sebeok, 1954). However, that theory involves only one aspect of functioning, the processing of isolated words. It does not involve the interpretation of phrases and sentences. A *compound* bilingual is said to process second language words through the mediation of first language words, having learned the second language through translation. The *coordinate* bilingual, however, processes second language words without first language mediation, having learned the second language through direct experience. The possibility that different process models may result as a consequence of the mode of acquisition is still a question worthy of consideration and Osgood's compound-coordinate word processing distinction may well be a valid one.

Acquisition conditions and development

Natural vs. planned language situations
When a child learns a first language, we may say that the child learns the language under natural conditions. Such a learning situation generally differs greatly from artificial ones, with the most common one used in second language learning being the school classroom. Not all second language learning, however, takes place in the classroom. A second language can be learned under natural conditions. For example, children who are taken to live in foreign countries may learn a second language without formal instruction by associating with speakers of the foreign language, e.g. playmates, and household personnel. Thus, a second language can be learned under either natural or planned conditions.

The planned condition of the classroom in which a second language is learned may be said to include the following major differences with reference to the natural condition:

Characteristics of the planned second language learning situation

1. *Psycho-social demands of classroom*. The school classroom requires adjustment of the learner to group processes, classroom discipline, and procedures. The learner receives only a limited amount of individual attention. Regular attendance is required.
2. *Preselected language data*. The teacher generally introduces preselected target language items. Spontaneity is limited. A planned curriculum is followed with the teacher attempting to realize certain goals regarding the language that is to be learned.
3. *Grammatical rules presented*. The teacher may describe a rule in the native language to explain a grammatical structure. The learner is expected to understand, assimilate, and later apply the abstract rule.
4. *Unreal limited situations*. Situations for language use in the classroom are limited in variety and scope as compared to those outside of the classroom. The situations which are employed are often simulated.

5. *Educational aids and assignments.* In order to assist learning and achieve teacher goals, books, writing, or a language lab, for example, may be used. Work assignments may be given to be completed in the class or at home.

Given such differences between the natural and planned learning situations, we may expect the development of second language acquisition to vary depending on the situation. Thus, the particular content of the second language grammar, the order in which structures and morphemes are acquired, and the type and range of situations for appropriate language use will vary depending on the type of learning situation. In normal first language learning, the learner proceeds through one-, two-, and multi-word stages, using function words only late in development, producing ungrammatical (from a mature speaker view) utterances, with typical early utterances including a high proportion of requests, demands, commands, and refusals. While a similar course of development may be expected from a person learning a second language under natural conditions, this is not what would be expected from the planned learning situation. Initial learners introduced to and trained in producing grammatical statements, e.g. *The book is on the table* and *This is a pen*, are not exposed to language problems in the same way as a first language learner who utters requests before statements and produces utterances like *Book table* and *No like fish*.

Empirical research

The number of empirical research studies comparing the development of first and second language acquisition are few. Milon (1974) compared the development of negation in an 8-year-old Japanese boy learning English in essentially a natural situation. His findings paralleled those of Klima and Bellugi (1966) on first language acquisition (reported in Chapter 8). Some studies have been done comparing the order of acquisition of a selected number of morphemes, similar to those reported by Roger Brown (1973) concerning first language learning. In one study, Dulay and Burt (1974) used Spanish and Chinese speaking children from six to eight years old as subjects while another by Bailey, Madden, and Krashen (1974) used 17- to 55-year-old adults from a variety of native language backgrounds. Both studies involved classroom situation learning. The Dulay and Burt study showed a relatively high agreement on acquisition order within the group of second language learners. However, there was only a low degree of agreement with the order of first language learners. The fact that there is little agreement between first and second language order of acquisition in this study is not surprising since the second language learners learned in a classroom situation. That the article and copula were second and third in order of acquisition for the second language learners undoubtedly reflects the teaching situation (what was taught, what was *demanded*). The findings of the Bailey, Madden, and Krashen study were similar to those of Dulay and Burt. The order of acquisition for second language adult learners was similar to that of the child learners. That the second language learners in the Dulay and Burt and the Bailey, Madden, and Krashen studies showed a fair degree of agreement in order may reflect, in large part, common teaching and classroom practices. Whether or not persons learning a second language under natural conditions would arrive at the same order remains a question open for empirical study. The one naturalistic study which I am aware of, however, shows little commonality of results with the second language classroom studies on the order of morpheme acquisition. That study (Hakuta, 1976) concerned a five year old Japanese girl who came to the U.S. and learned English from neighborhood children and from attending a kindergarten (no English lessons were given). Interestingly, the obtained order did not correspond with the Brown first language acquisition study either. Clearly, more research is needed before definite conclusions can be drawn. The prospect of settling this issue soon, however, is not to be expected. Research must take into account what particular first and second languages are involved since facilitation and interference effects will vary depending on what pairs of languages are involved. A Frenchman learning English, for example, would be expected to have less trouble learning the use of such morphemes as auxiliaries, verb endings relating to person and number, and prepositions than would a Japanese since French has similar morphemes but Japanese does not.

Acquisition models

Depending on the language data to which the learner is exposed and the nature of the response that the teacher requires, the analytical challenge and solution for a learner in a planned situation will vary significantly in many respects from the natural one. This being the case, two different acquisition models will be required for the understanding of second language acquisition, one for the natural and the other for the planned learning situation. Furthermore, within each basic model category, other more refined models will be necessary. Thus, for the natural situation, different models would need to be developed for each pair of first and second languages, e.g. English and Chinese, Japanese and Hindi. The nature of prior learning always affects the course of future learning to some extent. A Frenchman learning English will not have the same problem in learning the use of the article as will a Japanese whose language does not have the article. Facilitation and interference effects would have to be considered. Similarly, for the planned situation different models will be necessary depending not only on the particular two languages involved but on the sort of planned situation (teaching method) selected. The course of development in the acquisition of a second language would not be the same for those learning through the Audiolingual method, Grammar-Translation, or the Silent Way. Since even within such methods there is a wide variety of practices, further model differentiation would be required.

The particular nature of any particular second language acquisition model will change, of course, through time. The learner is constantly acquiring new knowledge, and adjusting and correcting old knowledge. One of the models for studying what the nature of the competence of the learner might be at any one time involves an analysis of the learner's errors in conjunction with other aspects of the utterances he or she makes. This approach, Error Analysis, is similar to that taken by first language acquisition researchers: the grammatical knowledge of a learner is inferred through an analysis of utterances and the errors contained in them.

The evolving transitional second language system has been given various names by theorists, e.g. *interlanguage* (Richards, 1972; Selinker, 1972), *approximate system* (Nemser, 1971), and *idiosyncratic dialect* (Corder, 1971). No details of the system and its functional relationship to first language knowledge, however, have been postulated. While various useful procedures for identifying word errors have been proposed, e.g. Corder (1971; 1973); Richards (1974); Burt and Kiparsky (1972); and Schachter, (1974) no systematic interlanguage models of second language competence have yet been proposed. One reason for this is a lack of data, for there is only a small number of second language acquisition studies. (See Hatch, 1978, for a collection of research studies on second language acquisition.) More importantly, however, is the fact that, as yet, no ready-made model is available into which empirical data may be integrated or tested, although a number of important considerations for inclusion in such a model have been discussed by the interlanguage theorists. Until such models are available, there is no way of integrating various second language research data into a comprehensive whole.

Prior to the influence of Chomsky's mentalistic theorizing on the nature of language and its acquisition, most psychologists employed behavioristic stimulus and response associationistic learning principles in explaining acquisition. Second language learning was seen as an accumulation of associations between new learning (second language) and old learning (first language) and was viewed within a transfer of training learning paradigm. Whether the old learning facilitated (positive transfer) or interfered with (negative transfer) the new learning was of prime consideration. The mentalistic view of the Gestaltists, and more recently, Chomsky, that learners acquire abstract principles and rules through an abstract analysis of data employing hypothesis testing was not considered. (Just as in first language learning, the learner must use strategies which assist in the identification of content words and morphemes, assign possible relations within a propositional framework, and determine the critical structural features which signal those words and relations.) Errors, thus, were conceived of as the result of interference between first and second language associations. The hypothesizing and analytical procedures employed by the learners were not considered a factor in learning. The mentalistic orientation of most theorists today, however, considers the hypothesizing and abstract analyzing of speakers as a principal factor in learning, although the precise nature and operation of that factor in terms of strategies, etc. remains vague. This situation is likely to continue given the relatively meager understanding that theorists have of a more simple but related problem, that of first language acquisition.

The transfer of training paradigm has appeared in second language research under the title of Contrastive Analysis. First and second languages were compared in terms of their phonology, syntax, and vocabulary, then, on the basis of the analysis and transfer principles, errors or degree of difficulty in learning the second language were predicted. In the main, most contrastive analyses have involved phonological comparisons. This is understandable since individual phoneme inventories are limited and largely known while syntactic and vocabulary inventories are vast and largely unknown. Not unexpectedly, the Contrastive Analysis approach has not proven successful in these regards and for the most part has been abandoned. (See H. Douglas Brown, 1980, for a perceptive review and evaluation.) Such an approach is much too simplistic given what theorists now understand to be a very complex language learning process.

As far as teaching and curriculum are concerned, because Contrastive Analysis (and any other theory) fails to predict difficulty with any degree of exactness, the inference should not be drawn that comparisons of the native and target languages are not useful. Analysis of differences between languages often do highlight potential problems for learners such that teachers who are alerted to such potential problems may be able to assist the learner better. An intuitive approach must suffice until theory that adequately predicts difficulty and isolates its cause is provided.

Rule learning: induction, explication, and correction

Inductive and explicative processing

In learning a second language, rules may be acquired in either of two ways, through induction or explication. Of these ways, induction is the primary means, for, aside from other considerations which will be discussed, it is not possible to learn the rules of a language entirely through explication given the current state of knowledge. Nothing close to a complete description of a language exists. Even for English, probably the most researched of all languages, only a fragment of the grammar is available and linguists are often in disagreement about that. Given this, it is clear that cases of successful second language learning all must have involved to a great degree the basic rule learning process of induction. The traditional device of presenting a learner with actual language data such as that of a story is one example where inductive processing, often unknowingly, is given a chance to operate.

The process of induction is one whose essence is learning through self-discovery. The learner is not told the rule. Actually, the process involves two distinct aspects after the learner has been exposed to relevant language data, language data being words, phrases, and sentences in conjunction with a meaningful context. First, the learner abstracts a rule based on those data and second, the learner develops a basis for its application. For example, given such data as *John danced then John sang* and *John danced then he sang*, a learner first recognizes that the two sentences are related and that *he* is a replacement for *John*. Next the learner develops the conditions for the application of the rule, e.g. which of the two *John*s in the sentence may be pronominalized and what might be the basis for pronoun selection. With such a rule, the learner then will be able to produce and understand sentences involving pronominalization.

As was noted in the previous chapter, rule learning through induction is the essential means whereby children learn their first language. Children cannot learn rules through explication for two principal reasons: (1) Children would be unable to understand the language in which rules would be explained because they themselves do not have language. (Of course, few parents would even be able to formulate syntactic or phonological rules). Understanding the explanation of a rule would be possible only after the children had already acquired the essentials of the language with its complex syntax through induction. However, even with a high degree of language ability, young children would not be able to comprehend the explanation of a rule either with respect to the first or a second language. (2) Only with maturity, perhaps after seven years of age, are children able to understand an explanation that is by nature highly analytical and abstract. Even the relatively simple pronominalization rule for English requires a complex explanation. Even the following simplification would be impossible for a child to understand: 'A noun phrase may be pronominalized if there has been some sort of prior reference to that noun phrase in language (as in *John* sang then he danced) or if the referent of the noun phrase has appeared in the environment (as in a situation where a woman walks by and smiles, upon which it is appropriate to say *She smiled*).' As if this were not abstract enough, in addition the rule must provide information as to pronoun selection, including number (*I* vs. *we, he* vs. *they*, etc.), gender (*he* vs. *she* vs. *it*, etc.) and syntactic function (*I* vs. *me* vs. *my, he* vs. *him* vs. *his*, etc.).

While learning syntactic rules through explication requires two essentials, basic knowledge of the language in which the explanation is given and advanced cognitive development, these may not be sufficient for learning to occur. Syntactic rules may be so complex and abstract that few people other than students of linguistics would be able to comprehend them, let alone be able to remember them in detail so as to able to apply them correctly. However, there are simple rules to be found in any language which could be taught without difficulty. A mature Japanese person studying English as a second language could be told, for example, that there is a Subject + Verb + Object order of consituents in English (the verb follows both the subject and object in Japanese) or that English requires count nouns to have a plural marker added when more than one is involved (plural marking occurs but is not obligatory in Japanese). On the basis of these descriptions, a learner may formulate relevant usable rules. In such cases, explication may be a faster means of learning than induction, where induction requires that a learner be exposed to sentences along with some indication as to meaning. Thus, rules which are simple, easy to comprehend and are closely related to the surface elements of a sentence may well be more effectively learned through explication than through induction. The inclusion of a number of relevant examples along with the rule explanation undoubtedly will further facilitate learning for with examples the learner will be given the opportunity to learn through induction and to remedy any lack of understanding he or she may have had regarding the rule explanation.

Although rules which are learned through explication involve conscious processing, in time such processing may become unconscious to the degree that inductive processing is, with the result that language may be dealt with effortlessly and without hesitation. With use, consciously learned rules can become unconscious, much the same as arithmetic rules for multiplication, division, etc. become unconscious with extensive use over time. For example, while the answer to a problem like '434 divided by 7' is easily computed, the precise specification of each of the steps involved is by no means easy. The figures must be lined up, certain digits must be selected for comparison, values must be compared, data in the multiplication table must be employed (in a veiy complex way), etc. Although each step was consciously learned in school, with constant use, the process has dropped below awareness. Language rules taught through conscious explication can become unconscious in a similar way. Many people who learn rules of a second language through explication may undergo such an experience.

Besides arithmetic, mathematics, and other school subjects such as history, biology, and physics, it is well to keep in mind that people acquire a great deal of knowledge through explication in their ordinary daily life. Sets of ordered instructions dealing with such diverse topics as the playing of a game, the cooking of a soup, the bathing of a baby, and the finding of someone's home are often communicated and learned through explication. This is not to deny that such knowledge may also be acquired by induction. However, for such cases, the explicative means may well be the more efficient one.

The analytical processes of induction and explication attain their optimal level of operation at different ages. The fact that children learn most of the complexities of a language prior to the age of 5 years establishes that young children have a level of inductive ability that is sufficient for learning language.

It would seem that with age there is no decline in that inductive ability. Actually, it may even be that it increases with age. The inductive ability which the younger child uses to learn language is continually used by older children and adults in acquiring new and complex intellectual systems. We may observe that older children and adults acquire music systems and structures, e.g. those of songs, suites, and symphonies, by induction. Learning occurs through being exposed to unanalyzed data in its natural form. The learner assigns it a structure, just as in language learning. It is worth noting in passing that the learning of music and language are similar, too, with respect to the relationship of understanding and production. Production is based on understanding. In the case of music, however, production often is minimally developed. We may also observe that adults are forever constructing abstract systems through induction to account for the observations which they make about the world. These include theological, biological, physical, or social concerns, such as explaining life and death, the changing of the seasons, and the intentions of other persons. Perhaps it is only with old age that the inductive ability of persons may decline.

The dependency of explication on the prior acquisition of language and a degree of abstract intellectual maturity establishes that only somewhere between the ages of six and nine years would such a processing ability begin to become operational. I would speculate that an adequate operational level of that ability would develop in the next three or four years between the ages of 10 and 13 years. It seems to me that the heavy explicative learning of such highly abstract and complex subjects such as mathematics, physics, and chemistry by students in high school and college indicates that it is after age 13 that the ability to learn through explication is developed to its optimum. This development of explicative processing, and that for inductive processing, too, has important implications for language teaching. These will be discussed in a later section of this chapter.

ROLE OF CORRECTION.   Before concluding this section, the role of corrective feedback in inductive and explicative processing should be given some consideration. When a language learner, first or second, is given correction for errors in form, correction is communicated in one of two essential ways, one by repetition, the other by explanation. The first, repetition, is non-specific and requires the use of induction if the correction is to be made. The second, explanation, is specific and, if correction is to occur, the use of explication by the learner is required. For example, suppose a learner says *Nobody don't like me*. A mature speaker might respond with *Nobody likes me*, a repetition, or with an explanation like 'You don't put *do* or a negative marker like *not*, as you do with certain negative sentences, when negation appears with a noun.' Undoubtedly, more mature speakers would be able to respond better to correction by explanation than would young children. Both categories of learners, on the other hand, have the ability to respond to correction by repetition. However, because repetition alone neither identifies the error in the sentence nor specifies what is required for its correction, such correction may be ineffective. Then, too, any correction by repetition will be ineffective if the learner has not yet attained a necessary level of competence. For example, if an utterance like *Why bird no sing*? is corrected by *Why didn't the bird sing*?, the correction may have no effect even if the corrected utterance were reproduced because the learner has not yet achieved an appropriate level of knowledge such that the information could be analyzed and assimilated. The same, of course, will be true for correction through explanation. To explain to a learner how to form relative clauses, *The school which I went to is big* when that learner is still struggling with simple noun phrases can hardly be expected to be effective. Given the nature and development of the explicative process, it is clear that correction by explanation will be more effective with older learners. It may be, too, that older learners will benefit more than younger learners with respect to repetition. An older learner who does not understand why a repetition is given may request an explanation or in some way inform the instructor as to what his or her level of language competence is. A child cannot do this. Furthermore, as Schachter[1] has demonstrated, a repetition may be misinterpreted by a learner since it may be used to signal a number of functions, including confirmation, e.g. Learner: *Bird no sing*? Instructor: *Yes. The bird didn't sing*, or even *Yes. Bird no sing*. Typically, repetitions are not used to correct form but to convey other information. That being the case, many repetitions intended as corrections may not be perceived as such by learners. In my opinion, the reason that the few empirical research studies that have been done on the effect of correction (of any type) have shown little positive results involves two main factors. They are: the studies were not of a sufficiently long term nature to demonstrate an effect, and the type of feedback given was ambiguous and insufficiently informative. With adequate research studies, I believe that a beneficial effect for correction will be shown.

Even so, such an effect will constitute only a small portion or rule learning. Most of such learning will involve self-correction to an overwhelming degree. For learners are exposed to many more sentences than they produce, and it is on the basis of their understanding of the sentences to which they have been exposed that they formulate rules for production. Sentence production involves only a small part of their learning, and the incidence of those which are corrected involves an even smaller portion.

Memory and motor skills: role and age change

Two factors, *memory* and *motor skills*, are essential to acquiring the ability to understand and produce speech in a second language. Without memory, one could not begin to learn language and without motor skills one would have no means for producing speech. Since a complete loss of either capacity does not occur in the course of normal life, the question as to whether or not a change in these essential capacities may occur through age arises. This section will address itself to a consideration of the role of these capacities in language learning and possible effects on them with age.

Memory

One cannot learn the meaning-sound correspondence of words and the grammatical rules of a language without some memory capacity. A learner who perceives an object, e.g. a cat, and hears it referred to in a language, e.g. 'neko' in Japanese, will not be able to learn that word unless an association between the perceived object and sound form is established such that when the object is experienced it elicits the sound form or when the sound is experienced it elicits a representation of the object. In my opinion, this associative learning capacity begins to decline quite early in life beginning perhaps around the age of five years. By the age of 10 years, a substantial portion of this associative learning ability has been lost, not so much that learning cannot take place but enough that significantly more frequent exposure is required for learning which required only a small amount of exposure at age 5 or earlier. With age, associative learning requires increased exposure and practice. Thus, while it is not uncommon for a young child to hear a word once or twice and remember it the next day, older persons are not able to do so. Casual observation indicates that it is easier for young children to memorize long poems, songs, and stories in their entirety than it is for older children and adults. While it is undoubtedly the case that older children and adults develop heuristics and strategies which assist their memory, such devices play little role in natural language learning, although they do in memory experiments where, for example, series of paired-associate items are given to be learned and where a number of consecutive trials are presented. In real life, one may hear a word one day and not hear it again for another week. One may hear a phrase or a sentence and not hear another having a similar structure for several days. The language data which must be remembered in real life for the most part occur as unrelated individual items. Any buildup in the frequency of occurrence of any one item extends over a period of time. Repetition is not common. Of course, to the extent that a language learning situation incorporates learning tasks which are similar to those of verbal learning experiments, e.g. where a list of vocabulary items is to be learned, then heuristic devices could be developed to assist memory. However, even in such cases, the initial imprint of an item is crit‑ical. One cannot begin to use heuristics unless one has some experience to manipulate. Any decline in the ease of retaining such an experiential imprint will ultimately alter the rate of acquisition.

In the learning of grammatical rules by induction, long-term memory is essential. The language data which a learner receives must be stored so that other similar data can be compared and analyzed. So must the rule which is discovered by the analysis (or learned by explication) be stored for future use. Thus, unless a number of words, phrases, and sentences are stored in their entirety, along with their situational contexts, the discovery of underlying rules is not possible. That persons actually do store entire language items in their exact form is indicated by a variety of evidence. We remember items from all sources of language experience, conversations, stories, and songs. Items like, 'How are you,' 'I am fine,' 'Have a nice day,' 'A stitch in time saves nine,' 'Look before you leap,' and, 'I regret that I have but one life to give for my country' are familiar to many English speakers as are long lists of idioms such as 'to take for a ride,' 'cut it out,' 'kick the bucket,' 'needle and thread' (not 'thread and needle'), 'once in a blue moon,' and 'salt and pepper' (not 'pepper and salt'). It seems to me, although no supporting evidence is available, that the capacity to learn and store such language items decreases with age as it does in the learning of words with the result that more exposure and practice is needed with increased age. One reason why 'You can't teach an old dog new tricks' (at least not without increased difficulty) may thus be due to a decline in memory. Another reason may be a decline in motor skill ability. It is that factor which is the next topic of discussion.

Motor skills

The ability of persons to develop and control the muscles of the body is an essential component of the speech production process. In order to produce speech, muscles must control the movement of the jaws, lips, tongue, vocal chords, and other speech articulators. In general, new motor skills become more difficult to acquire after the early teens. This is true in sports, for example. A 25-year-old who has never played basketball or baseball and who has never exercised the particular motor activities involved in those sports would have great difficulty perfecting the necessary skills as compared to a 15-year-old. Given a five year training period, it is undoubtedly much easier to develop a good player beginning from 15 years of age than it would be for one beginning at 25 years of age.

The research evidence which is available shows, as might be expected, that pronunciation ability decreases with age, e.g. Asher and Garnica (1969). It has been frequently observed that children in immigrant families acquire perfect or near-perfect accents while their older teenage siblings or parents generally do not, even when the mature speakers have mastered other aspects of the language. Actually, there is no controversy on the issue of decline of pronunciation ability with age for most persons, although there is with respect to syntax and other aspects of language (McLaughlin, 1977). However, because the number of research studies which have been conducted concerning the acquisition of pronunciation is small (Oyama, 1976), definite age norms which chart the progress of decline are not available. Perhaps somewhere around 10 years of age is when a significant decline in the ability to develop new articulatory motor skills may begin.

Motivation, attitude and other relevant factors

A number of factors which affect second language acquisition operate only in certain types of learning situations. The question of motivation for learning a second language is not likely to arise in a natural type of setting where language is but one aspect of the world that the learner is living in. In such a situation, the learner is exposed to language in the ordinary course of living. The planned learning situation such as the classroom, however, presents a very different problem. There is an element of choice involved in attending class, listening to the teacher, participating in activities, and in doing assignments. The amount of exposure which one receives and the amount of attention and effort which one may devote to learning may be affected by one's motivation. Dislike of a teacher, for example, could seriously affect language learning unless it is balanced by a high degree of motivation that enables one to persist. Similarly, a negative attitude toward the target language or its speakers, or the other members of the class could also affect one's determination and persistence to be involved in the class and its activities (Gardner & Lambert, 1972; Oller, Hudson & Liu, 1977; Chihara & Oller, 1978; Oller, Baca & Virgil, 1978). This same negative attitude could impair memory functions and detract from focusing on the target language. In the same way, any of a host of personality and sociocultural variables could have deleterious effects (H. Douglas Brown, 1980). Many such variables, such as status and cultural background, become more potent with the age of the learner and are important considerations in the classroom learning situation.

There is no reason to suppose as some theorists have that some sort of special motivation or purpose is necessary for second language learning. Thus, while the goal of wanting to learn a language for the purpose of integrating and identifying oneself with the second language people and culture has been thought by some theorists to be better than that of learning for the purpose of using language as an instrument for some end, (e.g. furthering one's career or gaining knowledge, Gardner & Lambert, 1972), accumulated research evidence indicates that both these integrative and instrumental motivations work equally well (H. Douglas Brown, 1980). The same could be said for variables such as liking a teacher. In an actual classroom situation any one of a number of variables could affect motivation. Teachers are generally well aware of this possibility and thus often devise ways to increase positive motivation and attitudes.

Optimal age for second language learning
At what age can a second language be learned the fastest? Do younger children learn faster than older children? Do older children learn faster than adults? While there is little controversy regarding the area of pronunciation, in which children are believed to be better learners than adults, there is much controversy with regard to the more substantive areas of language, i.e. grammatical rules, vocabulary, and pragmatics. The limited research which has been done tends to show that performance in these areas improves with age, with older children and adults doing better than younger children (see McLaughlin (1977), for a review of such research). However, because such research has mainly involved learners in classroom situations where the criterion test items are often of a very limited nature, e.g. certain morphemes and transformations, the conclusions which one might draw regarding the general issue under consideration must be restricted. Given that in classroom situations older persons tend to do better than younger persons, the issue remains as to whether or not this would also be the case in learning in a natural type of situation. A four-year-old child, for example, who has great difficulty in learning in the typical classroom situation (unless the classroom itself is designed to simulate the natural situation), would have little difficulty in learning under natural conditions. Adjusting to the psychosocial demands of the classroom and the methods of instruction requires a period of adjustment on the part of children, perhaps two or three years.

Unfortunately, no research is available which compares children and adults learning a second language under natural conditions. This is not surprising since the opportunities for studying children and adults in a comparable situation, where amount of exposure to the second language, amount of interactive use of the second language with speakers, and other relevant variables are controlled, are not common. However, until such research is done, one critical dimension of the children vs. adult learning issue cannot be resolved.

Although the question of whether children or adults are better language learners has not been given an answer supported by empirical evidence, this has not prevented theorists from speculating on what that conclusion might be and then providing a theoretical justification of that speculative conclusion. Lenneberg is the most prominent of such theorists. Based on his belief that children are better language learners than adults (for which he offers no substantiation), Lenneberg presented a theoretical explanation for that assumed outcome (Lenneberg, 1967; 1969). His explanation concerns the biological maturation of the brain and the fact that language tends to become located in the dominant left hemisphere of the brain (lateralization). As the brain matures, language learning is permitted to occur and directs its localization. When brain maturation ceases, however, around the age of puberty, and localization is completed, then language learning becomes difficult. Lenneberg presented a number of arguments in support of his brain maturation lateralization theory. Empirical research, however, has since shown those arguments to be weak or invalid. Lateralization, for example, appears to be established by age four or earlier (Krashen, 1973; Berlin et al., 1972; Harshman & Krashen, 1972). This being the case, lateralization cannot be meaningfully related to the critical age of puberty which Lenneberg proposes. That Lenneberg's explanation and justification for his puberty critical age hypothesis is invalid does not, it should be noted, invalidate his claim that puberty is a critical age. Moreover, evidence could be discovered which would support puberty as being a critical age for language learning to occur. Lenneberg could be right but for the wrong reasons.

My own speculations suggest that the optimal age for second language learning will vary according to two main factors, both of which have been described in detail earlier: (1) The intellectual, memory, and motor skill abilities of learners; and (2) The type of learning situation, natural or classroom. Table 4 considers these factors and their effects at various ages. According to the table, with regard to the functioning level of abilities, we observe that the *Inductive Processing* ability does not change with age. On the other hand, the *Explicative Processing* ability increases its power with age, becoming somewhat functional somewhere between six and nine years of age. *Memory*, however, peaks and then declines after nine years, although not so much that language learning cannot occur. *Motor Skills* also peak and then decline after nine years, although not so much that pronunciation is completely impaired.

With regard to the estimated capacity of learners to respond to the natural and classroom learning situations, we see very different outcomes over time. For the *natural* situation, there is a decline in the sort

TABLE 4. Optimal learning age predictions based on essential learning abilities and situational requirements

	Younger Children Under 6 Years	Older Children 6–9 Years	Older Children 10–13 Years	Adults Over 13 Years
Abilities: Level of functioning				
Inductive Processing	Optimal	Optimal	Optimal	Optimal
Explicative processing	Inadequate	Somewhat Adequate	Adequate	Optimal
Memory	Optimal	Optimal	Decline Adequate	More Decline Adequate
Motor skills	Optimal	Optimal	Decline Adequate	More Decline Somewhat Adequate
Situations				
Natural: Social interaction	High	Medium	Medium	Low
Classroom: Skills and adjustment	Low	Medium	High	High

Predictions
For the natural situation   —1. Younger children will do best.
                            2. Older children will do better than adults.
For the classroom situation —1. Older children will do best.
                            2. Adults will do better than younger children.

of social interaction which promotes language interchange, a principal basis for language learning. While it is often relatively easy for a young second language learner to interact socially in play with young native language speaking children, such is not the case for older children and adults where language has a critical role in their social relations. The adult especially may, in daily life, have great difficulty in participating in good language learning social interactions with native speakers. Even when the adult learner is able to get a job where there is social interaction with native speakers, the use of language in that interaction is severely limited. (The person would not have been hired for the job had substantial language knowledge been required.) Then, too, there are other factors which operate in the case of adults that have considerably less importance for children, e.g. the adult learner is generally more inhibited to speak for fear of making embarrassing errors or of being judged unintelligent. With respect to older children, it would seem that they would have a better opportunity than adults to be involved in language beneficial social interactions due to their attending school. Of course, at school much will depend, too, on other factors such as the attitudes of the native speakers and the second language learners to one another.

When the *classroom* situation is considered, the reverse seems to be the case for the various age groups. There is improvement with age for the classroom skills and adjustments which are essential for most language teaching methods. (These skills and adjustments were noted earlier in the chapter.) The Natural Method could be one exception here to the extent it is successful in simulating the natural learning situation.

To the extent that the foregoing analysis has identified the essential contributing variables in second language learning and has correctly assessed their function and effect at various ages, a number of predictions can be made.

For the natural situation:

1. *Younger children will do best.* Although all age groups are optimal in terms of Inductive processing, because of memory decline and poorer quality social interaction, the older groups will do worse than the young children. The younger children will also do better in pronunciation because of the decline of motor skills in the older groups.
2. *Older children will do better than adults.* For adults, the greater decline in memory and motor skills, along with poorer social interaction for learning, will result in poorer performance as compared to older children.

For the classroom situation:

1. *Older children will do best.* Older children and adults will do better

than younger children because of increases in classroom adjustment skills and explicative processing, even though they experience some decline in memory. Because the adult decline in memory will probably have a greater effect than the gain made in explicative processing, the older children will do better. Younger children will do best in pronunciation because of a decline in motor skills on the part of the older groups.

2. *Adults will do better than younger children.* The lack of adequate explicative processing and classroom skills and adjustment on the part of younger children will allow adults to do better despite a decline in memory. The younger children will do better in pronunciation, however, because of the adult decline in motor skills.

The above predictions, it should be noted, concern groups of persons. There is no doubt that there is great variation among individuals; some will be endowed with more or less of some essential ability than others. What the analysis does predict with respect to individuals, however, is that the same sequence of changes in an individual's capacity will occur, although the age range may vary.

Language and mind issues

In this section, two important issues will be briefly discussed. One concerns the Rationalism-Empiricism controversy in second language acquisition, the other concerns the relationship of language to thought in the case of persons who have acquired a second language.

Rationalism vs. empiricism in second language acquisition

In accounting for second language acquisition, the issue of whether or not innate ideas are involved appears just as it does in first language learning. The issue, insofar as Rationalist theory is concerned, however, is more complex for second language learning. One may ask such questions as: Do innate ideas vary in the intensity of their influence or force over time?; Does Chomsky's LAD system of innate language ideas atrophy with age?; or, Are the ideas incorporated into the first language sufficient for the second without having to resort to the original operations of LAD? Actually, there has been little or no speculation on what the role of LAD might be in second language learning. Chomsky does not address himself to this problem but focuses rather on first language learning as do other rationalist supporters such as McNeill. This is not surprising since the problem of second language acquisition is much more complex and would require a more detailed specification of the LAD theory for first language acquisition than the mere outline of the theory that Chomsky has provided to date.

With respect to Empiricist theory, contemporary second language theorists have been greatly confused. This has been mainly due to a misconception which pervades the field which is the synonymous treatment of Empiricism and Behaviorism. Theorists fail to distinguish Empiricism, which is a mentalist school of thought in the tradition of Aristotle, Locke, and Piaget, from that of Behaviorism, which is an anti-mentalist school of thought. (One source of confusion is the ambiguous word *empiricist*, where one meaning is that of subordinating theory to fact – Behaviorists use the word in this sense – and the other meaning is that of the mentalist philosophical school.) These theorists are unaware that Behaviorism, under the leadership of its founder John B. Watson (1924), arose in the 20th century as a reaction to the mentalistic theorizing of the Empiricists. (See Chapter 5 for a detailed discussion of the Rationalist, Empiricist, and Behaviorist schools.) As a result of their failure to distinguish Empiricism and Behaviorism, second language theorists have erroneously rejected Empiricism because of the deficiencies of Behaviorism. Diller (1971) is one such theorist who does this. There is no question that Empiricist theory is as viable as Rationalist theory in accounting for the acquisition of language. (See Chapters 1 and 5 concerning deficiencies in Behaviorist theorizing, and see Chapters 5 and 8 for a discussion of language acquisition according to the Empiricists.) Both types of mentalistic theories are undoubtedly sufficiently flexible (*vague* may be the more accurate description!) so as to be able to provide a general accounting of phenomena. Whether or not specific problems may arise in second language acquisition which would provide a basis for selecting between the competing theories remains to be seen. However, given that these theories have survived active competition with one another since the beginning of recorded history, one should not be too hopeful in this regard.

Language and thought relations in bilinguals

Does learning a second language affect the system of thought? On the basis of the detailed arguments presented in Chapter 6, it was concluded that the acquisition of a language does not affect the essentials of the thought system. A language system is simply a means for the expression of thought. Given this view, learning a second or more languages will provide a learner with different means for expressing thoughts. The system of thought, however, will not be affected by any of the variety of the labelling systems (languages).

Some research has been done on the effect on cognitive abilities as a result of learning a second language. The findings have not been consistent, probably because different measures of those functions were used. Some studies show positive effects, some negative effects and some no effect (McLaughlin, 1977). Until there is some agreement, however, in defining the essential functions of thought (e.g. the operation of inductive and deductive reasoning) and an objective means is devised for their measurement, research studies may be expected to provide inconsistent results on this important issue.

Second language teaching methods

In this section a number of the principal methods of second language teaching are described, analyzed, and assessed. These are: Grammar-Translation, Natural Method, Direct Method, Audiolingual Method, Cognitive Code, Silent Way, Community Language Learning, Suggestopedia, Comprehension Primary, and Drama.

Principal methods and their characteristics

Essentially, the various methods involve at their foundations one or more of four basic ideas: translation, situational context participation, linguistic analysis, and learning psychology. *Translation* involves providing comparable native language words, phrases, and sentences for unknown target language items. For example, an unknown language item in the target language is rendered in the native language. In the case of pure translation, no discussion of grammatical points would follow. *Situational Context Participation* involves the use of the target language in actual or simulated situations in which the student participates. Language items are not learned outside of situational context. *Linguistic Analysis* concerns the application of linguistic knowledge either indirectly through the selection, organization, and grading of target language materials or directly in the actual teaching of students. In the latter case, students may be taught linguistic terminology, e.g. *noun, verb, subject, direct object*, etc., or taught abstract and complex syntactic rules such as those involved in passivization and negation. Whether it is best that syntactic rules and other linguistic complexities be learned directly by explication or learned indirectly through induction involves a consideration of *Learning Psychology*, and Philosophy, too.

Of course, teaching methods differ on a number of other characteristics in addition to those just outlined. What sorts of *skills* are emphasized, e.g. aural, oral, reading, or writing, whether *spontaneous language* materials in the target language regularly occur, and what unique or *special features* may be involved are just a few of such additional characteristics which must be considered. Table 5 presents a summary of the methods and their principal characteristics. Thus, for example, reading across, we see that Grammar-Translation employs translation, is not involved with situational context participation, uses linguistic knowledge, teaches rules by explication, emphasizes reading and writing, does not involve the use of spontaneous language, and is generally oriented to language which appears in literature.

It is important to observe that the characteristics which have been assigned the various methods in the table cannot be treated as absolutes. There is no method that is without variation. Theorists and practitioners of any method may vary on certain important aspects. For example, with regard to the Audiolingual method, some advocates would

TABLE 5. Principal methods and characteristics

Method	Meaning provided by	Linguistic analysis guide	Intended rule learning means	Skill emphasis	Spontaneous language use	Special features
a. Grammar-translation	Translation	Yes	Explication	Literacy	No	Oriented to literature.
b. Natural method	Social, demonstration, pictures	No	Induction	Speech	Yes	First language situation simulated.
c. Direct method	Social, demonstration, pictures	Yes	Induction	Speech	Partly	Reaction against grammar-translation.
d. Audiolingual method	Demonstration, pictures	Yes	Induction mainly	Speech	No	Mechanical drill orientation.
e. Cognitive code	All means	Yes	Induction & explication	Literacy & speech	Partly	All skills learned simultaneously; error tolerated.
f. Silent way	Demonstration	No	Induction	Speech	No	Teacher mainly silent but leads.
g. Community language learning	Translation	Partly	Induction & explication	Speech mainly	Yes	Group interacts and leads; teacher advises.
h. Suggestopedia	Translation	Partly	Induction	Speech mainly	No	Attempts memory improvement; mystical and musical.
i. Comprehension primary	Social, demonstration, pictures	Varies	Induction	Speech	No	Speech understanding precedes production.
j. Drama	Translation, social	No	Induction	Speech mainly	Partly	Students produce and act in plays.

explain rules while others would not, some would use written materials while others would not. Still, the characteristics assigned to the various methods, by and large, tend to typify those held by most of their advocates.

The methods and their background
For a detailed treatment of the three oldest methods, Grammar-Translation, the Natural Method, and the Direct Method, the reader is referred to the works of Kelly (1969), Titone (1968), and Darian (1972).

Grammar-translation
The Grammar-Translation (GT) method essentially involves two components, the explicit study of grammatical rules and vocabulary, and the use of translation. Translation is the oldest of the components and is probably the oldest of all teaching methods having been used in ancient Greece and Rome and elsewhere in the ancient world. The grammar aspect was rather minimal in those times since grammatical knowledge itself was limited. With the growth of grammatical knowledge, however, the grammatical component played a greater role in teaching, eventually dominating the translation aspect. By the end of the 18th century in Europe it had become a full partner in the method, even to the extent of being included in the name. The growth of the grammatical component continues to the present day. Rules are explained by the teacher, then memorized, recited, and applied by the student.

The aim of the GT method has changed over the years. Originally it had two principal aims, the study of the literature of the second language and the development of analytical skills through the study of grammar. The latter aim, which was motivated by Cartesian grammarians who believed that a universal logic underlay all languages, has largely disappeared. The orientation to literature and the attendant emphasis on reading and writing have been modified somewhat. Vernacular expressions are often introduced and some attention is given to pronunciation and listening. The overwhelming direction, however, is toward books, particularly the classics of a language.

The grammar aspect of the GT method has changed over the centuries in accord with the linguistic knowledge and theory of the time. The 20th century, for example, has seen three main changes in grammatical explanation: the neo-grammarian prescriptivist approach in the early part, the structural linguistic approach in the middle part, and the transformational approach in the latter part of the century. The adaptability of the GT method to radical changes in linguistics is one principal factor that accounts for its viability over the ages. The continuing improvement in the production of attractive, interesting, and comprehensive textbooks is another factor in that regard.

Natural method

The Natural Method (NM) developed as a reaction to Grammar-Translation and grew most vigorously in France with inspiration from the work of Rousseau (1780) and other theorists such as Comenius (1568) and Pestalozzi (1801). The NM began to form early in the 19th century and by the latter part of that century the method had become firmly established through the writings of those such as Sauveur (1878) and Gouin (1880). The method took its name from what it considered to be the natural way to learn a language, by exposure to language that is used in ordinary personal communicative situations. Its model was the child's learning a first language, where grammar is not taught and translation is irrelevant. Learning was through conversations, demonstrations, and other forms of direct language experience. The teacher used only the target language much the same as a parent speaks to the child in the language that the child is to learn. The teacher either did or did not use previously prepared materials depending on whose version of the method was being employed. Books were generally not used, and reading and writing might be introduced only when students had reached an advanced level.

Direct method

The Direct Method (DM) also developed as a reaction against Grammar-Translation. As with the Natural Method, it, too, emphasized the learning of speech, acquiring meaning in environmental context and learning grammar through induction. The advocates of the DM, while approving of the Natural Method, sought to improve upon it by providing systematic procedures based on scientific knowledge of linguistics and psychology. There was considerably less use of spontaneous language as a result. Materials were preselected and graded (from simple to complex and from high to low frequency of occurrence), and oral pattern drills and dialogs for memorization were devised on the basis of current scientific knowledge. Some practitioners used translation. Reading and writing might be introduced only after the speech aspect of what was introduced had been acquired. The DM became established toward the end of the 19th century and reached the height of its influence in the first quarter of the 20th century through such advocates as Palmer (1922) and Jespersen (1904). With the advent of the Audiolingual Method, the DM has almost disappeared, with the exception of Berlitz schools and CREDIF in France. On the other hand, it should be recognized that a number of current methods such as Community Language Learning and Comprehension Primary reflect the essential

ideas of the DM and may be viewed as versions of it. The work of
Newmark and Reibel (1970) also may be considered in this regard.

Audiolingual method

The Audiolingual Method (AM) is the direct successor to the Direct
Method, for aside from incorporating structural linguistic theory and
behavioristic psychology into its foundation, the AM significantly differs from DM only in emphasis. The Natural Method component to
which the Direct Methodists had always given prominence was greatly
downplayed by AM theorists. They preferred drill to the natural use of
language in context. It was this lack of attention to the communicative
use of language that stimulated the growth of a number of contemporary methods which do emphasize the environmental aspects, e.g. Community Language Learning, Silent Way, Comprehension Primary, Drama, and Total Physical Response. The AM was developed during
World War II and reached its height of influence during the 1950s and
1960s. Theorists like Fries (1949), Lado (1957), and Wellmers (1953)
were in the forefront of the movement.

Cognitive code

Cognitive Code (CC) arose in the 1960s as a reaction to the Audiolingual Method. Theorists who are associated with this orientation, e.g.
Chastain (1971), Donaldson (1971), and Ausubel (1964), are typically
mentalist in their philosophy, advocates of generative grammar in their
linguistics, and eclectic in their methodology. Other than advocating
the teaching of grammatical rules through both inductive and explicative means and the non-sequencing of speech and literacy skills, they
have developed little in the way of a distinctive method.

Silent way

The Silent Way (SW) was developed by Gattegno (1972) and takes its
name from the fact that there is more silence than usual in the course
of a class. This is mainly due to the teacher being almost entirely silent.
The primary aim is for students to develop a productive speaking competence. Listening comprehension is secondary and reading and writing
are hardly dealt with at all. Classes begin with the naming of objects
with single words and phrases and then proceed to the naming of situations with sentences. On this basis, other communicative language
forms are developed. For conveying meaning, a set of colored rods is
typically used, e.g. the words *rod, blue*, and *red* may be introduced in
this way as may the phrases *red rod* and *blue rod* and the sentences *The
red rod is on top of the blue rod* and *The blue rod is longer than the red
rod*.

In the pure application of the method, the teacher never utters any word but points to individual printed letters which, in combination, indicate to the student how a word might be pronounced. The teacher may provide corrective feedback in the form of headshakes or hand movements. The teacher will point to an object then to the printed letters. On this basis, the student develops the meaning-sound connection that is necessary for vocabulary learning. By moving the rods and doing various things with them, the teacher creates many situations and events which the student must name. In the less pure application of the method, the teacher will utter a word, phrase, or sentence only once or twice. Even with this modification, the speech exposure to which the student is provided is minimal since, for most of the time, it is the student who must provide the speech input. As might be expected, this provides great pressure on the student since the teacher requires the student to respond. It is on this issue of the primacy of speech production that most other situationally oriented methods differ with the SW. Comprehension Primary, which is discussed below, is one such method that takes an opposing view on what the teaching order of speech production and understanding skills should be.

Community language learning

Community Language Learning (CLL), or Counselling Learning, as it is sometimes called was originated in the 1960s by Curran, a counselor-therapist and priest who regarded the second language learning situation from the point of view of small group dynamics and counselling (Curran, 1972, 1976). The teacher takes the role of a counselor while the learner takes the role of a client. The clients are to interact independently with one another while the counselor's role is only to foster that interaction. In effect, this reduces to the counselor translating into the target language whatever it is that the clients wish to say to one another. The clients sit in a circle and converse using only the target language. The counselor stands behind the client who is to speak. The client tells the counselor in the native language what it is that he or she wants to say, and the counselor provides the translation. The client then utters that target language translation to one or more of the other clients who, in turn, are obliged to respond. Discussion of grammatical points and the language were kept to a minimum.

Since Curran's original CLL proposal (and his fantastic unsubstantiated claims for the method's success), numerous versions of the method have arisen, some of which differ so greatly that perhaps all they have in common is the establishing of some sort of small group interaction. For example, the sentences uttered by the group may be recorded, transcribed, and then given to the students for study and memorization. The students raise questions about the grammar and other aspects of language and the teacher provides detailed explanations. Here, CLL does not differ in fundamentals from the traditional Grammar-Translation method. The initial group interaction, however, serves to maintain a certain distinctiveness for CLL.

Suggestopedia

According to Georgi Lozanov, the founder of Suggestopedia (SP), in *24 days* second language students can learn 1800 words, speak within the framework of a whole essential grammar, and read any text (Lozanov, 1979). Lozanov holds that this and other similarly remarkable achievements can be gained through a state of 'hypermnesia' in which memory powers and other abilities related to language learning are increased remarkably. How the hypermnesic state is brought about is the essence of Lozanov's method. This is done through relaxing and building the confidence of the learner thus breaking down the 'anti-suggestive barriers.' Relaxation is brought about by the playing of music (10 classical pieces including a Haydn symphony), comfortable armchairs, and specially decorated and arranged rooms. Other possible relaxers such as alcoholic beverages or sex are discouraged. The confidence of the learner is built up by what the teacher says and does. The teacher is to suggest things to the learner and to act in a highly authoritarian and confident way.

Teaching involves the presentation of dialogs and vocabulary which the student is to study and memorize. The materials are presented first in written then spoken forms. A translation is offered along with the written form. The unique aspect of teaching lies in the way materials are then presented in conjunction with certain learner behavior and environmental events. The teacher reads each dialog aloud, in a special way, three times to the students who are relaxing in their armchairs. On the first reading, the students follow by reading. On the second and third readings the students listen only. It is on the third reading, that the specially selected classical music (no other music is permitted) is played in accompaniment to the reading.

Despite the enthusiasm of Lozanov's supporters (e.g. Bancroft, 1978; Stevick, 1976) for the method, I am in complete accord with Scovel's (1979) negative evaluation of it: '... suggestopedy, taken as a self-contained method for language instruction, offers at best nothing much that can be of benefit to present day, eclectic EFL programs, and at worst nothing more than an oversold package of pseudoscientific gobbledygook!' (p. 258)

Comprehension primary

Comprehension Primary (CP) is a name which I have given to a number of methods which share certain characteristics, among them Postovsky's (1974) 'Delayed Oral Practice,' Winitz and Reeds' (1975) 'Comprehension Strategy,' and Asher's (1974) 'Total Physical Response'. The essential view is that speech understanding should become established before speech production is introduced. (The opposite of the notion employed by the Silent Way.) The rationale for this view is that it is the way a child learns a first language, i.e. a child is exposed to the speech of others in some sort of meaningful context and is thus given the opportunity to understand speech before any meaningful utterance is produced. In essentials, CP may be usefully considered as a version of the Direct Method since materials are selected, graded, and sequenced so that grammatical rules may be learned by induction. To date, the materials which have been developed for CP are mainly suitable for students who are at an elementary level in learning a second language.

Drama

Learning language through involvement in drama has a lengthy tradition. The Jesuits, for example, used it in the Middle Ages to teach Latin. Then, as now, it was recognized that it is important for learners who are to have some social command of speech to have some experience with it in some sort of communicative environmental context. In considering drama from the point of view of language learning, two different types of materials and situations must be noted. One, the more obvious, concerns remembering or creating the lines in the play and their rendition in the context of a performance. Such lines may be fixed, as in a published play, or spontaneous, as in a creative drama. The other type, less obvious and perhaps more important, concerns the linguistic interaction among students and teacher which relates to producing the play. Discussion involving the selection of a cast, the preparation of sets, and numerous other aspects of the production will be required. To the extent that discussion in the target language is demanded, important aspects of the language will be acquired. Some of the proponents of the drama method, e.g. Via (1981), even contend that it is this unplanned communicative language learning situation that provides the method with its greatest amount of success.

Assessment of methods

A brief outline of the advantages and disadvantages of the various methods and the current status of each are shown in Table 6. Such an assessment, it is well to observe, does not include the important consideration of goal or purpose in learning a second language. One method may be preferred over another on the basis of national aim, for example. One country may assess its principal need to be one of gaining knowledge through reading in the second language, while another may regard personal communication as its highest priority. Individuals, too, have their own aims, such as the reading of literature or the meeting of people. Certain teaching methods are better designed to meet certain

TABLE 6. Assessment of principal methods

a. *Grammar-translation*

   Advantages: Large classes can be taught; non-fluent teachers can be used; appropriate for all linguistic levels of students (introductory, intermediate, and advanced); students can acquire significant aspects of a language by book alone without the aid of a teacher.

   Disadvantages: Linguistically trained teachers required; most subject matter impersonal, remote; inappropriate for illiterates such as young children and certain immigrants; little language for interpersonal communication; exposure to spontaneous speech is limited.

   Current status: Thriving. The most widely used and relatively successful of all methods.

b. *Natural method*

   Advantages: Provides fluent natural speech ability in context; appropriate for all student linguistic levels; much exposure to spontaneous speech.

   Disadvantages: Small group only; difficult to provide a variety of interesting situational activities in classroom; fluent teachers required.

   Current status: Almost extinct. Most often employed with young children.

c. *Direct method*

   Advantages: Provides useful language knowledge for speech in context; appropriate for all student linguistic levels; some exposure to spontaneous speech.

   Disadvantages: Small group only; difficult to provide a variety of interesting and situational activities in classroom; fluent teacher required.

   Current status: Almost extinct, except for Berlitz, CREDIF in France, and some places in South America.

d. *Audiolingual method*

   Advantages: Medium-sized classes; provides much practice in listening and speaking; appropriate for all student levels.

   Disadvantages: Fluent teacher required; repetition often boring and inhibiting regarding rule hypothesizing; little exposure to spontaneous speech.

   Current status: While declining due to the shattering of its structural linguistic and behavioristic bases, it is still widely used.

e. *Cognitive code*

   Advantages: Large classes; tolerance of errors. Mixture of skills may reinforce learning; appropriate for all student levels.

   Disadvantages: No specified method.

   Current status: Dissipating into eclecticism.

f. *Silent way*

   Advantages: Stimulates rule hypothesizing; language learned in situational context.

   Disadvantages: Small group only; specially trained fluent teachers required; very strenuous situation for students; proper pronunciation difficult without a model; lack of a language model limits progress much beyond introductory level.

   Curent status: Cultish. Holds little general appeal for both teachers and students.

g. *Community language learning*

   Advantages: Language used in context for personal interaction.

   Disadvantages: Small group only; conversation often forced or stilted; fluent linguistically trained teachers needed.

   Current status: Broadening theory and practice is making it less distinctive. May be incorporated into other methods.

h. *Suggestopedia*
   Advantages: Relaxing for lovers of Haydn and certain other classical composers.
   Disadvantages: Small group only; disturbing to those who do not like Haydn
   or certain other classical composers; expensive; no provision for intermediate and advanced levels.
   Current status: Cultish. Fantastic learning claims are unsupported. May soon
   be extinct, except in Sofia and Toronto.

i. *Comprehension primary*
   Advantages: Allows for vocabulary and rule learning by observation without
   strain of production.
   Disadvantages: Teacher must provide language input that is both interesting
   and varied for a long period of time; no provision for intermediate and
   advanced levels.
   Current status: Struggling. May develop into a version of the Direct Method,
   the underlying ideas of which are well-founded and deserve to be pro-
   moted.

j. *Drama*
   Advantages: Stimulates discussion during the production of the play so that
   natural language is used in context.
   Disadvantages: Small group only; difficult for reticent students.
   Current status: Struggling. Particularly useful as a supplemental method.

---

of these needs than others. Then, too, there is the matter of practical-
ity. A country with limited finances and a limited number of fluent
teachers, for example, may well find the Grammar-Translation method
more suitable than, say, the Silent Way, a method which is applicable
only to small groups and requires specially trained teachers who are
fluent in the target language.

All things considered, it is undoubtedly the case that over the years
more second language knowledge has been acquired through the Grammar-Translation method than through all other methods combined.
This is really a remarkable achievement when one considers that the
knowledge of grammar which teachers have to impart is relatively
small. Even for a language like English that has been well researched,
there is relatively little certain knowledge available. This, of course,
was even more true in the past. Clearly, the grammatical knowledge
which was learned had to have been based on something other than the
limited and often inadequate grammatical explanations which were
given. That 'something,' in my opinion, is the text selection which was
included in every lesson. For exposure to that set of sentences which
are interrelated to form a meaningful discourse, in conjunction with a
translation, allowed for grammar learning by induction. This situation
illustrates an important point about teaching methods, which is that
methods may operate (successfully) in ways that are unknown or unin-
tended. For example, although Pattern Practice was originally used by
Audiolingualists who believed that, given sentences like *John is happy*
and *Is John happy?*, learners would learn associations among word

classes, it is quite possible that through this means, a transformational rule was actually being learned. The effectiveness of a method, therefore, requires empirical validation independent of the motivating theory and its supposed effects. A method may be effective despite an invalid rationale while another may be ineffective despite a sound rationale. In the final analysis, a method can be judged successful only if it is successful. Unfortunately, so little empirical research has been done on the effectiveness of teaching methods that a neutral observer has little basis for making an objective assessment in this regard.

Note

1. Talk presented by Jacquelyn Schachter on the function of correction at the Department of English as a Second Language, University of Hawaii, December 1980.

Chapter 10

Reading principles and teaching

This chapter focuses on the nature and teaching of reading. A number of principles for the optimal learning of reading are presented as is a reading program and research based on those principles. Following this presentation, the issues of reading readiness and early reading are considered.

Since, in order to properly understand reading, certain essentials regarding writing systems and their relationship to speech is necessary, a brief discussion of this problem is presented first.

Writing systems and speech

Writing systems are designed to represent the individual words of a language. Only indirectly, through individual words, are other higher units of language, such as the phrase and sentence, represented. Writing systems, as systems of visual symbols, provide a means for writing words as economically as possible. Although there are many different writing scripts in use throughout the world today, e.g. in India (Devanagari), Egypt (Arabic), Israel (Hebrew), China (Characters), Japan (Characters, Kana), U.S.S.R. (Cyrillic), and Canada (Roman), there are only two basic principles according to which the systems of visual symbols are constructed. The visual symbols represent either a speech sound (phoneme or syllable) or a morpheme. English, for example, essentially uses a sound based writing system, where symbols are used to represent individual phonemes of the language, e.g. the letter t represents the phoneme /t/, the letter a represents the phonemes /a/ and /æ/, and the combination of letters th represents the phonemes /θ/ (_th_in) or /ð/ (_th_is). While English also uses some morpheme symbols, e.g. _1_ for the word _one_, _2_ for the word _two_, + for _plus_, and & for _and_, the writing system is predominantly a sound based one where symbols represent the phonemes of the language. There are systems, however, which are designed to represent the syllables of the language, e.g. the syllabaries of Japan and Korea. The word *karate*, for example, can be written in Japanese *katakana* as カ ラ テ , where the syllable 'ka' is represented by カ , 'ra' is represented by ラ , and 'te' is represented by テ. Any word of the language can be represented by combining the kana symbols.

On the other hand, Chinese is essentially a system where symbols represent morphemes of the language, a morpheme being a string of speech sounds which carries a meaning, e.g. *dog, tree*, and *war* are words composed of single morphemes while words like *anti-war* and *dogs* are composed of two morphemes each (*anti* + *war*, and *dog* + Plural). Although clues as to the pronunciation of the morpheme may be added, the principal aim of the system is to represent the morpheme. Thus, for example, consider the Chinese word *kowtow* (Cantonese pronunciation) which means kneeling and touching the ground with the forehead to show submissive respect to a superior. The word is written 叩頭 consisting of two morphemes, 叩 (*kow*) meaning 'knock' and 頭 (*tow*) meaning 'head.' While it is true that the Chinese symbols had their origin in pictures, e.g. 人 for *person*, relatively few of the many thousands of symbols used currently retain a pictorial indication. The relationship between symbol and morpheme, therefore, is essentially conventional rather than pictorial.

Although the writing system of a language is based on speech, a comparison of what is written and of what is said often shows marked differences. Aside from the desire of some cultures to preserve ancient prestige dialects, one of the principal causes of such differences between speech and writing involves not the nature of the language itself but the use of language. Consider the case of English. The vocabulary and syntax of the English language does not essentially differ in speech and writing. No vocabulary item that appears in speech may not appear in writing or vice versa. Similarly, no syntactic construction, e.g. relative clause, passivization, or pronominalization, appears exclusively in either of these domains. Only a single grammar is in use. It is how grammar is used, along with the establishment of certain writing preferences and conventions, which provides for differences in the observed output between speech and writing. For example, the false starts and sentence fragments which are common to speech are not permitted in writing, and certain syntactic constructions are preferred, e.g. the use of the passive may be encouraged while sentences ending with a preposition and the splitting of infinitives may be discouraged. Then, too, the organization of a written presentation may follow other prescribed lines. Nonetheless, it is clear that both speech and writing involve essentially the same grammar. Thus, in this respect, speech cannot be said to involve one kind of language, and writing another.

Optimal principles for the learning of reading

On the basis of this writer's knowledge of theory and research in reading and of psycholinguistics in general, five fundamental principles have been formulated which would provide for optimal results in the teaching of reading to children. These are: (1) Reading should involve only meaningful words, phrases, and sentences; (2) Reading should depend on speech understanding and not speech production; (3) Reading should not depend on teaching new language or concepts; (4) Reading should not depend on teaching writing; and (5) Learning to read should be enjoyable. Discussion of these principles will involve the most critical issues in the teaching of reading.

Reading should involve only meaningful words, phrases, and sentences

In reading, the essential task for a reader is the recovery of meaning (Smith, 1971; Gates, 1928; Huey, 1908). Whether a reader can say or write the words which are written is incidental to the reading process. Reading is a form of communication the goal of which is the reception of information through written forms. A teaching program, consequently, should direct itself to the realization of that goal. Towards this end, only the written forms of a word, phrase, or sentence for which the child knows the meaning in speech should be selected for teaching. Written forms, the speech counterparts of which are not known by the child are to be avoided. Actually, research evidence shows that meaningful words are easier to learn than meaningless items such as letters. For example, one study with English speaking preschool children showed that written words were learned twice as fast as letters (Steinberg, 1978; Steinberg et al. 1979). Interestingly, when a separate experimental group was presented written words and letters, e.g. *finish, dollar, a*, and *n*, but instead had the written words called by phonic letter names (e.g., *finish* was called 'a') and the letters called by the speech word names (e.g., *a* was called 'finish'), the results were reversed. These findings show that the visual complexity of what is written plays only a minor role in learning and that what is most important is what is said along with a written form. Meaningful spoken words lead to much greater learning than do meaningless letter names. In research with Japanese children in Japan, similar results were found. Children learned meaningful complex Chinese characters (*kanji*) faster than meaningless simple syllable symbols (*kana*) (Steinberg & Yamada, 1978 –79). (With the reversal of speech word and syllable names, superior performance also went with the speech word name.) Again, what was crucial was the meaningfulness of what was said along with a written form. This is not to say that the visual complexity of a written form has no effect on learning. Undoubtedly, it does. Its effect, however, is minor with respect to that of the meaningfulness of co-occurring stimuli such as spoken words.

In selecting written words, phrases, or sentences that are to be taught, it is not enough that such items be familiar to the child. It is also important that they relate to some sort of personal context, i.e. to objects, experiences, action, situations, or events in the child's immediate environment, e.g. *car, television, hot, juice, Let's go to the store.* Items from stories which the child likes and is familiar with would also qualify in this regard. It is not advisable to teach isolated items or prescribed vocabularies, even though the child may know the meaning of such items. For without a personal context, such items have relatively little interest for the child and consequently are more difficult to learn and remember. Such a principle as this, it is worth noting, has been included in a number of reading methods, e.g. Ashton-Warner (1963) and Schulwitz (1977). At times in the past, whole word teaching was not as successful as it might have been because so often the items taught were not meaningful or did not relate to the child's personal and immediate life experiences, e.g. the program of Bloomfield (1942). Teaching meaningful items in a meaningful personal context provides the best foundation for the teaching of reading.

While it is necessary for children to know letter-sound correspondences in order to be able to sound out and recognize novel written words (words which they have not learned), it is *not* necessary and may actually be detrimental to teach such correspondences directly. Children can learn the requisite correspondences on their own, without being taught. What they must be taught, however, is to read a number of whole words, for it is on the basis of these whole words that the child will discover the letter-sound system that relates the component parts of spoken and written words.

Given the remarkable analytical capacity which all children display in learning the syntax and phonology of a language (see Chapter 8 for details), it should be recognized that the induction of the systematic letter-sound correspondences which are inherent in whole word data is a much less formidable task. In language, for example, parents do not teach their children all the component sound segments of a word. What they do is utter the whole word. They say whole words like *pushed, grandma, strong*, and *friend*, and leave it to the child to do the segmenting. The fact that children produce words which they have never heard such as *breaked, comed, mouses*, and *brung* through sound substitutions (see Chapter 8) demonstrates that they do learn sound segmentation on their own. Clearly, in dealing with the speech they receive, children apply great analytical skill. They take whole data (words, phrases, sentences) as input and search for regularities then formulate rules which underlie those data.

Some research has been devoted to the problem of learning letter-sound correspondences by induction. Gates (1928) determined, on the basis of relatively long-term studies with a large number of English speaking elementary school children, that the sound values of letters could be learned without instruction simply through the learning of whole words. Other, more recent, long-term case studies with preschool children also support the findings of Gates. For example, Söderbergh (1971) found that her Swedish speaking female subject learned all of the letter-sound correspondences necessary for reading without direct instruction and without any special order of materials, as did Steinberg and Steinberg (1975) with their English speaking subject. The same was found for the subject in the Weeks (1981) study where English orthography was learned.

However, findings which have been obtained from some short-term experiments (generally a few hours per subject) have been less conclusive. For example, while Bishop (1964), Skailand (1971), and Steinberg (1981) found evidence of letter-sound inductions. Jeffrey and Samuels (1967) and Silberman (1964) found in their research that little or no spontaneous induction occurred. In examining these latter studies and others like them, though, it is evident that a number of important variables often were not dealt with adequately. For example, some studies did not give learners a sufficient amount of time for training and for arriving at a solution. Thus, the one short session given in the Jeffrey and Samuels' experiment may well have been insufficient, as indicated by Gibson and Levin (1975: 291). Studies were deficient, too, in other respects as well: (a) learners were not given any clue as to the left-to-right directionality of the writing nor given sufficient time to discover the directionality on their own; (b) the limited number of whole words given for learning did not contain a sufficient number of recurring target elements; (c) subjects were required to respond quickly and were not given time to think about (so as to analyze) the written words which they had learned; and (d) individual phonemes which are difficult to pronounce is isolation, such as /p/ and /n/, were required to be uttered as evidence of learning.

One danger of phonics methods which directly teach sounds for letters is that such instruction draws the child's attention to meaningless sounds and away from meaningful concepts. Such methods, whether they teach letter-sound correspondences in isolation or teach such correspondences in the context of whole words (so-called 'decoding'), draw attention to the identification of sound elements which comprise words. Then, too, the linguistic fact that individually uttered sounds usually do not naturally blend to form words (Bloomfield, 1961, presents an added barrier to learning. For example, the individually pronounced segments in *picked*, *dog*, and *clock*, do not, in combination, provide the intended whole word. Thus, for *picked*, /pə/ + /i/ + /kə/ + /də/ provides /pəikədə/ and not /pikt/. Clearly, a child could not recover words by this method if the designated sounds of letters are directly combined. In order to be successful, the child must devise and apply complex phonological transformations to the combination of sounds so as to derive the intended word, e.g. in the latter part of *picked*, the child must mentally delete the vowel of /ə/ from the syllable /kə/ in order to recover the consonant /k/, so that it can be combined with the final consonant /d/ which itself must be devoiced to /t/.

Rather than attempting to teach children to recognize novel words by requiring them to pronounce sounds for letters and then blending those uttered sounds, it would be better if children learned the sound values of letters mentally by induction, and then blended those sounds mentally to form words. As was noted earlier, since children who learn to speak develop the ability to segment sounds mentally and to combine them mentally, they already have the requisite skill for performing such operations.

Related to the issue of teaching letter-sound correspondences directly, there is that of teaching children to discriminate the letters of the alphabet from one another, i.e. to distinguish the perceptual shape of *o* from *c* from *d*, etc. One way this could be done is to teach children the names of the letters, *ay, bee, cee*, etc. Such teaching is unnecessary and not particularly advisable for the same reasons given for not teaching letter-sound correspondences. After learning some of the initial letters, *a, b*, and *c*, there is not much to interest a child in *p, q, r*, etc. Then, too, focusing on the names of letters detracts from their symbolic function, to represent words of the language. It is better to teach whole words and let children discover for themselves the individual letters. This is the same process of induction which children apply in segmenting whole speech words into phonemes and syllables.

There is some empirical evidence that children can learn to read whole words without having any prior knowledge of the shapes of individual letters. In a reading program teaching only whole words to preschool children (two-, three-, and four-year-olds) over a period of about four months, 17 children learned a mean of 16 words and 2 phrases or sentences although they were not able to identify any letters at all by name (Steinberg, 1980). One of these was a three-year-old who learned 31 words and 2 phrases and sentences. Then, too, during this same period of time, one four-year-old learned as many as 86 words and 20 phrases and sentences, although he was able to identify only three lower case letters and five upper case ones.

In the past, those who advocated beginning the teaching of reading with whole words were divided on the question of whether whole word teaching was sufficient. Gray (1948) believed that instruction on letter-sound correspondences should be given, after a large number of whole words were learned. Gates (1928), on the other hand, believed that whole word teaching was sufficient, i.e. that no other instruction was necessary. While empirical research of a long-term nature with a variety of types of subjects is necessary to firmly establish which of these approaches is superior, this writer is of the belief that Gates' view on the matter is correct.

There is, of course, some irony to this proposal for teaching reading through whole words. For, it advocates that English writing, which mainly has an alphabetic character, be treated for teaching purposes as though it were a word (morpheme) writing system like Chinese. Actually, all fluent English readers eventually learn to identify whole words as if they were Chinese characters. Experimental evidence as far back as the last century (Cattell, 1885) shows that fluent readers use a whole word strategy in identifying words. The recent work of Goodman (1973), Kolers (1970), and others reinforce this view. They find that the prediction of meaning (not the decoding of letter-sound correspondences) is the major strategy used in the identification of words. Since it is the case that learning to recognize whole words is necessary to be a fluent reader, therefore, the learning of whole words right from the start may be easier and more effective for readers in the long run. Children have the memory capacity for this, for, as was noted in the chapter on child language acquisition, young children have a prodigious memory, acquiring thousands of vocabulary items. Likewise, the memorization of thousands of written forms should provide no special problem for children.

Reading should depend on speech understanding and not on speech production

It is not necessary for children learning to read to be able to speak or enunciate clearly. Reading can be learned without speaking. For example, it is often observed that persons with speech disabilities, such as cerebral palsy, learn language and learn to read. These persons acquire language by listening to others speak, and they learn to read by associating that language knowledge with written forms. Thus, whether or not a child can say 'dog' or 'hippopotamus' is not essential for the child learning to read such items. A recent piece of research with a hearing-mute Japanese girl to whom reading was taught, dramatically illustrates this principle (Steinberg & Chen, 1980). The girl was mute since birth and was able to utter only a few sounds and a couple of recognizable words, 'papa' (father), and 'mamma' (baby word for food). Because she could hear, she learned to understand language. She was three years and nine months of age when the teaching program began. Over a period of 11 months, this girl learned to read at least 78 words, 47 being composed of complex kanji (Chinese characters) and 31 of kana (syllable symbols). All the items that she learned were written on cards. To verify if she knew any item, one just needed to say, for example, 'jitensha' (bicycle) or 'enpitsu' (pencil) and she would pick out the appropriate card. Or, if the card with the word written on it was shown to her, she would point to the object to which it referred. Only about 10 minutes per day had been devoted to instruction.

While children do not have to produce speech in order to learn to read, it is important that they be able to understand the speech that is spoken to them. For, if the child knows what is meant when someone says 'TV,' 'car,' 'the red truck,' and 'Open the door,' the child will have little difficulty in learning to read the written representations of such items. A child who is not able to understand a speech word will have greater difficulty in learning the written representation of that word than the child who already understands that word in speech. Written items selected for teaching, therefore, should only be those that the child understands in speech.

Reading should not depend on teaching new language or concepts

A reading program should not include the teaching of language. If language is to be taught, it should be done in a curriculum component other than that of reading. There is more than enough material that a child can be taught to read without giving the child the additional burden of learning language. A three-year-old child, for example, already has acquired thousands of vocabulary items and understands a great number of sentences composed of those items. Rather than spending time teaching new vocabulary and other aspects of language, it would be better to teach the reading of those words and structures which the child already knows.

Although some understanding of language is necessary for the teaching of reading, a complete mastery is not. Partial language knowledge is sufficient. Actually, this is a principle that is already followed in teaching reading to children, e.g. vocabulary items which a Grade 1 child does not know such as *eclipse, process*, and *tantamount*, or complex structures like passives *The dog had been bitten by the cat* or embedded sentences like *The boy who pushed the girl the policeman shouted at ran away* are not introduced. Instead, children are presented written items for which speech equivalents are already known.

Neither does a reading program require a component for the teaching of concepts or reasoning. Again, there is more than enough to deal with without giving children and teachers additional and unnecessary burdens. Actually, by two or three years of age children have already acquired a high degree of conceptualization. Their use of language demonstrates this clearly. For example, suppose, after going to the doctor, a child utters the sentence *The needle hurt*. In saying this the child is describing a complex conceptual relationship where the insertion of a needle is regarded as the cause of the child's experiencing pain. This instance of causation demonstrates only a few of the many basic concepts which young children have at their disposal. (Chapter 8 presents data which shows how well developed young children's conceptualization actually is.)

Since children already have acquired a wide variety of concepts before being taught to read, there is no need to explicitly teach new concepts. Then, too, even if certain concepts had not been acquired, there is doubt as to whether they could actually be taught. After all, philosophers have puzzled for centuries over the meaning of such words as *cause, effect, same*, and *similar*. It should be noted, too, that simply saying the word for an idea, e.g. *cause, effect*, etc., does not bring to mind or provide the idea in question. There is no conceptual content in the acoustic speech signal itself. Then, again, not knowing these words does not necessarily indicate an absence of the ideas in question. For, although young children may use sentences which involve the ideas of cause and effect, they may not know the particular sound forms which signal those ideas, i.e. 'cause' and 'effect.'

Concerning reason and logic, there is no basis for believing that teaching in this area is required for reading. Consider the following: *If some Buddhists are Communists, and if some Communists are Maoists, then some Buddhists are Maoists*. One can easily read and understand the meaning of each of the component simple sentences without being certain whether the conclusion is a valid one. For, in order to assess the validity of this argument, certain methods and operations must be applied to the set of propositions (as represented by sentences) which comprise the argument. Such an ability is distinct from that of reading. By the way, the conclusion that some Buddhists are Maoists is not a valid one.

Besides, certain elemental logic and reasoning are acquired without explicit teaching. One does not have to go to school to learn that if all dogs have a nose and if Spot is a dog, then it necessarily follows that Spot has a nose. Actually, logic is acquired at a very early age. It is not uncommon for a three-year-old child to say to another, 'You have more candy!' Implied here is the argument, *Since you have more candy than me, and since we should have an equal amount, therefore, you should give me some to make it equal*. Research indicates, too, that non-standard English dialect speakers are as adept in reason and logic as are standard English speakers (Labov, 1970b).

It should be emphasized here that the recommendation not to teach concepts and thinking only concerns the inclusion of such topics as a curriculum component in a reading program. The recommendation does not apply to situations where, in the natural course of events, teachers explain new ideas and stimulate children to think. Such endeavors are natural and proper. What is unadvisable, rather, is the inclusion and development of such endeavors in a special sub-program or curriculum which is designed to teach reading.

As far as a reading program is concerned, children should be taught to read the language that they can understand. In this way, their cognitive conceptual capacity will never be exceeded and the reading material will always fall within their intellectual scope.

Reading should not depend on teaching writing

While reading is essentially a skill in which only the eyes are used, writing requires, additionally, the use of the muscles of the hand. The muscles of the fingers must be precisely trained before they have the control necessary for producing written symbols. Because appropriate physical maturation and muscular development are prerequisites for writing and because such prerequisites do not develop early, young children have difficulty in controlling a writing implement, and, they fatigue easily. Such difficulties, however, are not present for reading. The visual ability of the child develops before the first year, when the child learns to identify objects, faces, etc.

Children learning to write are usually trained by copying or tracing written figures which are present as models. However the ultimate goal of writing is to be able to write meaningful messages when no written model is present, i.e. to write from memory. This being so, it must be realized that one cannot write from memory unless one first has acquired certain knowledge through perception, i.e. one must have stored in memory the visual shapes of particular words or letters, or have learned the orthographic rules for generating written symbols from speech. We often have difficulty in writing accurately (one form of spelling) because our visual memory of particular words is vague or because the orthographic rules do not provide us with a unique solution. For example, in English, the nouns, *lode* and *load* both have the same speech form of /lōd/. Writing, therefore, as the skill of recalling and composing words which are realized in written form, requires knowledge that is gained by reading.

Although reading is independent of the skill of writing, it does not follow that teaching writing may not sometimes benefit a learner in reading. Indeed, writing may help a learner to remember a word. However, because writing involves a motor skill which requires fine hand coordination which young children do not have, it is advisable that writing instruction be reserved for a later time when children have become fluent readers. Even then, however, reading should never be made contingent on writing progress for reading can be learned much faster than writing.

At this point, it may be useful to bring together into a single model the essential relations of thought, language, reading, writing, and motor control which have been heretofore discussed or implied. The following schema represents, for normal persons, the dependency relations among the various linguistic knowledge and skill areas:

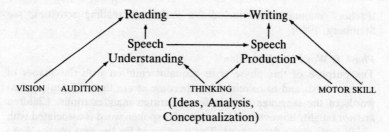

Thus, according to the schema, *Reading* is not dependent on *Speech Production* or *Writing*. Rather, *Reading* is dependent on *Speech Understanding* and *Vision* where the source of *Speech Understanding* is considered to be *Thinking* and *Audition*.

Learning to read should be enjoyable

Reading should be made an enjoyable activity for children. This can be done by providing instruction in the form of interesting games and activities. As a consequence, not only will children learn to read, they will want to read. Children who are interested, intellectually stimulated, and who enjoy what they are doing will learn willingly and will not mind applying some effort.

To foster these goals, no teaching activity should be included which children find boring or tedious. An activity should be terminated as soon as the child's attention starts to wander. In this regard, it is probably best to intersperse reading activities with other types of activities. In this way, a reading activity will always appear fresh and be more readily welcomed. The application of generous and frequent encouragement and praise will also help to maintain interest and motivation on the part of the child.

A teaching program and some results

A four-phase teaching program

Children may be taught to read according to the following four phase program which embodies the previously discussed guiding principles: (1) Word familiarization; (2) Word identification; (3) Phrase and sentence identification; and (4) Text interpretation. Each phase involves meaningful language and is ordered such that a preceding phase serves as a prerequisite for the succeeding one. Prior phases may be continued along with succeeding phases, however. For example, Word identification may continue even though the child is in the Phrase and sentence identification and Text interpretation phases. The essential ideas in each phase, along with a few illustrative games and activities are offered below. (For more details concerning these phases along with a teachers' manual which includes a variety of reading activities, see Steinberg, 1980).

Phase 1: Word familiarization

The purpose of this phase is to acquaint children with the shapes of written words and to have children become aware that different spoken words of the language have different written manifestations. Children are *not* taught, however, which particular spoken word is associated with which particular written word. This is reserved for the next phase, Word identification.

For instructional purposes, one may attach word cards to objects around the room, e.g. *chair, television, wall, flower*, and *table*. The words should be ones which the child understands. Such cards are placed at the child's eye level wherever possible. Just the exposure of such cards in the course of the day will, even without instruction, serve to promote learning.

A number of activities may be done with the word cards around the room. Three such activities, in sequential order of difficulty, are: Room object pointing, Word card sticking, and Room object matching. In Room object pointing, the child points to the written word and the object to which it is attached. Pointing to written words brings the words to the child's attention and gives them importance. The children will come to realize that different words are associated with different objects. The child is not required to learn which particular word goes with which particular object. In Word card sticking, the child is given a word card and asked to place it on an object that is named. Again, the child sees that different words go on different objects. This activity sets the stage for the next activity, the important one of Room object matching.

In Room object matching, the child is given a word card and is asked to find another like it. This obliges the child to inspect written words so as to determine whether they are the same or different. By doing this, the child becomes familiar with the shapes of letters and learns to look for their differentiating features. Since the task requires only that the child compare two forms at a time, both of which are present, and make a judgment of same or different, only short-term memory is involved. Other interesting variations of the matching activity may be devised. For example, two dice with the same words on each (e.g. *dog, girl, apple*, etc.) could be rolled with the aim of getting a match.

Phase 2: Word identification

In this phase, the child learns which particular written words are associated with which particular spoken words or objects. The difference between this phase and the preceding one is that this one requires the use of long-term memory. Here the child must store a particular visual configuration and remember what particular spoken word it represents. For example, when seeing the written word *apple* in isolation the child is expected to be able to point to the object 'apple' (or its picture) or to say 'apple.'

Various games and activities can be devised to teach (and test) the child to identify particular written words. For example, word cards can be removed from objects in the room and the child could be asked to place them on the correct objects. A game could be made with a pair of dice, one with pictures and one with words. The dice are rolled with the aim of getting a match in terms of picture and word.

Once the child begins to learn some written words, most of which will be nouns, then other types of words, particularly verbs and adjectives should be introduced, e.g. actions (*run, touch*), colors (*red, yellow*), and states (*happy, angry*). Function words such as prepositions and articles would never be included. Such words should only be introduced in context through phrases and sentences. More abstract (but familiar and meaningful) words may be introduced (*good, friend*), and words can be written on demand from the child.

Phase 3: Phrase and sentence identification
This phase is similar to that of the preceding Word identification one, except that larger linguistic units are dealt with. Its goal is for the child to read the largest basic linguistic unit, the sentence. In teaching phrases and sentences it is not necessary that phrase teaching precede sentence teaching. Rather, whichever unit is of interest for a particular situation is what should be taught, e.g. *a big dog, Diane fell.*

The written phrase and sentence should include all words without any simplification, e.g. if *That dog is barking at the boy* is the appropriate sentence, it should not be changed to *Dog bark boy*. The presence of the other sorts of words such as *that, is,* and *at,* and the suffix *-ing*, provides a learning opportunity for the child. In time, such words will be learned without specific training. It is not necessary that the children always know how to read every key word (noun, verb, and adjective) in a phrase or sentence, before that unit is taught. However, to avoid learning problems, the number of unknown key words should be kept to a minimum. It is best not to create phrases and sentences for their own sake but to make them fit the events and situations which occur in the immediate environment. For example, *Diane fell*, would be of great interest if it indeed was the case that Diane, someone the child knows, did fall.

Phase 4: Text interpretation
Text involves the largest meaningful written linguistic unit. It consists of a sequence of two or more sentences that are related to one another. Stories and poems are prime examples of texts. Learning to

read text is probably the most interesting of all reading activities for children since there is an excitement that a story can generate which the reading of isolated words, phrases, and sentences cannot. As the child progresses in reading text, books may have fewer pictures and more text. Thus, over time, there will be less dependence on pictures and more dependence on the text. It is the purpose of his phase to provide children with the knowledge and skill that will enable them to read text fluently.

In teaching the reading of a book, the following is one possible procedure: (1) Read the book to the child, with the child looking at the pages. Point to the words in a sentence as they are spoken. (The child must be exposed to the written and spoken word simultaneously.) Answers any questions; discuss the plot and characters. (2) After the book has been completed in this manner, return to the beginning of the book. This time, each sentence is read aloud and pointed to one at a time, with the child asked to imitate by doing his or her own saying and pointing. (3) After the book has been completed in this manner, return to the beginning. This time have the child do all of the saying and pointing. Give assistance when needed.

Activities which do not involve books may also be introduced. For example, stories with as few as two or three sentences may be composed, e.g. Story A: (1) *Sara dropped the egg.* (2) *It landed on her brother's head.*; and Story B: (1) *The dog was hungry.* (2) *Harry didn't know what to feed it.* (3) *He gave it some bubble gum.* Each sentence of a story is written on a card. The task for the child is to arrive at an order of sentences so that they form a story. (The child may or may not be told the story beforehand.) Such an activity will foster in the child an awareness of order and the semantic relatedness of sentences.

It should be emphasized that although the child is taught to read books at this stage in the teaching sequence, this is not to imply that the introduction of books should wait until this time. On the contrary, books should be read and stories told just as soon as a child can understand what is being said. Such activities will make the child familiar with the nature of books and build the child's interest so that the child will be prepared when text reading is introduced.

Some results of the reading program

To date, this program has been administered in only four research studies. Nonetheless, the four studies represent a variety of circumstances and conditions. Two studies involved English reading while the other two involved Japanese reading. One of each of the two studies involved parents teaching children at home, the other of the two involved teachers teaching children in school. All children were four years of age or less when they began to learn to read. Some were even less than two years old.

With English – in the home
This research involves a single subject, my son (Steinberg & Steinberg, 1975). My wife and I began introducing words to him before he was 12 months of age. As was noted earlier, at 12 months of age he was able to correctly identify four written words, *car, baby, boy* and *girl*, (without being able to say any of them), while at 24 months he was able to identify 48 words, phrases, and sentences, e.g. *blow, cake, hooray, come on, I see*, and *Peter's room*, although he could say only 15 of them. By two and a half years of age, he could read 181 different items and at three and a half years, he could read short sentences in a text fluently and with natural intonation. On the average about 10 to 15 minutes daily was spent in instruction.

At 4 years 11 months of age, standardized tests placed his reading at generally beyond the third grade level. Since he had only been taught to read at home, such findings may be plausibly attributed to the effects of the reading program. The later findings (all based on independently administered standardized tests) show that he was able to maintain a three grade or more lead in reading over his grade mates. At about eight years old and a third grader, his reading achievement equalled or bettered sixth graders on vocabulary and comprehension, and eleventh graders on speed and accuracy. And at about 12 years old and a seventh grader, he scored higher than most tenth graders and as well as twelfth graders in terms of vocabulary, comprehension, speed, and accuracy.

With English – in the nursery school
The reading program was introduced to two-, three- and four-year-old children in a disadvantaged area on the island of Oahu in Hawaii (Steinberg, 1980). During an average of 17.2 weeks of instruction, with an average of 10 to 12 minutes of instruction daily, the subjects learned a mean of 28.7 words and 6.3 phrases and sentences. Overall, the older children learned more than the younger children. It is worth noting that a three-year-old child who rarely spoke learned 29 words and 12 phrases and sentences during 20.4 weeks of exposure and that the highest achiever was a boy who learned 94 words and 41 phrases and sentences during 23.6 weeks of exposure. That the children achieved what they did, coming as they did from welfare families and living in neighborhoods where the reading level in school is low, indicates the viability of the reading program.

With Japanese – in the home
The four phase reading program has been administered to three Japanese children in Hiroshima (Steinberg & Yoshida, 1981). The parents have spent about 15 minutes per day on the average in teaching the children.

The children are from two upper middle income families, two girls (sisters) and one boy. When the program was initiated, the sisters were 18 months and 29 months of age while the boy was 20 months of age. The girls were more linguistically advanced, being able to utter sentences. The boy could only utter a few words although he could understand many words and some phrases and sentences. During the first five months of the program, the boy learned a remarkable total of 311 words (Chinese character *kanji* and syllabic *kana*) and 62 phrases and sentences, while the girls learned 189 words and 86 phrases and sentences. (The progress of the girls is identical because the mother paced the older girl to the slower pace of the younger girl.) The boy was in the Word familiarization phase for the first seven weeks of the program, and it was only at the eighth week that he began to identify particular items. In that week, he learned a surprising number of 46 words, 31 of which were *kanji*. In terms of his ability to say these items, his mother noted that in the early weeks of the Word identification phase he could pronounce only a small number of the items. It was further noted that after just the first few weeks of identifying words, he began to remember written items after just one or two presentations. Similar findings were noted for the girls.

After just one week of Word familiarization, the girls began to identify their first words. They began with 10 words the first week, 5 of which were *kanji*. Their progress was much more gradual and less explosive than the boy's. Evidently, there are great individual differences in the rate of learning. After about two years, the children were given a standardized reading test. Each child scored between Grades two and three in overall achievement on sentence comprehension and vocabulary. Their ages at the time of the testing were: 4 years 2 months for the boy, and 3 years 11 months and 4 years 11 months for the girls. It should be noted that this test probably underestimates the true reading ability of the children since the test is designed for more socially and cognitively mature children.

With Japanese – in the nursery school
A project involving the reading program was introduced to a class of two-year-olds and a class of three-year-olds in a middle income neighborhood in Hiroshima (Steinberg & Sakoda, 1981). Over the eight month period during which the program was applied, the following results were obtained. Both the two- and three-year-olds proceeded from the Word familiarization to the Word identification phase within the first month of the reading program. During the eight month course of the program, the two-year-olds learned a total of 97.3 words (71.0 *kanji*) and 3.0 phrases and sentences on the average, while the three-year-olds learned a total of 99.3 words (81.3 *kanji*) and 1.93 phrases and sentences. While the high degree of similarity might indicate that the

learning capacity of the two age groups was much the same, it is the researcher's opinion that the three-year-olds would have done much better had the quality of instruction for the older class been as good as that for the younger class.

Implications of results
The results of the English and Japanese studies provide evidence in support of the effectiveness of the four phase teaching program and of the validity of the principles on which it is based. While much more long-term research is necessary with a variety of subjects and a variety of orthographies before a firm conclusion can be drawn, the findings strongly suggest that guiding principles and the teaching program are optimal and universally applicable.

Readiness and early reading

Since ideas on the nature and teaching of reading make themselves particularly manifest in discussion concerning reading readiness, it may be instructive to consider prevalent views on this topic. Both research and standardized tests are discussed in this regard.

Readiness research

Concern with readiness to read emerged strongly in the 1920s (Dickson, 1923; Holmes, 1927). One of the most influential studies around that time was that of Morphett and Washburne (1931) who claimed that reading should be postponed until a mental age of 6.5 years was attained. Other reports of this period concurred (Biegelow, 1934; Dean, 1939; Witty & Kopel, 1936).

There were dissenting views, however. Gates and Bond (1936), for example, found that at the end of first grade the correlation between reading achievement and mental age was only +.25. The authors insightfully concluded that 'the optimum time of beginning reading is not entirely dependent upon the nature of the child himself, but is in large measure determined by the nature of the reading program' (p. 684). Contemporary theorists such as Durkin (1970); Spache and Spache (1969), and Adelman (1970) have taken similar positions. Any special motivation for wanting to read, it might be noted here, is not an important variable for young children. Preschoolers will engage in any activity which interests them regardless of its long term goals.

Readiness testing

Rather than trying to predict reading readiness or achievement from the standpoint of some global variable like mental age, tests direct themselves to specific knowledge and skills. In assessing the adequacy of readiness tests, a close inspection of the specific content of those tests is necessary. In this regard, let us consider a typical test, the Gates–MacGinitie (1968) Readiness Skills test. It is widely used for kindergartners and first graders. The test involves a battery of seven subtests. A description of five of the most important subtests (quoted from the test manual) is now presented along with my assessment.

(1) *The Listening Comprehension subtest* measures the child's ability to understand the total thought of a simple story. The subtest includes 20 stories (plus a sample story), each with a corresponding panel of three pictures in the test booklet. The examiner reads these stories aloud to the children. Each story is followed by a question, and the child is to mark the one picture in each panel that best answers the question. (p. 1)

Understanding and remembering the essentials of an entire story are required here. The research cited above shows that significant reading skills can be acquired long before such a criterion can be met. Children learned to read words, phrases, and sentences at least a year or two before they would have been able to meet the standards of this subtest.

(2) *The Following Directions subtest* measures the child's skill in following increasingly more complex directions. This subtest has 14 items (and a sample), consisting of one or more directions which the examiner reads aloud. Corresponding to each set of directions is a panel of four pictures to be marked by the child as he carries out the directions. (p. 1)

A typical item on the subtest is 'Move your finger up to the next door, and put an X on the little dog that is followed by a big dog and another X on the big dog that stands between two little ones.' The authors instruct the examiner, 'Do not repeat the instructions for this or any of the following items in this subtest; read directions clearly only once. Pause after each item, *but do not* pause between parts of the directions within an item.' (p. 9. Emphasis in original.) It is doubtful whether any of the young children in the research projects described above could have responded to such complex instructions even after having acquired the ability to read a number of words, phrases, and sentences.

(3) *The Letter Recognition subtest* is designed to measure the child's recognition of letters of the alphabet. It consists of 18 items (and a sample), with four letters of the alphabet in each item. The examiner names one letter which the child must recognize and mark. (p. 1)

It is implied here that failure to perform indicates that a child is not ready to learn to read. Yet, as research cited above shows children can learn to read words, phrases, and sentences without knowing the name of a single letter of the alphabet. Knowing the names of letters is not essential to the reading process.

(4) *The Visual-Motor Coordination subtest* measures the child's skill in completing printed letters. Seven letters (plus a sample) are shown as models, and a part of each letter is also printed in the adjoining column. The child is to complete each letter in the adjoining column, following the model. (p. 1)

Few of the young children who acquired significant reading skills would have been able to do this. The ability to write, as was noted earlier, is irrelevant to the task of reading.

(5) *The Auditory Blending subtest* provides information about the child's ability to join the parts of a word, presented orally, into a whole word. The 14 items (plus a sample), consist of three pictures in each item, saying it in two or three parts, and the child marks the corresponding picture. (p. 2)

The examiner pronounces elements like: *br*, *i*, and *cks* (for *bricks*), *p*, *ai*, and *nt* (for *paint*), and *n* and *ap* (for *nap*). A one second pause is inserted between elements. The child is asked, for example, 'Put an X on *br* and *i* and *cks*.' This task, which is relevant for only certain decoding methods, is a particularly difficult one for children. (1) Many of the sounds pronounced by the examiner are strange and artificial; e.g. consider what *br*, *cks*, *n*, and *nt* sound like in isolation. Such sounds do not occur alone in natural speech. Furthermore, the phonetic quality of consonants and vowels when pronounced in isolation differs greatly when pronounced in a word. For example, the initial consonant sound of /p/ in *pop* differs from the sound of /p/ in the final position; so much so that the final /p/ is likely to be interpreted in isolation as a /b/ (Steinberg, 1969). (2) The child is required to hold in memory a number of strange sounds in sequence. (3) The strange sounds have to be blended to form a word, which is not something that children usually do outside of the teaching and test situations. Furthermore, as was noted earlier, most isolated sound sequences actually do not blend naturally to form the target word. Considering how complex and unnatural the task of this subtest is, it is not surprising that children under the age of five (and many above) generally cannot pass it.

The foregoing shows that none of the major subtests of the Gates–MacGinitie reading readiness test is a valid measure of readiness. Unfortunately, this test is typical of current readiness tests. The widely used *Van Wagenen* (1933–58) and *Metropolitan* tests (1933–66), for example, not only require knowledge and skills like those of the Gates–MacGinitie, but they also demand such prerequisites as: *general knowledge*, e.g. 'What animal has humps on its back?'; *understanding analo-*

gies and complex sentence structure, e.g. 'You wear a hat on your head and a glove on your _____ '; and, *knowledge of antonyms*, e.g. 'When I say east, you say _____ .' Again, most of the subjects would have had to wait years before being able to pass such tests.

That research has not demonstrated the value of this and other readiness tests is not surprising. Reviews and specific studies of the diagnostic and predictive power of standardized reading tests indicate that the tests are of dubious value (Brandt, 1974). For instance, Askov et al. (1972) examined the *Metropolitan Readiness Tests* and found that readiness scores predicted success and failure in the opposite direction for approximately 70 per cent of the children. Other reviews by Hobson (1959), Bollenbacher (1959), and Dunn (1953) also raise serious questions about the predictive validity, reliability, and classroom usefulness of available standardized readiness tests. Clearly, current readiness tests, based as they are on a faulty conception of the nature of reading, language, and the capacity of children, do not measure the true abilities which are required in the learning of reading.

Early reading

The research cited above on teaching reading to preschool age children, along with the studies of Söderbergh (1971), Weeks (1981), Doman (1964), Terman (1918), and Fowler (1962), demonstrates that children can be taught to read at an early age. Of course, the degree of success depends on the method that is applied. The teaching program outlined above is particularly suited for young children focusing, as it does, on whole meaningful words in a personal context, with such items being taught through the medium of games and other interesting activities. It is worth noting that none of the successful studies on early reading used phonics type methods. All used a whole word approach. That such should be the case is not coincidental for what these studies do is to exploit the optimal means which children have for the learning of reading. With the four phase reading program described and on the basis of the research that has been done with it, it would appear that by about 24 months of age, normal children are ready to benefit by reading instruction. By that age the children have acquired some knowledge of speech understanding, which is the foundation for the teaching of reading.

There are a number of important advantages of teaching reading to children in their preschool years.

(1) Reading satisfies and stimulates a child's natural curiosity. It provides enjoyment and, as a source of knowledge, enriches the child. The earlier a child discovers this, the more enriched and more deeply attracted to reading the child will become.

(2) The warm supportive informal atmosphere of the home or the preschool provides an excellent situation for learning. In such a situa-

tion, a positive attitude toward reading can be established without the difficulties that are often encountered in elementary school.

(3) Young children are docile and impressionable. They are not as apt as older children to reject the instruction of teachers or to be negatively influenced by peers.

(4) Young children learn quickly and easily. They have a remarkable rote-memory learning ability and can easily acquire a multitude of written words. The older the children get, the more they require additional exposure and practice.

In addition to the advantages noted above, there is an important overall one. Having children learn to read early could have the effect of improving the educational level of children in all areas of knowledge. That being the case, society as a whole would benefit significantly.

References

ADELMAN, H. (1970) Learning to read in the classroom. *The Reading Teacher* **2** 28

ARDREY, ROBERT (1970) *The Social Contract* Dell Publishing: New York

ARISTOTLE (4th Cent. B.C.) *On the Soul* (De anima) (*Great Books of the Western World*) Encyclopaedia Britannica: Chicago, 1952

ASHER, J. (1974) Learning a second language through commands: the second field test. *Modern Language Journal* **58** 24–32

ASHER, J. J. and GARNICA, R. (1969) The optimal age to learn a foreign language. *Modern Language Journal* **53** 334–41

ASHTON-WARNER, SYLVIA (1963) *Teacher* Simon & Schuster: New York

ASKOV, M., OTTO, W. and SMITH, R. (1972) Assessment of the de-Hirsch predictive index test of reading failure, in Aukerman, R. (ed) *Some Persistent Questions on Beginning Reading* International Reading Association: Newark, Del.

AUSTIN, J. L. (1962) *How to Do Things with Words* Oxford University Press: New York

AUSUBEL, DAVID (1964) Adults versus children in second-language learning. *Modern Language Journal* **48** 420–24

BAILEY, N., MADDEN, C. and KRASHEN, S. (1974) Is there a "natural sequence" in adult second language learning? *Language Learning* **24** 235–43

BANCROFT, JANE (1978) The Lozanov method and its American adaptations. *Modern Language Journal* **63** 4, 167–75

BERKELEY, GEORGE (1710) *A Treatise Concerning Principles of Human Knowledge* (*Great Books of the Western World*) Encyclopaedia Britannica: Chicago (1952)

BERLIN, C. S., LOWE-BELL, R., HUGHES, I. and BERLIN, H. (1972) Dichotic right-ear advantages in males and females – ages 5 to 13. *Journal of the Acoustical Society of America* **53** 368 (Abstract)

BEVER, THOMAS G. (1970) The cognitive basis for linguistic structures, in Hayes, J. R. (ed) *Cognition and the Development of Language* Wiley: New York, pp. 279–362

BEVER, THOMAS G. (1972) Perceptions, thought, and language, in Freedle, Roy O. & Carroll, John B. (eds) *Language Comprehension and the Acquisition of Knowledge* Wiley: New York

BIEGELOW, E. (1934) School progress of underage children. *Elementary School Journal* **35** 186–92

BIERWISCH, MANFRED (1971) On classifying semantic features, in Steinberg, D. D. and Jakobovits, L. A. (eds) (1971)

BISHOP, CAROL (1964) Transfer effects of word and letter training in reading. *Journal of Verbal Learning and Verbal Behavior* **3** 215–21

BLOOM, LOIS M. (1973) *One Word At a Time: The Use of Single Word Utterances Before Syntax* Mouton: The Hague

BLOOMFIELD, LEONARD (1961) Teaching children to read, in Bloomfield, Leonard and Barnhart, Clarence L. (1961) *Let's Read* Wayne State University Press: Detroit. Article written in 1942

BLOUNT, B. G. (1972) Parental speech and language acquisition: some Luo and Samoan examples. *Anthropological Linguistics* **14** 119–30

BOLLENBACHER, J. (1959) Murphy-Durrell reading readiness test, in Buros, O. (ed) (1959)

BRAINE, MARTIN D. (1963) The ontogeny of English phrase structure: the first phase. *Language* **39** 1–13

BRAINE, MARTIN D. (1971) The acquisition of language in infant and child, in Reed, C. (ed) *The Learning of Language* Appleton-Century-Crofts: New York

BRANDT, M. E. (1974) Reading readiness redefined. Unpublished M.A. thesis, University of California: San Francisco

BROWN, H. DOUGLAS (1980) *Principles of Language Learning and Teaching* Prentice-Hall: Englewood Cliffs, N.J.

BROWN, ROGER (1973) *A First Language: The Early Stages* Harvard University Press: Cambridge, Mass.

BROWN, ROGER and BELLUGI, URSULA (1964) Three processes in the child's acquisition of syntax. *Harvard Educational Review* **34** 133–51

BROWN, ROGER and BERKO, JEAN (1960) Word association and the acquisition of grammar. *Child Development* **31** 1–14

BROWN, ROGER, CAZDEN C. and BELLUGI, U. (1969) The child's grammar from I to III. Vol. 2 of Hill, J. P. (ed) *Minnesota Symposium on Child Psychology* University of Minnesota: Minneapolis, Minnesota

BROWN, ROGER W. and LENNEBERG, ERIC H. (1954) A study in language and cognition. *Journal of Abnormal and Social Psychology* **49** 454–62

BUROS, O. (1959) *Fifth Mental Measurement Yearbook* Gryphen Press: Highland Park, N.J.

BURT, MARINA (1971) *From Deep to Surface Structure* Harper & Row: New York

BURT MARINA and KIPARSKY, CAROL (1972) *The Gooficon: A Repair Manual for English* Newbury House: Rowley, Mass.

CARROLL, JOHN B. (ed) (1956) *Language, Thought, and Reality: Selected Writings of Benjamin Lee Whorf* MIT Press: Cambridge, Mass.

CATTELL, J. M. (1885) Ueber der Zeit der Erkennung und Bennenung von Schrifzeichen, Bildern und Farben. *Philosophische Studien* 2 635–50

CHARNIAK, E. (1972) *Toward a Model of Children's Story Comprehension* MIT Artificial Intelligence Laboratory: Cambridge, Mass.

CHASTAIN, KENNETH (1971) The audio-lingual habit theory versus the cognitive-code learning theory: some theoretical considerations, in Lugton, Robert C. and Heinle, Charles H. (eds) (1971)

CHIHARA, TETSUO and OLLER, JOHN W. (1978) Attitudes and attained proficiency in ESL: a sociolinguistic study of adult Japanese speakers. *Language Learning* 28 55–68

CHOMSKY, CAROL (1969) *Acquisition of Syntax in Children from 5–10* MIT Press: Cambridge, Mass.

CHOMSKY, NOAM (1955) *The Logical Structure of Linguistic Theory* MIT Library: Cambridge, Mass.

CHOMSKY, NOAM (1957) *Syntactic Structures* Mouton: The Hague

CHOMSKY, NOAM (1959) Review of Skinner's *Verbal Behaviour. Language* 35 26–58. Also in Fodor, J. and Katz, J. (eds) (1964)

CHOMSKY, NOAM (1961) On the notion 'rule of grammar', in Fodor, J. and Katz, J. (eds) (1964)

CHOMSKY, NOAM (1962) Explanatory models in linguistics, in Nagel, E., Suppes, P. and Tarski, A. (eds) *Logic, Methodology, and Philosophy of Science* Stanford University Press: Stanford, California

CHOMSKY, NOAM (1963) Formal properties of grammars, in Luce, R., Bush, R. and Galanter, E. (eds) *Handbook of Mathematical Psychology*, Vol. 2 Wiley: New York

CHOMSKY, NOAM (1964) Current issues in linguistic theory, in Fodor, J. and Katz, J. (eds) (1964)

CHOMSKY, NOAM (1965) *Aspects of the Theory of Syntax* MIT Press: Cambridge, Mass.

CHOMSKY, NOAM (1966) *Cartesian Linguistics* Harper & Row: New York

CHOMSKY, NOAM (1967a) The formal nature of language, in Lenneberg, E. *Biological Foundations of Language* Wiley: New York. Also in Chomsky, Noam (1972) *Language and Mind* (enlarged edn) Harcourt Brace Jovanovich: New York

CHOMSKY, NOAM (1967b) Recent contributions to the theory of innate ideas. *Synthese* 17 2–11

CHOMSKY, NOAM (1968) *Language and Mind* Harcourt, Brace & World: New York (Enlarged edn, 1972)

CHOMSKY, NOAM (1970) Remarks on nominalization, in Jacobs, R. A., and Rosenbaum, P. S. (eds) *Readings in English Transformational Grammar* Ginn & Co.: Waltham, Mass.

CHOMSKY, NOAM (1971) Deep structure, surface structure, and semantic interpretation, in Steinberg, Danny D. and Jakobovits, Leon A. (eds) (1971)

CHOMSKY, NOAM (1975a) Conditions on rules of grammar. Article based on lectures presented at the Linguistic Institute, University of South Florida

CHOMSKY, NOAM (1975b) *Reflections on Language* Pantheon: New York

CHOMSKY, NOAM (1975c) *The Logical Structure of Linguistic Theory* Plenum: New York

CHOMSKY, NOAM & HALLE, M. (1968) *The Sound Pattern of English* Harper & Row: New York

CLARK, RUTH (1977) What's the use of imitation? *Journal of Child Language* **4** 341–58

CLARK, H. H. (1973) Space, time, semantics, and the child, in Moore, T. E. (ed) *Cognitive Development and the Acquisition of Language* Academic Press: New York

COMENIUS (JAN AMOS KOMENSKY) (1568) *Didactica Magna*. (1896, 1967) *The Great Didactic of John Amos Comenius* (In English) Russell & Russell: New York

CORDER, S. PIT (1971) Idiosyncratic dialects and error analysis. *International Review of Applied Linguistics* **9** 147–59

CORDER, S. PIT (1973) *Introducing Applied Linguistics* Penguin: Harmondsworth, England

CROSS, T. G. (1977) Mother's speech adjustments: the contributions of selected child listener variables, in Ferguson, C. and Snow, C. (eds) (1977)

CURRAN, CHARLES A. (1972) *Counseling-Learning: A Whole-Person Model for Education* Grune & Statton: New York

CURRAN, CHARLES A. (1976) *Counseling-Learning in Second Language* Apple River Press: Apple River, Illinois

DARIAN, STEVEN G. (1972) *English as a Foreign Language: History, Development, and Methods of Teaching* University of Oklahoma Press: Norman, Oklahoma

DEAN, C. (1939) Predicting first grade reading achievements. *Elementary School Journal* **33** 609–16

DEPAULO, B. M. & BONVILLIAN, J. D. (1975) The effects on language development of the special characteristics of speech addressed to children. Unpublished paper, Harvard University

DERWING, B. (1973) *Transformational Grammar as a Theory of Language Acquisition* Cambridge University Press: London

DERWING, B. (1977) Against autonomous linguistics, University of Alberta, Department of Linguistics. Mimeo

DESCARTES, RENE (1641) *Meditations on First Philosophy*, (*Great Books of the Western World*), Encyclopaedia Britannica: Chicago. 1952

DE VILLIERS, JILL G. & DE VILLIERS, PETER A. (1978) *Language Acquisition*

Harvard University Press: Cambridge, Mass.

DICKSON, U. E. (1923) *Mental Tests and the Classroom Teacher* World Book: New York

DILLER, KARL C. (1971) *Generative Grammar, Structural Linguistics and Language Teaching* Newbury House: Rowley, Mass.

DILLER, KARL C. (1978) *The Language Teaching Controversy* Newbury House: Rowley, Mass.

DOMAN, G. (1964) *How to Teach Your Baby to Read* Random House: New York

DONALDSON, WEBER D. (1971) Code-cognition approaches to language, in Lugton, Robert C. and Heinle, Charles H. (eds) (1971)

DRACH, K. M. (1969) The language of the parent: a pilot study. *Working paper No. 14* University of California: Berkeley, California

DULAY, HEIDI and BURT, MARINA (1974) Natural sequences in child second language acquisition. *Language Learning* 24 1, 37–53

DUNN, S. (1953) Murphy-Durrell reading readiness test, in Buros, O. (ed) *Fourth Mental Measurement Yearbook* Gryphen Press: Highland Park, N. J.

DURKIN, D. (1970) A language arts program for pre-first grade children: two-year achievement report. *Reading Research Quarterly* 5 534–65

ENGELKAMP, J. (1975) The interaction of semantic features of transitive verbs and their objects. *Psychological Research* 37 299–308

FERGUSON, CHARLES A. (1964) Baby talk in six languages. *American Anthropologist* 66 103–14

FERGUSON, CHARLES A. (1977) Baby talk as a simplified register, in Ferguson, C. A. and Snow, C. (eds) (1977)

FERGUSON, CHARLES A. and GARNICA, O. K. (1975) Theories of phonological development. Vol. 1 in Lenneberg, Eric H. and Lenneberg E. (eds) (1975)

FERGUSON, C. A. and SNOW, C. (eds) (1977) *Talking to Children: Language Input and Acquisition* Cambridge University Press: New York

FILLENBAUM, S. (1971) On coping with ordered and unordered conjunctive sentences. *Journal of Experimental Psychology* 87 93–8

FILLENBAUM, S. (1974a) Pragmatic normalization: further results for some conjunctive and disjunctive sentences. *Journal of Experimental Psychology* 102 574–8

FILLENBAUM, S. (1974b) Or: some uses, *Journal of Experimental Psychology* 103 913–21

FILLMORE, C. (1968) The case for case, in Bach, E. and Harms, R. T. (eds) *Universals in Linguistic Theory* Holt, Rinehart & Winston: New York

FILLMORE, C. (1971) Types of lexical information, in Steinberg, Danny D. and Jakobovits, Leon A. (eds) (1971)

FILLMORE, C. (1977) The case for case reopened, in Cole, P. and Sadock, J. (eds) *Syntax and Semantics: Grammatical Relations, Vol. 8* Academic Press: New York

FODOR, J. and KATZ, J. (eds) (1964) *The Structure of Language: Readings in the Philosophy of Language* Prentice-Hall: Englewood Cliffs, N. J.

FODOR, J. A., BEVER, T. G. and GARRETT, M. F. (1974) *The Psychology of Language* McGraw Hill: New York

FORSTER, K. I. and RYDER, L. A. (1971) Perceiving the structure and meaning of sentences. *Journal of Verbal Learning and Verbal Behavior* **10** 285–96

FOSS, D. J. and HAKES, D. T. (1978) *Psycholinguistics: An Introduction to the Psychology of Language* Prentice-Hall: Englewood Cliffs: N. J.

FOWLER, W. (1962) Teaching a two-year-old to read. *Genetic Psychology Monographs* **66** 181–283

FRANK, PHILIPP (1953) *Einstein, His Life and Times* Knopf: New York. Quotation appears in Hayakawa (1954)

FRAZIER, LYN and FODOR, JANET DEAN (1978) The sausage machine: a new two stage parsing model. *Cognition* **6** 291–325

FRIES, CHARLES C. (1949) *Teaching of English* George Wahr Publishing: Ann Arbor, Michigan (1957)

FRIES, CHARLES C. (1952) *The Structure of English* Harcourt, Brace & World: New York

FURTH, HANS (1966) *Thinking Without Language* Free Press: New York

FURTH, HANS (1971) Linguistic deficiency and thinking: Research with deaf subjects, 1964–1969. *Psychological Bulletin* **76** 1, 58–72

GARDNER, B. T. and GARDNER, R. A. (1969) Teaching sign language to a chimpanzee. *Science* **165** 664–72

GARDNER, B. T. and GARDNER, R. A. (1975) Evidence for sentence constituents in the early utterances of child and chimpanzee. *Journal of Experimental Psychology: General* **104** 244–67

GARDNER, ROBERT and LAMBERT, WALLACE E. (1972) *Attitudes and Motivation in Second-Language Learning* Newbury House: Rowley, Mass.

GARNICA, O. K. (1977) Some prosodic characteristics of speech to young children. *Working Papers in Linguistics*, No. 22 Ohio State University: Ohio

GATES, ARTHUR I. (1928) *New Methods in Primary Reading* Teachers College, Columbia University: New York

GATES, ARTHUR I. and BOND, G. (1936) Reading readiness: a study of factors determining success and failure in beginning reading. *Teachers College Record* **37** 679–85

GATES, ARTHUR I. and MACGINITIE, W. (1968) *Readiness Skills* (Teacher's Manual) Macmillan: New York

GATTEGNO, C. (1972) *Teaching Foreign Languages in Schools: The Silent Way* (2nd edn) Educational Solutions: New York

GIBSON, ELEANOR J. and LEVIN, HARRY (1975) *The Psychology of Reading* MIT Press: Cambridge, Mass.

GOODMAN, KENNETH S. (1973) Miscues: windows on reading, in Goodman, Kenneth S. (ed) *Miscue Analysis* ERIC Clearinghouse on Reading and Communication Skills: Urbana, Illinois

GOODMAN, NELSON (1965) *Fact, Fiction and Forecast* (2nd edn) Bobbs-Merrill: Indianapolis, Indiana

GOUIN, FRANCOIS (1880) *L'art d'enseigner et d'etudier les langues* Librairie Fischbacher: Paris. English version: *The Art of Teaching and Studying Languages* (1892) Philip: London

GRAY, WILLIAM S. (1948) *On Their Own in Reading* Scott Foresman: Chicago

GREENBERG, J. H. (1963) Some universals of grammar with particular reference to the order of meaningful elements, in Greenberg, J. H. (ed) *Universals of Language* (2nd edn) MIT Press: Cambridge, Mass.

GREENFIELD, P. M. and SMITH, J. H. (1976) *The Structure of Communication in Early Language Development* Academic Press: New York

GREGOIRE, ANTOINE (1937) *L'apprentissage du langage: les deux premières années* Librairie E. Droz: Paris

HAKUTA, KENJI (1976) A case study of a Japanese child learning English as a second language. *Language Learning* 26 2, 321–52

HARSHMAN, R. and KRASHEN, S. (1972) An 'unbiased' procedure for comparing degree of lateralization of dichotically presented stimuli. *Journal of the Acoustical Society of America* 52 174 (Abstract)

HATCH, EVELYN M. (ed) (1978) *Second Language Acquisition: A Book of Readings* Newbury House: Rowley, Mass.

HAYAKAWA, S. I. (ed) (1954) *Language, Meaning, and Maturity* Harper & Row: New York

HAYES, J. R. (ed) (1970) *Cognition and the Development of Language* Wiley: New York

HILGARD, ERNEST R. & BOWER, GORDON (1966) *Theories of Learning* (3rd edn) Appleton-Century-Crofts: New York

HOBSON, J. (1959) Lee-Clark reading readiness test, in Buros, O. (ed). See also Bollenbacher (1959)

HOLMES, M. C. (1927) Investigation of reading readiness of first grade entrants. *Childhood Education* 3 215–21

HUEY, EDMUND B. (1908) *The Psychology and Pedagogy of Reading* Macmillan: New York. Reprinted by MIT Press: Cambridge, Mass. (1968)

HUMBOLDT, WILHELM VON (1836) Über die Verschiedenheit des menschlichen Sprach baues undihren Einfluss arf die geistige Entiwickelung des Menschengeschilectis. *Linguistic Variability and Intellectual Development* University of Miami Press: Coral Gables, Florida (1971)

HUME, DAVID (1748) *An Inquiry Concerning Human Understanding (Great Books of the Western World)* Encyclopaedia Britannica: Chicago (1952)

HUTTENLOCHER, JANELLEN (1974) The origins of language comprehension, in Solso, R. L. (ed) *Theories in Cognitive Psychology* Lawrence Erlbaum Associates: Potomac, Md.

JACKENDOFF, R. (1972) *Semantic Interpretation in Generative Grammar* MIT Press: Cambridge, Mass.

JACKENDOFF, R. (1977) X̄ syntax: a study of Phrase Structure. *Linguistic Inquiry Monograph No. 2* MIT Press: Cambridge, Mass.

JAKOBSON, ROMAN (1968) *Child Language, Aphasia, and Phonological Universals* Mouton: The Hague

JEFFREY, W. E. and SAMUELS, S. J. (1967) Effect of method of reading training on initial learning and transfer. *Journal of Verbal Learning and Verbal Behavior* **6** 354–8

JESPERSEN, OTTO (1904) *How to Teach a Foreign Language* G. Allen: London

JESPERSEN, OTTO (1933) *Essentials of English Grammar* University of Alabama Press: University, Alabama.

JOHNSON, D. E. (1974) Toward a theory of relationally-based grammars. Unpublished doctoral dissertation, University of Illinois: Urbana, Illinois

KANT, IMMANUEL (1781) *Critique of Pure Reason* (*Great Books of the Western World*) Encyclopaedia Britannica: Chicago (1952)

KATZ, J. (1972) *Semantic Theory* Harper & Row: New York

KATZ, J. and FODOR, J. (1963) The structure of a semantic theory. *Language* **39** 170–210. Also in Fodor, J. and Katz, J. (eds) (1964) *The Structure of Language* Prentice-Hall: Englewood Cliffs, N. J.

KAY, P. and MCDANIEL, C. K. (1978) The linguistic significance of the meanings of basic color terms. *Language* **54** 3, 610–46

KELLY, LOUIS G. (1969) *25 Centuries of Language Teaching* Newbury House: Rowley, Mass.

KLIMA, EDWARD S. and BELLUGI, URSULA (1966) Syntactic regularities in the speech of children, in Lyons, J. and Wales, R. J. (eds) *Psycholinguistics Papers* Edinburgh University Press: Edinburgh, pp. 183–208

KOBASHIGAWA, B. (1969) Repetitions in a mother's speech to her child. *Working paper No. 14* University of California: Berkeley, California

KOLERS, PAUL (1970) Three stages of reading, in Levin, Harry and Williams, Joanna (eds) *Basic Studies on Reading* Basic Books: New York

KORZYBSKI, ALFRED (1933) *Science and Sanity: An Introduction to Non-Aristotelian Systems and General Semantics* (4th edn) The International Non-Aristotelian Publishing Co.: Lakeville, Conn. 1958

KRASHEN S. D. (1973) Lateralization, language learning, and the critical period: some new evidence. *Language Learning* **23** 63–74

LABOV, W. (1970a) The study of language in its social context, *Studium Generale* **23** 1–43

LABOV, WILLIAM (1970b) The logic of non-standard English, in Alatis, James (ed) *Report of the Twentieth Annual Round Table Meeting on Linguistics and Language* Georgetown University Press: Washington, D. C. Pp. 30–87

LADO ROBERT (1957) *Linguistics Across Cultures* University of Michigan Press: Ann Arbor, Michigan

LAKOFF. GEORGE (1971) On generative semantics, in Steinberg. Danny D. and Jakobovits. Leon A. (eds) (1971)

LAKOFF. G. and THOMPSON. H. (1975) Dative questions in cognitive grammar, Papers from the Parasession on Functionalism, Chicago Linguistic Society

LAMENDELLA. J. (1969) On the irrelevance of transformational grammar to second language pedagogy. *Language Learning* 19 3 & 4, 255–70

LANTZ. DELEE (1963) *Color Naming and Color Recognition: A Study in the Psychology of Language* Doctoral dissertation, Harvard University

LEECH. G. (1974) *Semantics* Penguin: Baltimore, Maryland

LENNEBERG. ERIC (1967) *Biological Foundations of Language* Wiley: New York

LENNEBERG. ERIC (1969) On explaining language. *Science* 163 635–43

LENNEBERG. ERIC H. and LENNEBERG E. (eds) (1975) *Foundations of Language Development: A Multidisciplinary Approach* Academic Press: New York

LENNEBERG. ERIC H.. REBELSKY. F. G. and NICHOLS. I. A. (1965) The vocalizations of infants born to deaf and hearing parents. *Human Development* 8 23–37

LEOPOLD, W. F. (1947) Speech development of a bilingual child: a linguist's record. Vol. 2, *Sound Learning in the First Two Years* Northwestern University Press: Evanston, I11.

LEOPOLD. W. F. (1953) Patterning in children's language learning. *Language Learning* 5 1–14

LIBERMAN. ALVIN M. (1957) Some results of research on speech perception. *Journal of the Acoustic Society of America* 29 117–23

LIEBERMAN. PHILIP (1967) *Intonation, Perception, and Language* MIT Press: Cambridge, Mass.

LOCKE. JOHN (1690) *An Essay Concerning Human Understanding* (*Great Books of the Western World*) Encyclopaedia Britannica: Chicago (1952)

LOZANOV GEORGI (1979) *Suggestopedy and Outlines of Suggestopedy* Gordon & Breach, Science Publishers: New York

LUGTON. ROBERT C. and HEINLE. CHARLES H. (eds) (1971) *Toward A Cognitive Approach to Second-Language Acquisition* The Center for Curriculum Development: Philadelphia

MACCORQUODALE. KENNETH (1970) On Chomsky's review of Skinner's *Verbal Behavior*. *Journal of Experimental Analysis of Behavior* 13 83–9

MACINTYRE. ALASDAIR (1970) Noam Chomsky's view of language. (Stuart Hampshire's interview of Noam Chomsky), in Lester, Mark (ed) *Readings in Applied Transformational Grammar* (1st edn) Holt, Rinehart & Winston: New York

REFERENCES

225

MCCAWLEY. J. (1968) The role of semantics in grammar, in Bach, E. and Harms, R. T. (eds) *Universals in Linguistic Theory* Holt, Rinehart & Winston: New York

MCCAWLEY. J. (1971) Where do noun phrases come from? in Steinberg, Danny D. and Jakobovits, Leon A. (eds) (1971)

MCLAUGHLIN. BARRY (1977) Second language learning in children. *Psychological Bulletin* **84** 3, 438–59

MCNEILL. DAVID (1966) Developmental psycholinguistics, in Smith, Frank and Miller, George (eds) *The Genesis of Language: A Psycholinguistic Approach* MIT Press: Cambridge, Mass., pp. 15–84

MCNEILL. DAVID (1970) *The Acquisition of Language* Harper and Row: New York

MCNEILL. DAVID and MCNEILL. NOBUKO B. (1968) What does a child mean when he says "no"?, in Zale, E. M. (ed) *Language and Language Behavior* Appleton-Century-Crofts: New York, pp. 51–62

Metropolitan Readiness Tests (1933–66) Harcourt, Brace & World: New York

MILL. JAMES (1829) *Analysis of the Phenomena of the Human Mind* A. M. Kelley: New York (1967)

MILL. JOHN STUART (1843) *A System of Logic, Ratiocinative and Inductive, Being a Corrective View of the Principles of Evidence and the Methods of Scientific Investigation* (8th edn) Longmans, Green and Co.: London 1930

MILON. JOHN P. (1974) The development of negation in English by a second language learner. *TESOL Quarterly* **8** 137–43

MORPHETT. M. C. and WASHBURNE. C. (1931) When should children begin to read? *Elementary School Journal* **31** 496–503

MOSKOWITZ. BREYNE A. (1971) Acquisition of phonology. Ph.D. dissertation, University of California at Berkeley

MOSKOWITZ. BREYNE A. (1978) The acquisition of language. *Scientific American* November 92–108

MOWRER. O. (1960) *Learning Theory and the Behavior Symbolic Process* Wiley: New York

NAKAZIMA. S. (1962) A comparative study of the speech developments of Japanese and American English in childhood. *Studies in Phonology* **2** 27–39

NEMSER. W. (1971) Approximate systems of foreign language learners. *International Review of Applied Linguistics* **9** 115–23

NEWMARK. LEONARD and REIBEL. DAVID (1970) Necessity and sufficiency in language learning, in Lester, Mark (ed) *Readings in Applied Transformational Grammar* (1st edn) Holt, Rinehart & Winston: New York

NEWPORT. E. L. (1975) Motherese: the speech of mothers to young children. Technical report no. 52, Center for Human Information Processing, University of California: San Diego

NIYEKAWA-HOWARD, AGNES (1972) The current status of the linguistic relativity hypothesis. *Working Papers in Linguistics* University of Hawaii **4** 2, 1–30

OLLER, JOHN W., BACA, LORI L. and VIRGIL, ALFREDO (1978) *Attitudes and attained proficiency in ESL: a sociolinguistic study of Mexican-Americans in the Southwest.* TESOL *Quarterly* **11** 173–83

OLLER, JOHN W., HUDSON, A. and LIU, PHYLLIS F. (1977) Attitudes and attained proficiency in ESL: a sociolinguistic study of native speakers of Chinese in the United States. *Language Learning* **27** 1–27

OSGOOD, CHARLES E. (1953) *Method and Theory in Experimental Psychology* Oxford University Press: New York

OSGOOD, CHARLES E. (1968) Toward a wedding of insufficiencies, in Dixon, T. R. and Horton, D. L. (eds) *Verbal Behavior and General Behavior Theory* Prentice-Hall: Englewood Cliffs, N. J.

OSGOOD, CHARLES E. (1971) Where do sentences come from? in Steinberg, Danny D. and Jakobovits, Leon A. (eds)

OSGOOD, CHARLES E. and SEBEOK, T. A. (1954) Psycholinguistics: a survey of theory and research problems. *Journal of Abnormal and Social Psychology* **49** (supplement)

OSGOOD CHARLES E., SUCI, GEORGE J. and TANNENBAUM, PERCY H. (1957) *The Measurement of Meaning* University of Illinois Press: Urbana, Illinois.

OYAMA, SUSAN (1976) A sensitive period for the acquisition of a nonnative phonological system. *Journal of Psycholinguistic Research* **5** 3, 261–84

PALERMO, DAVID S. and MOLFESE, D. L. (1972) Language acquisition from age five onward. *Psychology Bulletin* **78** 409–28

PALMER, HAROLD E. (1922) *The Principles of Language-Study* George G. Harrup: London. Reprinted (1964) Oxford University Press: London

PATTERSON, FRANCINE (1978) Conversations with a gorilla. *National Geographic* October 438–65

PESTALOZZI, JOHANN H. (1801) *Wie Gertrud ihre Kinder lehrt* (*How Gertrude Teaches Her Children*) George Allen & Unwin: London (1898)

PETERS, ANN (1980) The units of language acquisition. *Working Papers in Linguistics* **12** 1, 1–72 University of Hawaii

PETERS, ANN (1981) Language typology and the segmentation problem in early child language acquisition. *Proceedings of Seventh Annual Meeting of the Berkeley Linguistics Society*, Berkeley, CA.

PHILLIPS, JOHN L. JR. (1969) *The Origins of Intellect: Piaget's Theory* Freeman: San Francisco

PHILLIPS, J. R. (1973) Syntax and vocabulary of mother's speech to young children: age and sex comparisons. *Child Development* **44** 182–5

PIAGET, JEAN (1955) *The Language and Thought of the Child* World Publishing: Cleveland, Ohio

PIAGET, JEAN (1957) *Logic and Psychology* Basic Books: New York

PIAGET, JEAN (1968) Quantification, conservation, and nativism. *Science* **162** (Nov. 29) 976–9

PIAGET, JEAN & INHELDER, BARBEL (1969) *The Psychology of the Child* Basic Books: New York

PIKE, KENNETH L. (1954) *Language in Relation to a Unified Theory of the Structure of Human Behavior* Summer Institute of Linguistics: Glendale, California

PLATO (4th Cent. B. C.) *Dialogues* (*Great Books of the Western World*) Encyclopaedia Britannica: Chicago (1952)

POSTAL, P. (1970) On the surface verb 'remind.' *Linguistic Inquiry* **1** 37–120

POSTOVSKY, VALERIAN A. (1974) Effects of delay in oral practice at the beginning of second language learning. *Modern Language Journal* **58** 5–6, 229–239

PREMACK, A. J. and PREMACK, D. (1972) Teaching language to an ape. *Scientific American* **227** 92–9

PUTNAM, HILARY (1967) The 'innateness hypothesis' and explanatory models in linguistics. *Synthese* **17** 12–22

QUINE, W. V. O (1953) *From a Logical Point of View* Harper & Row: New York

QUINE, W. V.O. (1960) *Word and Object* MIT Press: Cambridge, Mass.

RICHARDS, JACK (1972) Social factors, interlanguage and language learning *Language Learning* **22** 159–88

RICHARDS, JACK (1974) *Error Analysis: Perspectives on Second Language Acquisition* Longman: London

ROUSSEAU, JEAN JACQUES (1780) *Emile ou de l'education* Garnier Frères: Paris (1964)

RYLE, GILBERT (1949) *The Concept of Mind* Hutchinson: London

SACHS, J., BROWN, R. and SALERNO, R. A. (1972) Adult's speech to children. Paper presented at the International Symposium on First Language Acquisition: Florence, Italy

SACHS, J. S. and TRUSWELL, L. (1976) Comprehension of two-word instructions by children in the one-word stage. *Papers and Reports on Child Language Development* **12** 212–20 Department of Linguistics, Standford University

SAPIR, EDWARD (1921) *Language: An Introduction to the Study of Speech* Harcourt, Brace & World: New York

SAPIR, EDWARD (1929) The status of linguistics as a science. *Language* **5** 207–14. Also in *Selected Writings in Language, Culture, and Personality* (ed) by D. G. Mandelbaum), University of California Press: Berkeley

SAUVEUR, LAMBERT (1878) *The Natural Method: Introduction to the Teaching of Ancient Languages* Holt: New York

SCHACHTER, JACQUELYN (1974) An error in error analysis. *Language Learning* **24** 2, 205–14

SCHANE, S. (1971) The phoneme revisited. *Language* **47** 3, 503–521

SCHANE, S. (1973) *Generative Phonology* Prentice-Hall: Englewood Cliffs, N. J.

SCHLESINGER, I. M. (1977) *Production and Comprehension of Utterances* Lawrence Erlbaum: Hillsdale, N. J.

SCHULWITZ, G. C. (1977) The teacher: fostering interest and achievement, in Ollila, L. (ed) *The Kindergarten Child and Reading* International Reading Association: Newark, Delaware

SCOLLON, RONALD (1976) *Conversations with a One Year Old. A Case Study of the Development Foundation of Syntax* University of Hawaii Press: Honolulu, Hawaii

SCOVEL, THOMAS (1979) Georgi Lozanov: Suggestology and outlines of Suggestopedy. *TESOL Quarterly* **13** 2, 255–67

SEARLE, JOHN R. (1969) *Speech Acts: An Essay in the Philosophy of Language* Cambridge University Press: London

SEARLE, JOHN R. (1975) Speech acts and recent linguistics. *Annals of the New York Academy of Sciences, Developmental Psycholinguistics, and Communication Disorders* **263** 27–38

SEITZ, SUE and STEWART, CATHERINE (1975) Imitations and expansions. Some developmental aspects of mother-child communications. *Developmental Psychology* **11** 763–8

SELINKER, L. (1972) Interlanguage. *International Review of Applied Linguistics* **10** 201–31

SHATZ, M. and GELMAN, R. (1973) The development of communication skills: modifications in the speech of young children as a function of the listener. *Monographs of the Society on Research in Child Development* **38** 152

SILBERMAN, HARRY F. (1964) *Exploratory Research on a Beginning Reading Program* System Development Corp.: Santa Monica, California

SINCLAIR, HERMINA (1970) The transition from sensory-motor behavior to symbolic activity. *Interchange* **1** 119–26

SINCLAIR-DE-ZWART, HERMINA (1969) Developmental psycholinguistics, in Elkind, D. and Flavell, J. H. (eds) *Studies in Cognitive Development* Oxford University Press: New York

SKAILAND, DAWN B. (1971) *A Comparison of Four Language Units in Teaching Beginning Reading* Far West Laboratory for Educational Research and Development: Berkeley, California

SKINNER, B. F. (1957) *Verbal Behavior* Appleton-Century-Crofts: New York

SKINNER, B. F. (1964) Behaviorism at fifty, in Wann, T. W. (ed) *Behaviorism and Phenomenology* University of Chicago Press: Chicago

SKINNER, B. F. (1971) Humanistic behaviorism. *The Humanist*, May–June, 35.

SKINNER, B. F. (1972) On having a poem. *Saturday Review* July 15, 32–5

SLOBIN, DAN I. (1975) On the nature of talk to children. Vol. 1, in Len-neberg, Eric H. and Lenneberg, E. (eds) (1975), pp. 283–98

SLOBIN, DAN I. (1979) *Psycholinguistics* (2nd edn) Scott, Foresman & Co.: Glenview, Illinois

SMITH, FRANK (1971) *Understanding Reading* Holt, Rinehart & Winston: New York

SMITH, M. K. (1941) Measurement of size of English vocabulary. *General Psychological Monographs* **24** 311–45

SNOW, CATHERINE E. (1972) Mothers speech to children learning language. *Child Development* **43** 549–65

SNOW, CATHERINE E. (1975) Language acquisition and mothers' speech to children. Ph.D. dissertation, McGill University

SNOW, CATHERINE E., ARLMAN-RUPP, A., HASSING, Y., JOBSE, J., JOOKSEN, J. and VORSTER, J. (1976) Mothers' speech in three social classes. *Journal of Psychological Research* **5** 1–20

SÖDERBERGH, R. (1971) *Reading in Early Childhood* (in Swedish). Also Georgetown University Press: Washington, D. C. (1977)

SPACHE, E. & SPACHE, G. (1969) *Reading in the Elementary School* Allyn & Bacon: Boston

STAATS, ARTHUR (1968) *Learning, Language, and Cognition* Holt, Rine-hart & Winston: New York

STAATS, ARTHUR (1971) Linguistic-mentalistic theory versus an explana-tory S-R learning theory of language development, in Slobin, D. I. (ed.) *The Ontogenesis of Grammar* Academic Press: New York

STEINBERG, DANNY D. (1969) Natural class, complementary distribution, and speech perception. *Journal of Experimental Psychology* **79** 2, 195–202

STEINBERG, DANNY D. (1975a) Semantic universals in sentence processing and interpretation. *Journal of Psycholinguistic Research* **4** 3, 169–93

STEINBERG, DANNY D. (1975b) Chomsky: From formalism to mentalism and psychological invalidity. *Glossa* **9** 2, 218–52

STEINBERG, DANNY D. (1976) Competence, performance and the psycholo-gical invalidity of Chomsky's grammar. *Synthese* **32** 373–86

STEINBERG, DANNY D. (1978) Why children can't read: Meaning, the ne-glected factor. Paper presented to the 86th annual meeting of the American Psychological Association , 1 September, Toronto, Canada

STEINBERG, DANNY D. (1979) Learning to read Japanese with implications for teaching English. *Working Papers in Linguistics* **11** 1, 99–119

STEINBERG, DANNY D. (1980) Teaching reading to nursery school children. Final Report, Office of Education, US Office of Education, Project No. 5336H90306, Grant No. G007903113

STEINBERG, DANNY D. (1981) Kana moji no kinooteki gakusyuu (Learning kana symbols by induction). *Shinrigaku Kenkyuu* (Japanese Journal of Psychology) **25** 2, 59–69

STEINBERG. DANNY D. and CHEN. SHING-REN (1980) A three-year-old mute-hearing child learns to read: the illustration of fundamental reading principles. (In Japanese) *Dokusyo Kagaku* (Science of Reading) **24** 4, 134–41. Also in *Working Papers in Linguistics* University of Hawaii (in English) 1980 **12** 2, 77–91

STEINBERG. DANNY D. and JAKOBOVITS. LEON A. (eds) (1971) *Semantics: An Interdisciplinary Reader in Philosophy, Linguistics, and Psychology* Cambridge University Press: New York

STEINBERG. DANNY D. and KROHN. ROBERT (1975) The psychological validity of Chomsky and Halle's vowel shift rule, in Koerner, E. F. K. (ed) *Current Issues in Linguistic Theory*, Vol. 1 John Benjamins B. V.: Amsterdam

STEINBERG. DANNY D.. KUSHIMOTO. KAYOKO. TATARA. NAOKO and ORISAKA. RITSU-KO (1979) Why children can't read: Meaning, the neglected factor. *Working Papers in Linguistics* **9** 3, 115–7

STEINBERG. DANNY D. and STEINBERG. MIHO T. (1975) Reading before speaking. *Visible Language* **9** 3, 197–224

STEINBERG. DANNY D. and SAKODA. KUMIKO (1981) Teaching two- and three-year-olds to read in nursery school. Submitted to *Dokusho Kagaku* (Science of Reading)

STEINBERG. DANNY D. and YAMADA, Jun (1978–79) Are whole word kanji easier to learn than syllable kana? *Reading Research Quarterly* **14** 1, 88–99

STEINBERG. DANNY D. and YOSHIDA. KYOKO (1981) Teaching one- and two-year-olds to read at home. Submitted to *Dokusho Kagaku* (Science of Reading)

STEVICK. EARL W. (1976) *Memory, Meaning, and Method: Some Psychological Perspectives on Language Learning* Newbury House: Rowley, Mass.

STROHNER. H. and NELSON. K. E. (1974) The young child's development of sentence comprehension: influence of event probability, nonverbal context, syntactic form, and strategies. *Child Development* **45** 567–76

TERMAN. L. M. (1918) An experiment in infant education. *Journal of Applied Psychology* **23**, 219–28

TITONE. RENZO (1968) *Teaching Foreign Languages: An Historical Sketch* Georgetown University Press: Washington, D. C.

TODD. P. H. III (1972) Learning to talk with delayed exposure to speech. Unpublished Ph.D. dissertation, University of California: Berkeley, California

TONKOVA-YAMPOL'SKAYA. R. V. (1969) Development of speech intonation in infants during the first two years of life. *Soviet Psychology* **7** 48–54

TWADDELL. W. (1935) On defining the phoneme, in Joos, M. (ed) (1958) *Readings in Linguistics* American Council of Learned Societies: Washington, D. C. Reprinted as *Readings in Linguistics I* Chicago University Press: Chicago.

VAN WAGENEN *Reading Readiness Scales* (1933–58) Van Wagenen Psycho-Educational Reseach Laboratories: Minneapolis, Minnesota

VELTEN, H. V. (1943) The growth of phonemic and lexical patterns in infant language. *Language* **19** 281–92

VIA, RICHARD A. (1981) Via-Drama: an answer to the EIIL problem, in Smith, Larry (ed) *English for Cross-Cultural Communication* Macmillan: London

VYGOTSKY, LEV S. (1934) *Thought and Language* (1962) MIT Press: Cambridge, Mass.

WANNER, ERIC (1980) The ATN and the sausage machine: which one is baloney? *Cognition* **8** 209–25

WANNER, ERIC, KAPLAN, RONALD & SHINER, SANDRA (1975) Garden paths in relative clauses. Manuscript, Harvard University

WATSON, JOHN B. (1924) *Behaviorism* Norton: New York (1970)

WATT, WILLIAM C. (1970) On two hypotheses concerning psycholinguistics, in Hayes, J. R. (ed) (1970)

WATT, WILLIAM C. (1974) Mentalism in linguistics. *Glossa* **8** 1, 3–40

WEEKS, THELMA (1981) *Encounters with Language* Early childhood literacy (ch. 5) Newbury House: Rowley, Mass. (in press)

WELLMERS, WILLIAM (1953) *Spoken English as a Foreign Language* American Council of Learned Societies: Washington, D. C.

WELLS, R. (1954) Meaning and use in linguistics today. *Word* **10** 235–50

WINITZ, HARRIS & REEDS, JAMES (1975) *Comprehension and Problem-Solving as Strategies for Language Training* Mouton: The Hague

WITTY, P. and KOPEL, D. (1936) Preventing reading disability: The reading readiness factor. *Educational Administration and Supervision* **28** 401–18

Author Index

Subject Index